CADENCE IV (A)

DR BASAK AND ACHARJYA

Made with ♥ on the Notion Press Platform
www.notionpress.com

Contents

Preface

According to the NEP rules set by the Central Board, new syllabus has been offered for University and College students. In this regard, the absence of a proper all- encompassing book catering to the specific needs of students has been felt.

Hence, it is our sincere effort to present before the student, a book that includes both the text as well as possible questions in the exact pattern and syllabi of the semester examinations. The texts have been included for preliminary reading and is supplemented by a through study of an exhaustive complimentary notes. It should be remembered that answers to questions have to both brief and complete, concise and to the point and this book attempts to address such a need of students preparing for the examination.

We are indebted to all our near and dear ones, our teachers and our colleagues for motivating us to undertake such a task.

CHAPTER ONE

THE GOOD-MORROW

The Good-Morrow
BY JOHN DONNE

I wonder, by my troth, what thou and I
Did, till we loved? Were we not weaned till then?
But sucked on country pleasures, childishly?
Or snorted we in the Seven Sleepers' den?
'Twas so; but this, all pleasures fancies be.
If ever any beauty I did see,
Which I desired, and got, 'twas but a dream of thee.
And now good-morrow to our waking souls,
Which watch not one another out of fear;
For love, all love of other sights controls,
And makes one little room an everywhere.
Let sea-discoverers to new worlds have gone,
Let maps to other, worlds on worlds have shown,
Let us possess one world, each hath one, and is one.
My face in thine eye, thine in mine appears,
And true plain hearts do in the faces rest;
Where can we find two better hemispheres,
Without sharp north, without declining west?
Whatever dies, was not mixed equally;
If our two loves be one, or, thou and I
Love so alike, that none do slacken, none can die.

<u>About the poet:</u>

John Donne was born in London in 1572 to a Roman Catholic family. Donne learned French and Latin during his studies at Hart Hall, Oxford (now Hertford College, Oxford University). Being Roman Catholic, Donne was not officially awarded his degree because that required pledging allegiance to Queen Elizabeth I, who was Protestant.

Roman Catholics were social outcasts in England's Protestant society. In 1593, Donne's younger brother was put in prison, where he died of the plague for hiding a Catholic priest. Donne's Catholic great-great-uncle Sir Thomas More was beheaded during the Reformation for refusing to take the Oath of Supremacy, opposing King Henry VIII's break away from the Catholic Church.

From 1591 to 1594, Donne studied law at Lincoln's Inn in <u>London</u>. Donne's father died just before this, leaving Donne an inheritance he mostly spent on travel. In his late teens, Donne lost his faith in the Roman Catholic church and chose to examine both Protestant and Catholic teachings, privately seeing himself as belonging, for a time, to neither.

After finishing at Lincoln's Inn, Donne travelled through Spain and Italy, failing to reach Jerusalem as intended, learning Spanish and Italian, and meeting persecuted Spanish Catholics. In 1596, Donne sailed with the Earl of Essex in failed naval expeditions to capture Spanish treasure ships and occupy the Azores Islands. After returning to England in 1597, Donne became the secretary of Sir Thomas Egerton, a man of great importance in the royal court.

Donne's hopes to one day become an essential public figure himself were ruined when, in 1601, he secretly married his boss' teenage niece, Anne More (1584–1617). In February 1602, Donne sent a letter revealing the marriage to Anne's father, Sir George More, another powerful figure in the royal court. In the letter, Donne explains that they married in secret because his 'present estate' was 'less than fit for her' and he knew he 'stood not right' in Sir George More's 'opinion'. Sir George More made sure Donne lost his job and was thrown into prison for conspiracy to marry without permission.

Donne was released when the marriage was proven valid.

Over ten years of financial hardship followed, with Donne failing to secure a new position in public office. During this time, his wife Anne More gave birth to one child almost every year. Donne and Anne relied on the support of friends and family for accommodation.

During this time, Donne studied theology and Christian law and wrote religious and love poetry. Donne shared his poetry privately with close friends. Donne's relationship with Anne's father eventually improved, and Anne's father offered the couple some financial support.

In 1610, Donne published an anti-Catholic pamphlet called *Pseudo-Martyr*, giving up Catholicism completely. *Pseudo-Martyr* defended pledging the Oath of Allegiance to King James I, something Catholics resisted. Donne encouraged Catholics to view taking the Oath of Allegiance as a political pledge to King James I in the pamphlet, which meant Catholics could take the Oath and thereby avoid persecution without giving up their faith. John Donne won King James I's favour with this pamphlet.

While King James I and friends of John Donne believed Donne's place was in the church, John Donne resisted taking Holy Orders for years, believing he belonged in public office. In 1614 with finances tight and no other option, Donne took Holy Orders when King James I commanded him to, becoming a priest with the Church of England (the Anglican Church) in 1615.

Less than two years later, Donne's wife died in childbirth. Five of their 12 children died young or in childbirth. Anne More's death had a powerful impact on Donne. He vowed never to marry again and felt driven in his role as priest.

In 1621, John Donne became the Dean of St. Paul's Cathedral in London, an important and well-paid position which he stayed in until his death. Donne's moving sermons earned him a great reputation as a preacher. In 1623, Donne became seriously ill and wrote his prose work *Devotions upon Emergent Occasions* (1624) while he was trying to recover, reflecting on life, death, sickness, and God's role.

In February 1631, Donne preached his final sermon called 'Death's Duel' and died a month later. John Donne posed for his memorial statue, and it can still be seen at St. Paul's Cathedral today.

<u>Definition and Characteristics of Metaphysical Poetry</u>

The word 'Metaphysical Poetry' is a philosophical concept used in literature where poets portray the things/ideas that are beyond the depiction of physical existence. Etymologically, there is a combination of two words 'meta' and 'physical' in word "metaphysical". The first word "Meta" means beyond. So metaphysical means beyond physical, beyond the normal and ordinary. The meaning are clear here that it deals with the objects/ideas that are beyond the existence of this physical world.

In the book **"Lives of the Most Eminent English Poets (1179-1781)"**, the author Samuel Johnson made the first use of the word Metaphysical Poetry. He used the term Metaphysical poets to define a loose group of poets of 17th century. The group was not formal and most of the poets put in this category did not know or read each other's writings. This group's most prominent poets include John Donne, Andrew Marvell, Abraham Cowley, George Herbert, Henry Vaughan, Richard Crashaw, etc. He noted I his writing that all of these poets had the same style of wit and conceit in their poetry.

The types of questions metaphysical poetry may make you ask yourself can be:

1. Is our world real or a projection?
2. Is there an afterlife?
3. Can souls time travel?
4. Is God out there?
5. Are we restricted in our bodies or free?
6. Is fate real?

There is just so many questions like that, which otherwise we might ignore. The thing that is obvious here is that none of these questions has a definite answer in science. It is all about belief and philosophy.

Definition of Metaphysical poetry:

Metaphysical poetry is a genre of poetry that deals with deep and profound subjects like spirituality, religion, etc. it is highly intellectual form of poetry and presents the world to its readers in a different way. It asks questions that science cannot answer. Metaphysical poetry prompts the readers to question their reality and existence. It takes one beyond the physical world and gives new perspectives through its imagery, wit and paradox.

Characteristics of Metaphysical Poetry:

- Intellectual and Philosophical Themes

- 1. Exploration of complex ideas: Metaphysical poets explored intricate philosophical, scientific, and theological concepts.
- 2. Use of abstract concepts: Poets employed abstract ideas, such as time, space, and eternity, to explore human experience.

- Imagery and Symbolism

- 1. Intricate metaphors: Metaphysical poets used complex, extended metaphors to convey their ideas.
- 2. Allegories and symbolism: Poets employed allegories and symbolism to add layers of meaning to their work.

- Unconventional Structure

- 1. Disregard for traditional forms: Metaphysical poets rejected traditional poetic forms, embracing irregular rhythms and stanzaic structures.
- 2. Experimentation with language: Poets pushed the boundaries of language, using innovative techniques such as conceits and wordplay.

- Emotional Intensity

- 1. Exploration of intense emotions: Metaphysical poets explored intense emotions, such as love, death, and spirituality, with urgency and passion.
- 2. Personal and introspective tone: Poets often adopted a personal, introspective tone, exploring their own thoughts and feelings.

- Other Key Features

- 1. Conceits: Extended metaphors that make surprising connections between seemingly disparate ideas.
- 2. Wit and wordplay: Poets used clever language, puns, and double meanings to convey complex ideas.
- 3. Paradox and irony: Metaphysical poets often explored contradictions and ambiguities.
- 4. Use of scientific and philosophical concepts: Poets incorporated ideas from astronomy, anatomy, and philosophy into their work.

- Use of Classical Allusions

- 1. References to mythology and classical literature: Metaphysical poets often incorporated allusions to classical mythology and literature into their work.

- Playfulness with Language

- 1. Puns and double meanings: Poets used wordplay to create complex, layered meanings.
- 2. Neologisms and invented words: Metaphysical poets sometimes created new words or used unusual vocabulary to convey their ideas.

- Exploration of the Human Condition

- 1. Mortality and transience: Poets often explored themes of death, decay, and the fleeting nature of life.
- 2. Love and relationships: Metaphysical poets examined the complexities of love, desire, and relationships.
- 3. Spirituality and faith: Poets explored themes of spirituality, faith, and the search for meaning.

- Use of Imagery and Sensory Details

- 1. Vivid and evocative imagery: Metaphysical poets used rich, sensory language to create powerful images in the reader's mind.
- 2. Use of metaphorical language: Poets employed metaphorical language to describe abstract concepts and ideas.

- Experimentation with Form and Structure

- 1. Unconventional stanzaic structures: Metaphysical poets often disregarded traditional stanzaic forms, creating innovative and complex structures.
- 2. Use of caesura and enjambment: Poets experimented with caesura (pauses within a line) and enjambment (the running on of a sentence or phrase from one line to the next without a pause).

<u>Context for understanding the poem:</u>

In the poem "The Good Morrow", John Donne explores the themes of love, relationships, and the nature of reality. Through his use of imagery, metaphor, and symbolism, Donne creates a rich and complex texture of meaning that rewards close reading and analysis.

One of the key contexts for understanding the poem is the cultural and social norms of Donne's time. In the early 17th century, when the poem was written, the concept of romantic love was still a relatively new and radical idea. The traditional view of marriage and relationships was based on social and economic considerations, rather than emotional or personal ones. Donne's poem challenges this traditional view, presenting a vision of love as a transformative and all-consuming force that transcends social and cultural norms.

Another important context for understanding the poem is Donne's own personal experiences and relationships. Donne was known for his complex and often tumultuous personal life, which included a secret marriage to Anne More and a period of imprisonment for his involvement in a scandalous love affair. These experiences likely influenced Donne's writing, including "The Good Morrow", which explores the complexities and challenges of romantic love.

The poem itself is a beautiful and intricate exploration of the nature of love and relationships. The opening lines, "I wonder, by my troth, what thou and I / Did, till we loved?" (lines 1-2), set the tone for the rest of the poem, which is characterized by a sense of wonder, curiosity, and awe. The speaker's use of metaphor and imagery, such as the comparison of his beloved's eyes to "two of the fairest morning suns" (line 11), creates a rich and vivid portrait of the beloved, and emphasizes the idea that love is a transformative and all-consuming force.

The poem also explores the idea of the "microcosm", which was a popular concept in Renaissance literature and philosophy. The microcosm refers to the idea that the individual is a miniature version of the universe, containing all the elements and principles of the macrocosm. Donne uses this concept to explore the relationship between the individual and the world, suggesting that the beloved is a microcosm of the universe, containing all the beauty, wonder, and complexity of creation.

In conclusion, "The Good Morrow" is a beautiful and complex poem that rewards close reading and analysis. Through its exploration of love, relationships, and the nature of reality, the poem creates a rich and vivid portrait of the human experience, and challenges the reader to think deeply about the complexities and challenges of romantic love.

Some Important lines and Analysis

I Wonder by my troth, what thou, and I
Did, till we lov'd? were we not wean'd till then?
But suck'd on countrey pleasures, childishly?
Or snorted we in the seaven sleepers den?
T'was so; But this, all pleasures fancies bee.

> If ever any beauty I did see,
> Which I desired, and got, t'was but a dreame of thee.[9]
> — Stanza 1 (lines 1–7)

This refers to the Seven Sleepers, the Catholic legend of seven Christian children, persecuted for their faith during the reign of the Roman emperor Decius, who fled to the shelter of a cave where they slept for more than 200 years. Donne, one of six or seven children and a baptised Catholic during a time of strong anti-Catholic sentiment from both the populace and the government, would certainly have been familiar with the story.[10]

> And now good morrow to our waking soules,
> Which watch not one another out of feare;
> For love, all love of other sights controules,
> And makes one little roome, an every where.
> Let sea-discoverers to new worlds have gone,
> Let Maps to other, worlds on worlds have showne;
> Let us possesse one world, each hath one, and is one.[9]
> — Stanza 2 (lines 8–14)

In this passage, the speaker experiences a sense of wonder, having awoken in bed with his lover; he makes the discovery that their love makes finding "new worlds" pale in importance. "[S]ouls" also awake, not just bodies, "as if called by love from the sleep of ordinary life and mere lust".[11]

> My face in thine eye, thine in mine appeares,
> And true plain hearts do in the faces rest,
> Where can we finde two better hemispheares
> Without sharpe North, without declining West?
> What ever dies, was not mixd equally;[9]
> — Stanza 3 (lines 15–19)

This passage shows the speaker communicating to his lover that they have proceeded from their former "childish" pleasures to this moment, where their souls have finally awakened; something "miraculous" has happened, because the speaker feels the sort of love that Paul the Apostle claimed would only be encountered in heaven.[12]

> If our two loves be one, or, thou and I
> Love so alike, that none doe slacken, none can die.[9]
> — Stanza 3 (lines 20-21)

While the version found in Songs and Sonnets includes this passage as the last two lines, other manuscripts and a later volume of poetry give the last lines as, "If our two loves be one, both thou and I/Love just alike in all, none of these loves can die"

<u>**Explanations**</u>

Lines 1-7:

I wonder, by my troth, what thou and I

Did, till we loved? Were we not weaned till then?

But sucked on country pleasures, childishly?

Or snorted we in the Seven Sleepers' den?

' Twas so; but this, all pleasures fancies be.

If ever any beauty I did see,

Which I desired, and got, 'twas but a dream of thee.

Explanation:

In this opening stanza, Donne reflects on the trivialities of life before the speaker and their beloved fell in love. The rhetorical question—"what thou and I / Did, till we loved?"—signals a profound transformation wrought by love, as if their previous existence lacked purpose or depth. The speaker compares their pre-love existence to childish indulgence in "country pleasures" and spiritual lethargy, as suggested by the reference to the "Seven Sleepers' den." He concludes that any past beauty he desired was merely a shadow or a dream of the perfection he now finds in his beloved.

Critical Commentary:

Donne frames love as a revelatory experience that redefines the speaker's perception of existence. The dismissive tone toward past pleasures contrasts sharply with the reverence for the present, underscoring the spiritual elevation brought about by mutual affection. The mention of "country pleasures" carries both an innocence and a carnal undertone, suggesting that their earlier life lacked the sanctity of true love. Furthermore, the "Seven Sleepers" allusion evokes a state of dormancy, aligning with the poem's broader theme of awakening. Through this, Donne elevates romantic love to a metaphysical plane.

Notes on Poetic Prowess:

Donne's use of metaphysical conceits is evident in the juxtaposition of everyday experiences with spiritual metaphors, heightening the complexity of his argument. The interrogation in the opening line creates an intimate yet reflective tone, drawing the reader into the speaker's internal contemplation. Moreover, the imagery of dreaming underscores the theme of transformation, as past joys are devalued compared to the vivid reality of love. Donne's ability to transition seamlessly from mundane to profound lends this stanza a remarkable fluidity and depth.

Poetic Devices:

Metaphysical Conceit: The comparison of pre-love existence to "unweaned" infancy and slumber.

Allusion: The Seven Sleepers, representing spiritual lethargy.

Tone: Reflective and philosophical, transitioning from critique to celebration.

Comparison with Other Poets:

The theme of love as an awakening recalls the work of Dante Alighieri, particularly in La Vita Nuova, where love serves as a divine force that reshapes perception and purpose. Similarly, Andrew Marvell's To His Coy Mistress also contemplates the urgency and transformative power of love, though with a greater emphasis on its temporal limitations. While Donne's speaker transcends time and space through love, Marvell's speaker seeks to conquer them, highlighting differing metaphysical interpretations of love.

Lines 8-14:

And now good-morrow to our waking souls,

Which watch not one another out of fear;

For love, all love of other sights controls,

And makes one little room an everywhere.

Let sea-discoverers to new worlds have gone,

Let maps to other, worlds on worlds have shown,

Let us possess one world, each hath one, and is one.

Explanation:

In this stanza, the speaker proclaims the dawn of a new existence, marked by the unity of two souls in love. The phrase "good-morrow to our waking souls" signifies a spiritual awakening, where love casts aside fear and distrust, creating a harmonious bond. Donne elevates their passion to a universal scale, suggesting that their shared room transforms into a boundless world through the intensity of their affection. The dismissal of "sea-discoverers" and explorers reflects the speaker's belief that external achievements pale in comparison to the inner discovery of true love.

Critical Commentary:

Donne's portrayal of love as an all-encompassing force reflects his metaphysical sensibilities, as the speaker suggests that emotional and spiritual fulfilment surpasses physical exploration. The stanza emphasises the transformative power of love, which turns a confined space into "everywhere," symbolising the infinite potential of mutual devotion.

Donne's rejection of worldly pursuits for the introspection and depth of love challenges the Renaissance ideals of discovery and conquest, reinforcing his unique perspective on human connection.

Notes on Poetic Prowess:

Donne's use of metaphor and hyperbole enhances the stanza's philosophical depth, particularly in equating a single room to the world's vastness. The rhythm and structure of the stanza mirror the speaker's contemplative yet confident tone, while the imagery of exploration creates a juxtaposition between the external and internal realms. Donne's ability to blend intellectual argument with emotive resonance is a hallmark of his metaphysical style.

Poetic Devices:

Hyperbole: "One little room an everywhere" amplifies the transformative power of love.

Symbolism: The "waking souls" represent spiritual awakening through love.

Tone: Triumphant and celebratory.

Comparison with Other Poets:

Celebrating love as a transcendent force echoes Edmund Spenser's Epithalamion, where love unites the earthly and the divine. Similarly, Donne's conception of love as a microcosm of the universe parallels Shakespeare's sonnets, particularly Sonnet 116, which describes love as an eternal and unchanging force. However, while Shakespeare emphasises love's steadfastness, Donne highlights its capacity to transform and elevate the human experience.

Lines 15-21:

My face in thine eye, thine in mine appears,

And true plain hearts do in the faces rest;

Where can we find two better hemispheres,

Without sharp north, without declining west?

Whatever dies, was not mixed equally;

If our two loves be one, or, thou and I

Love so alike, that none do slacken, none can die.

Explanation:

In this concluding stanza, Donne encapsulates the perfect unity achieved through love. The reflection of each lover in the other's eye symbolises mutual understanding and equality. The metaphor of "two better hemispheres" suggests that their love forms a complete and harmonious whole, free from the imperfections of the natural world. The speaker asserts that true love transcends mortality, which is rooted in equality and balance, ensuring its eternal nature.

Critical Commentary:

Donne's exploration of love's eternal and unifying qualities elevates the poem to its metaphysical climax. The notion that "whatever dies, was not mixed equally" implies that imbalance leads to decay, positioning their love as an exception due to its symmetry and mutuality. By likening their love to celestial hemispheres, Donne invokes cosmic imagery that reinforces the grandeur and universality of their bond. This final assertion of love's immortality aligns with the poem's spiritual awakening and transcendence theme.

Notes on Poetic Prowess:

The stanza's intricate balance of imagery and argument reflects Donne's mastery of the metaphysical style. The metaphor of the hemispheres not only suggests unity but also evokes a sense of perfection and harmony. The repetition of "none" in the final line reinforces the steadfastness and immortality of their love, creating a resonant conclusion. Donne's precision in combining intellectual depth with emotional sincerity ensures that the stanza leaves a lasting impression.

Poetic Devices:

Metaphor: The comparison of lovers to hemispheres conveys their unity.

Paradox: The idea that love's equality renders it immortal.

Tone: Affirmative and transcendent.

Comparison with Other Poets:

Donne's celebration of eternal love recalls the mystical tone of George Herbert's religious poetry, where divine love is portrayed as unending and perfect. Similarly, the metaphor of the hemispheres echoes John Milton's Paradise Lost, where the union of Adam and Eve is described in cosmic terms. While Milton focuses on the divine plan, Donne emphasises the human experience of love as a reflection of heavenly harmony.

Questions and Answers:

Question 1: Analyze the theme of love in "The Good Morrow". How does Donne portray the speaker's emotions and relationship with his beloved?

Answer: In "The Good Morrow", Donne portrays love as a transformative and all-consuming force that elevates the speaker and his beloved to a state of spiritual and emotional unity. The speaker's emotions are characterized by a sense of wonder, joy, and intimacy, as he gazes into his beloved's eyes and finds a world of meaning and connection. Donne uses metaphysical conceits and imagery to convey the speaker's emotions and relationship with his beloved, emphasizing the idea that their love is a sacred and inviolable bond.

Question 2: Discuss the use of metaphor and imagery in "The Good Morrow". How do these literary devices contribute to the poem's meaning and effect?

Answer: In "The Good Morrow", Donne employs a range of metaphors and images to convey the speaker's emotions and ideas. For example, the comparison of the beloved's eyes to the sun and the speaker's soul to a shipwrecked sailor creates a powerful and evocative image of the transformative power of love. Similarly, the use of metaphysical conceits, such as the idea that the speaker and his beloved are two hemispheres of a single sphere, emphasizes the idea of their love as a unified and harmonious whole. These literary devices contribute to the poem's meaning and effect by creating a rich and complex texture of imagery and ideas that draw the reader into the speaker's world of emotion and thought.

Question 3: Examine the speaker's attitude towards sleep and dreams in "The Good Morrow". What does this reveal about his character and relationship with his beloved?

Answer: In "The Good Morrow", the speaker's attitude towards sleep and dreams is one of disdain and dismissal. He argues that sleep and dreams are inferior to the reality of his beloved's presence, and that he would rather be awake and gaze into her eyes than sleep and risk losing her. This reveals a great deal about the speaker's character and relationship with his beloved, emphasizing his passion, devotion, and desire for intimacy and connection. It also suggests that the speaker is a romantic and idealistic figure, who values the beauty and wonder of his beloved above all else.

Question 4: Discuss the poem's use of philosophical and scientific imagery. How does this contribute to the poem's themes and ideas?

Answer: In "The Good Morrow", Donne employs a range of philosophical and scientific imagery, including references to astronomy, geography, and metaphysics. For example, the comparison of the beloved's eyes to the sun and the speaker's soul to a shipwrecked sailor creates a powerful and evocative image of the transformative power of love. Similarly, the use of metaphysical conceits, such as the idea that the speaker and his beloved are two hemispheres of a single sphere, emphasizes the idea of their love as a unified and harmonious whole. This contributes to the poem's themes and ideas by creating a rich and complex texture of imagery and ideas that draw the reader into the speaker's world of emotion and thought.

Question 5: Analyze the poem's structure and form. How does this contribute to the poem's meaning and effect?

Answer: "The Good Morrow" is a metaphysical poem that consists of 18 lines, divided into three stanzas of six lines each. The poem's structure and form contribute to its meaning and effect by creating a sense of intimacy, informality, and conversational tone. The use of enjambment and caesura creates a sense of flow and continuity, emphasizing the idea that the speaker's thoughts and emotions are interconnected and interdependent. The poem's structure and form also contribute to its musicality and rhythm, creating a sense of harmony and balance that reflects the speaker's emotions and ideas.

Question 6: Discuss the idea of the "microcosm" in "The Good Morrow". How does Donne use this concept to explore the relationship between the individual and the world?

Answer: In "The Good Morrow", Donne uses the concept of the "microcosm" to explore the relationship between the individual and the world. The microcosm is a Renaissance concept that suggests that the individual is a miniature version of the universe, containing all the elements and principles of the macrocosm. Donne uses this concept to argue that the individual is a complete and self-sufficient world, containing all the elements necessary for happiness and fulfillment. This idea is reflected in the poem's imagery and metaphors, which suggest that the speaker's beloved is a world unto herself, containing all the beauty and wonder of the universe.

Question 7: Analyze the use of paradox in "The Good Morrow". How does Donne use paradox to create a sense of tension and complexity in the poem?

Answer: In "The Good Morrow", Donne uses paradox to create a sense of tension and complexity in the poem. Paradox is a rhetorical device that involves the juxtaposition of two contradictory ideas or statements. Donne uses paradox to explore the contradictions and complexities of love and relationships, suggesting that love is both a source of joy and a source of pain, both a liberating force and a confining one. For example, the poem's opening lines, "I wonder, by my troth, what thou and I / Did, till we loved?", create a sense of paradox by suggesting that the speaker's life was incomplete and lacking in meaning until he fell in love.

Question 8: Discuss the idea of the "private sphere" in "The Good Morrow". How does Donne use this concept to explore the relationship between the individual and society?

Answer: In "The Good Morrow", Donne uses the concept of the "private sphere" to explore the relationship between the individual and society. The private sphere refers to the realm of personal and intimate relationships, as opposed to the public sphere of social and civic life. Donne uses this concept to argue that the individual's most important and meaningful relationships are those that take place in the private sphere, rather than in the public sphere. This idea is reflected in the poem's imagery and metaphors, which suggest that the speaker's beloved is a private and intimate world, separate from the public world of society.

Question 9: Analyze the use of imagery and symbolism in "The Good Morrow". How do these literary devices contribute to the poem's meaning and effect?

Answer: In "The Good Morrow", Donne uses imagery and symbolism to create a rich and complex texture of meaning. The poem's imagery and symbolism contribute to its meaning and effect by creating a sense of wonder and enchantment, and by suggesting that the speaker's beloved is a source of beauty, joy, and transcendence. For example, the poem's image of the beloved's eyes as "two of the fairest morning suns" creates a sense of wonder and awe, and suggests that the beloved is a source of light and illumination.

Question 10: Discuss the idea of the "union of opposites" in "The Good Morrow". How does Donne use this concept to explore the relationship between the individual and the world?

Answer: In "The Good Morrow", Donne uses the concept of the "union of opposites" to explore the relationship between the individual and the world. The union of opposites refers to the idea that two seemingly contradictory or opposing forces can be united or reconciled. Donne uses this concept to argue that the individual and the world are not separate or opposing entities, but are instead interconnected and interdependent. This idea is reflected in the poem's imagery and metaphors, which suggest that the speaker's beloved is a world unto herself, containing all the opposites and contradictions of the universe.

The poem, "Good Morrow " is written by John Donne. It is a classic love poem, likely written by the poet's wife, Ann Moore. The first two stanzas draw out the poet's love for this woman, proclaiming love itself as the all-important event in life.

The third stanza continues on a similar path, beginning with an image of the two lovers looking at each other proclaiming, "My face in thine eye, thine in mine appears". This line refers to the two lovers gazing closely at each other, seeing themselves in their lover's eyes. It can be considered on a literal or metaphorical level; eyes do offer literal reflections, and one can see oneself in another's eyes, but the metaphorical interpretation suggests that John and his love only see each other because they're so deeply in love.

"Where can we find two better hemispheres/without sharp north, without declining west?" Since a hemisphere is only half of a sphere (think of each hemisphere as being half of a globe), Donne is drawing a traditional yet poetic image of the two lovers only being half of the entire whole. Donne is not complete without his love, and she is not complete without him.

The poem continues, "Whatever dies, was not mixed equally". Donne is explaining that true love cannot die, but that true love also requires reciprocal effort. Each lover needs to contribute equally, and only if the love is true can it never die.

The poem concludes, "If our two loves be one, or, thou and I/Love so alike, that none do slacken, none can die". With this final line, Donne continues the previous thought of eternal love and mutuality. If he and his lover are able to love each other truly, wholly, and equally, they can transcend mortal death. Their love is more powerful than all, and it cannot simply die. It's also interesting to note Donne's usage of the word "die" as the final word of the poem. In a literal sense, the poem ends at the word "die", just like a life is ended at death. Yet, the poem transcends time and escapes its death by existing as a form of love and art. Like the love described in the poem itself, "The Good-Morrow" is eternal.

Critical analysis of the Poem

John Donne's The Good-Morrow is a metaphysical love poem that delves into love's transformative and unifying power. The speaker addresses his beloved, reflecting on how their lives before love were shallow and fragmented, likened to childish pleasures or a state of dormancy. The poem envisions love as an awakening, where the lovers' souls unite in a relationship that transcends physical boundaries and becomes a profound, almost spiritual connection. This setting, possibly an early morning conversation, uses the dawning day as a metaphor for the enlightenment that love brings, elevating it beyond physical attraction.

The poem exemplifies Donne's metaphysical style, combining intellectual depth with emotional intensity. Its three stanzas follow a logical progression, exploring the lovers' past, present, and future. Donne's conversational tone is enriched with philosophical ideas, presenting love as a force that redefines existence, creating a world where lovers are wholly sufficient for each other. The vivid imagery and intricate conceits enhance the poem's aesthetic appeal, with metaphors like the "Seven Sleepers' den" symbolising a dormant past and "two better hemispheres" representing their harmonious unity. Hyperbolic expressions, such as their "one little room" becoming "an everywhere," highlight the boundlessness of their love. The reflective imagery of the lovers' faces in each other's eyes emphasises equality and mutual understanding, while the poem's smooth rhythm mirrors the continuity of their shared experience.

Among Donne's works, The Good-Morrow holds a central place for its balanced and spiritual portrayal of love. Unlike the playful tone of The Flea or the stoic detachment of A Valediction: Forbidding Mourning, this poem celebrates love as an eternal and transformative force. For Donne, if you read him carefully, love remains a transformative force yet an elusive idea to 'attain'. Its blend of Donne's outwitting intellect, mistaken emotional sincerity, and philosophical insight ensures the poem's enduring appeal, making it a timeless masterpiece of metaphysical poetry.

The Good-Morrow as a metaphysical love poem

John Donne's The Good-Morrow is a metaphysical love poem that explores true love's transformative and all-encompassing nature. The speaker, presumably Donne himself or a persona modelled after him, addresses his beloved in a deeply intimate and reflective tone, marking the transition from an immature, fragmented existence to the spiritual and emotional unity achieved through their relationship. The poem opens with a rhetorical inquiry into their lives before love, suggesting that any prior pleasures were shallow, childish, or even illusory. The scene might be imagined as an early morning conversation between the speaker and their beloved, where the dawning of the day mirrors the awakening of their souls to love. This setting underscores the poem's central metaphor of love as an act of spiritual enlightenment, elevating it beyond mere physical attraction.

The style of the poem is characteristic of Donne's metaphysical tradition, marked by intellectual depth, emotional intensity, and an intricate use of conceits and paradoxes. Its structure comprises three tightly woven stanzas, each building upon the other to create a logical progression of ideas about the nature of love. Donne employs a conversational tone, yet his language is dense with philosophical and spiritual implications. The poem's central theme is the transformative power of love, which Donne portrays as a force that unites two souls, transcending physical and temporal limitations. In this context, love is not merely an emotion but a profound, almost divine experience that redefines existence and renders the external world insignificant.

The lyrical and aesthetic qualities of the poem are remarkable, as Donne masterfully balances intellectual argumentation with vivid imagery and emotional resonance. The poem employs hyperbole to magnify the significance of love, such as the claim that their "one little room" becomes "an everywhere," suggesting that love creates a boundless universe for lovers. The metaphors are striking and varied, from the "Seven Sleepers' den" symbolising a state of dormancy to the "two better hemispheres" that capture the harmonious perfection of their union. Donne's reflective imagery, such as the lovers' faces appearing in each other's eyes, reinforces the idea of mutual understanding and equality in their love. The enjambment and rhythm of the lines create a seamless flow, reflecting the continuous and evolving nature of the speaker's thoughts. Furthermore, the poem's balanced structure and intricate conceits are hallmarks of Donne's ability to weave complex ideas into compact lyrical forms.

Among Donne's famous works, The Good-Morrow is a quintessential example of his metaphysical ingenuity. While poems like A Valediction: Forbidding Mourning and The Flea also explore themes of love and connection, The Good-Morrow uniquely celebrates love as a transformative and eternal force. It lacks the playful eroticism of The Flea and the stoic detachment of A Valediction, instead offering a more balanced and spiritual portrayal of love. This poem, therefore, occupies a central place in Donne's oeuvre as a testament to his ability to combine intellectual rigour with profound emotional sincerity. Its introspective depth and philosophical resonance ensure its enduring appeal, making it one of the most celebrated poems of the metaphysical tradition.

To wrap things up, one can agree that "The Good-Morrow" exemplifies John Donne's mastery of metaphysical poetry, producing the classical amalgamation of wit and passion. Through its exploration of love as a transformative and eternal force, the poem (as is the case of Donne's every famous poem) transcends the conventional boundaries of romantic verse.

Donne's intricate conceits and philosophical insights invite readers to contemplate the nature of love, unity, and immortality. The interplay of physical and metaphysical elements reflects the poet's belief in love's capacity to elevate the human experience, making "The Good-Morrow" a timeless celebration of spiritual and emotional awakening.

CHAPTER TWO

Batter my heart, three-person'd God

Holy Sonnets: Batter my heart, three-person'd God
BY JOHN DONNE

Batter my heart, three-person'd God, for you
As yet but knock, breathe, shine, and seek to mend;
That I may rise and stand, o'erthrow me, and bend
Your force to break, blow, burn, and make me new.
I, like an usurp'd town to another due,
Labor to admit you, but oh, to no end;
Reason, your viceroy in me, me should defend,
But is captiv'd, and proves weak or untrue.
Yet dearly I love you, and would be lov'd fain,
But am betroth'd unto your enemy;
Divorce me, untie or break that knot again,
Take me to you, imprison me, for I,
Except you enthrall me, never shall be free,
Nor ever chaste, except you ravish me.

Critical Summary

"Holy Sonnet XIV" – also known by its first line as "**Batter my heart, three-person'd God**" – is a poem written by the English poet John Donne (1572 – 1631). It is a part of a larger series of poems called *Holy Sonnets*, comprising nineteen poems in total. The poem was printed and published for the first time in *Poems* in 1633, two years after the author's death. In the 1633 edition the sequence of the poems was different from that found in Herbert Grierson's edition from 1912; that is why Holy Sonnet XIV features as Holy Sonnet X in older publications. However, the majority of twentieth-century and later editions of Donne's *Holy Sonnets* are found to prefer and use the order proposed by Grierson and thus include the sonnet as the fourteenth in the cycle.

The speaker asks God to intensify the effort to restore the speaker's soul. Knocking at the door is not enough; God should overthrow him like a besieged town. His own reason has not been enough either, and he has engaged himself to God's enemy. He asks God to break the knots holding him back, imprisoning him in order to free him, and taking him by force in order to purify him.

In his holy sonnets, Donne blends elements of the Italian (Petrarchan) sonnet with the English (Shakespearean) sonnet. Here he begins in the Italian form *abba abba*, but his concluding idea in the third quatrain bleeds over into the rhyming couplet (*cdcd cc*) that completes the poem.

The poet begins by asking God to increase the strength of divine force to win over the poet's soul. He requests, "Batter my heart" (line 1), metaphorically indicating that he wants God to use force to assault his heart, like battering down a door. Thus far, God has only knocked, following the scriptural idea that God knocks and each person must let him in, yet this has not worked sufficiently for the poet. Simply to "mend" or "shine" him up is not drastic enough; instead God should take him by "force, to break, blow, burn" in order to help him "stand" and be made "new" (lines 3-4). This request indicates that the speaker considers his soul or heart too badly damaged or too sinful to be reparable; instead, God must re-create him to make him what he needs to be. The paradox is that he must be overthrown like a town in order to rise stronger.

Indeed, the second quatrain begins with that metaphor, with the speaker now an "usurp'd town" that owes its allegiance or "due" to someone else (line 5). He is frustrated that his reason, God's "viceroy" in the town of his soul, is captive to other forces (such as worldly desire) and is failing to persuade him to leave his sins behind.

The poet then moves from the political to the personal in the last six lines. He loves God, but he is "betroth'd unto [God's] enemy" (line 9), the Satanic desires of the selfish heart (if not the devil himself). He seeks God's help to achieve the "divorce" from his sinful nature and break the marriage "knot" (lines 10-11). In the final couplet, he gives voice to the paradox of faith: the speaker can only be free if he is enthralled by God (line 13), and he can only be chaste and pure if God ravishes him (line 14).

The poet uses this dissonance of ideas to point out just how holy—in this case, otherworldly and spiritual in a carnal world—God truly is. In other words, a relationship with God requires being reborn and rebuilt from the ground up, in but not of the world.

Finally, since the speaker here suggests being in the female role of betrothal and ravishment (a city too tends to be coded as female), we once again see that the speaker is putting himself in the position of the Christian church generally. In the New Testament, the church is metaphorically said to be married to God. Can it be that, in Donne's eyes, the church still needs to be utterly reformed, even after the Reformation?

EXPLANATIONS

1.**Batter my heart, three-personed God, for you**
   As yet but knock, breathe, shine, and seek to mend;
   That I may rise, and stand, o'erthrow me, and bend
   Your force to break, blow, burn, and make me new.

The sonnet starts with an imperative clause: "Batter my heart" and addresses the three-personed God. The three-personed God refers to the Holy Trinity: the Father, the Son, and the Holy Spirit. Addressing the Holy Trinity is an example of an apostrophe.

God is silent throughout the poem. Like the God in "Sonnet XIV: Batter my heart, three-person'd God, the Sun in The Sun Rising, Death in Death Be Not Proud, the beloved in A Valediction: Forbidding Mourning, etc., we have noticed the addressee is silent in most of Donne's poems and the speaker plays a dominant role.

The speaker asks the Holy Trinity to batter his heart for spiritual redemption. The clause "Batter my heart" is a strong and violent imagery that conveys the intensity of the urge of the speaker to be free from the evil influence of Satan.

Additionally, we need one thing to keep in mind the clause "Batter my heart" is an example of hyperbole. The speaker does not want God to beat him severely, rather he means to intervene forcefully in his soul. Overall, The first line of the poem highlights the theme of the sonnet: the cry for the rescue of the speaker's soul to the Holy Trinity.

The phrase "for you" indicates the Holy Trinity. He wants Him to break his heart forcefully as of now God has only knocked, breathed, shone, and sought to mend the heart of the speaker. It highlights that God has been trying to revive his soul but to no avail.

However, these attempts have not brought any significant change to the speaker that he needs for the transformation. Therefore, he wants the Holy Trinity to take a serious step, that is battering his heart to purify his contaminated soul.

This forceful approach to purifying the soul contrasts with the gentle approach that the speaker mentions in the second line "knock, breathe, shine, and seek to mend". The second approach emphasizes his desperation to be free from the bondage of sin.

The tone of the sonnet is authoritative. It is peculiar because usually in a devotional poem, the speaker remains humble and shows reverence to the almighty. For instance, many of George Herbert's poems like "The Collar" express the speaker's politeness to submit himself to God.

On the other hand, the speaker in Donne's "Sonnet XIV" does not sound humble in any way. The absence of words like "request", and "please" complements the argument.

Though he wants to surrender himself to the Holy Trinity his approach to spiritual revival is different from others. It is contradictory for wishing to be reverent and commanding at the same time.

We can interpret the clause "That I may rise, and stand" as the speaker's hope for redemption from sin, He may rise from sin and stand as a piteous being. There is always a possibility of hope though sin has already corrupted his soul.

He also acknowledges that without God's intervention, it is impossible to transform himself into a new being. Therefore, he says coercively "o'erthrow me, and bend/Your force to break, blow, burn, and make me new" to suggest an impactful intervention to his soul. It also highlights the mood of the poem.

Even if it causes pain to him; he is willing to endure anything to reach his goal of being free and purified. The use of the alliteration "break, blow, burn" in the fourth line conveys the sense of agitation of the speaker and the urgency of the situation.

These four lines as a whole express the speaker's desire for spiritual renewal and growth.

2.I, like an usurped town, to another due,
Labour to admit you, but Oh, to no end.
Reason, your viceroy in me, me should defend,
But is captived, and proves weak or untrue.

The second quatrain expresses the speaker's dreadful spiritual life. He uses the simile, "like an usurped town", to compare his state of soul to that of a devastating town that has been seized by an enemy. The comparison implies the speaker is under foreign control.

Consequently, his soul is owed to another. The word "another" in the fifth line possibly refers to Satan or sin or the speaker's pride that is resisting him from coming into contact with God's grace.

The speaker is trying his best to allow God to enter his soul and purify him as he is certain that God is the only one who can rescue him. The phrase "to no end" means there is no progress in his effort of overcoming sin. The phrase "but oh" emphasizes the sense of disappointment in the speaker.

He expresses discontent, not for the fruitless struggle, but also expresses dissatisfaction for the reason, God's viceroy. The reason should have saved him from spiritual degeneration. The speaker uses the metaphor of a viceroy.

It is the job of reason to work on behalf of the best interest of a person. Similarly, the primary task of a viceroy, whom the speaker personifies as a ruler of the speaker's soul, is to guide him in his spiritual life.

The viceroy should be the ruler of the speaker's soul. But it has failed to prevent the speaker from the temptations of sin, Instead of becoming immune to the foreign power, the evil force has weakened the reason in the speaker and proved untrue to its role: resisting the soul from becoming corrupted.

Unlike the expectation, the reason has failed to do his job and other force has imprisoned him.

Here it seems the speaker whines to God for not preventing him at the right moment and he is doubting his reliability over God.

3.Yet dearly I love you, and would be loved fain,

But am betrothed unto your enemy:

Divorce me, untie or break that knot again,

Take me to you, imprison me, for I,

In this quatrain, the speaker affirms that he loves him dearly. The adverb "dearly" reinforces his deep love for God. He also expects that God would accept him and would gladly love him.

Since reason is weaker than sin, therefore, the speaker needs God's assistance.

He "would be loved fain" expresses the speaker's faith in God that despite his attachment to sin, God would love him.

The problem is the speaker is now engaged with God's enemy. We can interpret it as indulgence in sinful activities. He has engaged himself with God's enemy and his spiritual state is similar to that of an engaged person who cannot estrange from the other easily. The speaker is unable to break the bond of his entanglement with the enemy.

He ardently asks God to break the bond that he has been developing with God's enemy. The use of the imperative sentence, "Divorce me, untie or break that knot again" maintains a commanding tone and reinforces the desperation of the speaker.

The use of "again" could refer to a previous attempt by God where he rescued the speaker. Unfortunately, he has again indulged and made his life worse. Now, he wants to break any kind of association with the enemy and wants to be connected with Him again.

The speaker does not mean to divorce with sin rather it is a metaphorical expression that suggests the speaker's desire to be separated from sin and to be united with God.

The speaker is so serious about his situation that he goes on to use another imperative clause: "Take me to you", and "imprison me" to suggest his willingness to surrender to God. He thinks it is better to be imprisoned in God's custody than to be captive of sin. He wants God's protection for he wants to feel secure.

The last two lines of the third quatrain of the sonnet continue to express the speaker's longing for a profound change in his spiritual life with the help of God.

4.Except you enthrall me, never shall be free,
Nor ever chaste, except you ravish me.

If God does not help him, he shall never be free. He wants to be controlled by God's love and grace.

Unless God takes control of his soul by force and purifies the soul and frees it from corruption, he would never become morally pure.

The repetition of "except you" in the last two lines of the sonnet stresses the speaker's belief that without God, he can never be free and pure.

The speaker uses the violent image "ravish me" to convey the seriousness of his urge to be sanctified by God.

Short Questions and answers

1. What is the main theme of the poem?

Answer: The main theme of the poem is the speaker's desire to be transformed by God's love and to be made new in Christ.

2. What does the speaker mean by "batter my heart"?

Answer: The speaker is asking God to break down his heart and to transform him, to make him new and to give him a new heart.

3. What is the significance of the image of the "siege" in the poem?

Answer: The image of the siege represents the speaker's desire to be overwhelmed and transformed by God's love, and to be made new in Christ.

4. What is the main idea of the poem's first stanza?

Answer: The main idea of the poem's first stanza is the speaker's desire to be transformed by God's love and to be made new in Christ.

5. What does the speaker mean by "ravish me" in the poem?

Answer: The speaker means that he wants God to overwhelm him with His love and to take control of his life.

6. What is the significance of the image of the "prisoner" in the poem?

Answer: The image of the prisoner represents the speaker's feeling of being trapped in his own sin and imperfection, and his desire to be set free by God's love.

<u>**Essay Questions and answers**</u>

1. Analyze the use of imagery and symbolism in the poem. How do these literary devices contribute to the poem's meaning and effect?

Answer: The poem uses imagery and symbolism to convey the speaker's desire to be transformed by God's love. The image of the siege, for example, represents the speaker's desire to be overwhelmed and transformed by God's love. The use of imagery and symbolism creates a rich and complex texture of meaning that rewards close reading and analysis.

2. Discuss the theme of transformation in the poem. How does the speaker's desire to be transformed by God's love relate to the broader themes of the poem?

Answer: The theme of transformation is central to the poem, as the speaker desires to be made new in Christ. This desire for transformation is related to the broader themes of the poem, including the speaker's desire to be overwhelmed and transformed by God's love, and to be made new in Christ.

3. Analyze the poem's use of metaphor and simile. How do these literary devices contribute to the poem's meaning and effect?

Answer: The poem uses metaphor and simile to convey the speaker's desire to be transformed by God's love. The metaphor of the siege, for example, represents the speaker's desire to be overwhelmed and transformed by God's love. The use of metaphor and simile creates a rich and complex texture of meaning that rewards close reading and analysis.

4. Analyze the poem's use of paradox. How does Donne use paradox to convey the speaker's emotions and ideas?

Answer: The poem uses paradox to convey the speaker's emotions and ideas, such as the idea that he must be broken in order to be made whole, or that he must be taken captive in order to be set free. This use of paradox creates a sense of tension and complexity, and highlights the speaker's desperate desire for transformation.

5. Discuss the theme of surrender in the poem. How does the speaker's desire to surrender to God's love relate to the broader themes of the poem?

Answer: The theme of surrender is central to the poem, as the speaker desires to surrender to God's love and to be transformed by it. This desire for surrender is related to the broader themes of the poem, including the speaker's desire to be made new in Christ, and to be set free from his own sin and imperfection.

6. Analyze the poem's use of biblical imagery and allusion. How does Donne use biblical imagery and allusion to convey the speaker's emotions and ideas?

Answer: The poem uses biblical imagery and allusion to convey the speaker's emotions and ideas, such as the image of the siege, which is reminiscent of the biblical account of the siege of Jerusalem. This use of biblical imagery and allusion creates a sense of depth and complexity, and highlights the speaker's desire to be transformed by God's love.

Critical analysis of John Donne's Batter My Heart

Critics feel fairly certain that one group of John Donne's Holy Sonnets was published in 1633, a collection that included "Batter My Heart," sometimes listed as "Batter My Heart, Three Person'd God." It gained fame as a prime example of the style of Metaphysical Poets and Poetry with markedly unusual figurative language (figure of speech) or comparisons. Victorian readers found Donne's comparison of God's effect on his life to the violent act of ravishment, or rape, so disturbing that the poem basically disappeared from publishing until resurrected in the 20th century through the efforts of the poet T. S. Eliot and others. The sonnet's hysterical tone grows from the tradition of meditation, which may be used as an emotional stimulus. Typical of Donne, he heavily emphasizes the first-person pronouns I and me, enabling readers to visualize the speaker's involvement and the importance of the experience to him, while the strong but simple language does not distract the reader from the poem's theme of the importance in the Christian life of total surrender to God. While critics including the Donne expert Helen Gardner insist that a true assessment of Donne's "spiritual and moral achievement" may be gained only through his sermons, the sonnets best reveal his extreme capacity for passion and ecstasy.

From the opening line, "Batter my heart, three person'd God," the reader understands the speaker does not seek a Christian God who is gentle or compassionate. The three persons referenced constitute the holy trinity composed of Christ the Son, the Holy Spirit, and God the Father, and the speaker commands that all three attack his heart, the term Batter suggesting repeated blows. That line contains a caesura due to the semicolon that follows the apostrophe to God then continues with enjambment into the second line: "for, you / As yet but knock, breathe, shine, and seek to mend." This series of verbs reflects on various biblical characteristics of Christ, with knock representing a polite request to open a door. In Revelation 3:20 Christ states, in part, "Behold, I stand at the door, and knock: if any man hear my voice, and open the door, I will come in to him." Donne will extend this conceit throughout the sonnet.

The speaker does not want his deity to hesitate at the door. He explains, using paradox, that in order for him to "ride, and stand," God must "o'erthrow" him. As ore undergoing transformative purification into valuable metal, he needs God's "force, to break, blow, burn, and make me new." Donne moves into one of his favorite metaphors, expressing a single being as a larger geographic expanse, as the speaker continues, "I, like an usurp'd town, to another due, / Labour to admit you." He explains that another force has overtaken him, suggesting evil or the devil, and follows up on the previous reference to a knock on the door by stating he works to "admit" the deity, but to no avail: "but O, to no end." Although logic should move him to act, "Reason your viceroy in me, me should defend," reason has been taken captive by the opposing force, "and proves weak or untrue." The speaker offers a dual explanation for his incapacity to open the door to God's gentle prod. His use of logic lacks strength or proves false, causing the speaker to be "betroth'd unto your enemy." Here Donne compares the promise through law of a woman to a man to his promise to God's "enemy," or Satan. The comparison refl ects on the biblical comparison of Christ to a bridegroom, with the church his bride.

In the final four lines Donne builds to a mighty climax, avoiding the problem of a weak concluding couplet that some plagued some poets. He again turns to allusions to violence. Having introduced the idea of romantic love as a conceit, he extends that conceit, insisting that God "Divorce me, untie, or break that knot again." By Jewish law an engagement proved as strong a bond as a marriage, and the betrothal "knot" that tied two people together could only be broken through a second decree of law, a divorce. The speaker then begins the three lines that depict one of the most violent of attacks, a rape, made clear through the use of "ravish": "Take me to you, imprison me, for I / Except you'enthral me, never shall be free, / Nor ever chaste, except you ravish me." What some readers have missed is that Donne produces a double paradox, equating imprisonment with freedom and chastity with the act of sex, quite obviously not making a literal suggestion. In addition to the shocking allusion to violence, that a male would assume the role of the female as an object of attack was even more unusual, a fact of interest to later feminist and psychoanalytic critics.

Such outlandish expression proved a hallmark of metaphysical writing, and Donne would be eventually recognized as the most skillful of those who attempted it. While several centuries had to pass before society embraced his expression as art in its purest form, Donne's poetry at last received its due.

EASTER WINGS

Easter Wings

BY GEORGE HERBERT

Lord, who createdst man in wealth and store,
Though foolishly he lost the same,
Decaying more and more,
Till he became
Most poore:
With thee
O let me rise
As larks, harmoniously,
And sing this day thy victories:
Then shall the fall further the flight in me.
My tender age in sorrow did beginne
And still with sicknesses and shame.
Thou didst so punish sinne,
That I became
Most thinne.
With thee
Let me combine,
And feel thy victorie:
For, if I imp my wing on thine,
Affliction shall advance the flight in me.

Easter Wings is a poem by George Herbert which was published in his posthumous collection, *The Temple* (1633). It was originally formatted sideways on facing pages and is in the tradition of shaped poems that goes back to ancient Greek sources.

The Renaissance revival of interest in ancient Greek poetry brought to light a few poems preserved in the Greek anthology in which the shape of the lay-out mimics the poem's sense. Among these was one in the shape of wings by Simmias of Rhodes. The poem is in the form of an allusive riddle whose subject is Eros, the god of love, but where the only hint of his wings is contained in the adjective referring to him, "swift-flying". These poems and their like were later imitated in Renaissance Neo-Latin verse and the fashion then spread to vernacular literatures as well.

Stephen Hawes was the first English author to take this up in his intricate "A pair of wings" in about 1500. But whereas the Classical example is shaped so that the wings rise and fall from the centre, as happens also in Herbert's "Easter Wings", Hawes makes the lines diminish to wing tips in a crescent from the wider body of the poem's centre and backs it up with an alternative short poem lying behind the main text.

The speaker begins by stating that God created human beings to enjoy peace and abundance (line 1). However, humans lost this initial Paradise due to sin. Their situation became worse and worse (2-5). Then the speaker addresses God directly and asks to rise up to the sky like a lark (6-8). As an Easter poem, the image of birds and wings symbolizes Christ's resurrection. The speaker then calls for humanity to join Christ and celebrate the "victory" of resurrection over death (9). If they can succeed in this, then even the "Fall," the expulsion from Paradise due to sin, will have been worth it because it allowed believers to rise with Christ (10)

The second stanza tells a similar story from the perspective of the individual speaker. Even at a young age, he suffered (11-12). This was a punishment given by God, just like the punishment given to Adam and Eve (13). The speaker's life became increasingly diminished and his health began to suffer (14-15). As in the first stanza, half-way through, the speaker begins to address God directly. He asks to feel the victory of the resurrection and join God (16-18). Using the metaphor of "imping," a term from falconry that means adding feathers to an existing wing, the speaker asks to rise with Christ to the Kingdom of Heaven (19). If he succeeds, it is because of the great lows and pains he suffered taught him how to fly (20).

The shape of the poem mirrors its message. In each of the two wing-shaped stanzas, the story can be tracked through the length of the lines. When the lines are longest, at the beginning and the end of each stanza, the story is most hopeful. The thinnest lines represent the depth of the speaker's despair.

What is the poem about?

This poem is a prayer containing assorted elements: praise, confession, petition, admission of defeat, and anticipation of victory. It is a prayer about the general state of mankind and the particular state of the speaker. It is a prayer that sees the whole of Christian life as it deals with loss, decay, affliction, descent, sorrow, and sin alongside harmony, victory, ascent, advancement, and dependence. Above all, it is a petition to partake in the power of Easter wings to give flight to the fallen.

This is a pattern poem in that its shape reflects aspects of its meaning. The shape of the lines are like the movement of wings in flight and reflect the fall and rise of the lark's flight and also of the fall of man and the rise of the Easter event.

<u>EXPLANATIONS</u>

1.Lord, who createdst man in wealth and store,
Though foolishly he lost the same,
Decaying more and more,
Till he became
Most poore:
With thee
O let me rise
As larks, harmoniously,
And sing this day thy victories:
Then shall the fall further the flight in me.

Here the subject is mankind and the fall. After the descent from the creation through the fall to "most poor" at the mid-point of the stanza in line 5, the thoughts ascend with the speaker's petition to rise victoriously with the Lord on Easter. Finally, the opposites of fall and flight are united and reconciled as the stanza closes.

The speaker of "Easter Wings" addresses the Christian God as "Lord" at the opening of the first verse. "Man in wealth and store" is what this deity created. Everything Adam, the very first man, could require was present when he was formed. He had everything he should have been happy with food, shelter, and comfort. In the following lines, Herbert makes a subtle allusion to the Fall. He skips over the specifics of Adam and Eve along with the forbidden fruit. Rather, Jesus immediately addresses humanity's "foolishness" and the loss of all that God has made for them. Things started to "more and more" deteriorate till "man" was "pstanza

The joyful and upbeat vision decreases as the lines do. The poem's shortest lines are its darkest. Then, when they grow, everything brightens up again.

The speaker inserts themself into the poetry in the second part of this verse. He speaks to God, pleading with him to let him "rise" like a "lark." In this analogy, the speaker is compared to a bird that is exalted beyond human folly. The speaker wants to overcome Adam's decisions. Additionally, the speaker adds the Easter motif at this point in the poem. His desire is to rise with "thee." This alludes to the occasion that is customarily observed to commemorate Christ's resurrection. He requests permission to "sing" of his achievements and to climb to the extent that mankind was brought down in the final lines of the stanza.

With a direct approach to "Lord," the first stanza bemoans the state of humanity. By calling Adam "foolish," "weak," and "betray'd," it alludes to Adam's fall from grace and emphasises the weight of inherited sin as well as the loss of pristine innocence. The speaker feels "bound," unable to "reach" the divine, as a result of this fallen existence.

2.My tender age in sorrow did beginne
And still with sicknesses and shame.
Thou didst so punish sinne,
That I became
Most thinne.
With thee
Let me combine,
And feel thy victorie:
For, if I imp my wing on thine,
Affliction shall advance the flight in me.

The focus shifts to the particular situation of the speaker as sin and punishment diminish him to "most thin" in line 15. At that point, as at the mid-point in stanza 1, the lines begin to expand with the speaker's petition to combine with the Lord in victory "this day." And as in the last line of stanza 1, opposites (affliction and advancement) are united and reconciled at the fullest point of expansion. Biblical allusions. In the speaker's petitioning of the Lord for a renewal of strength, there are two possible biblical allusions: Isaiah 40:31 and Malachi 4:2.

The speaker of "Easter Wings" keeps using first-person pronouns in the second stanza. He claims that because of the previous man's decisions, he grew up into "sorrow." The actions of Adam and Eve continue to affect him. The vision grows increasingly melancholic as the lines get thinner. He talks about the sin, the illness, and the gloom in his own life. It seems impossible to escape until the lines begin to widen once more. In the middle of the second stanza, the poem reverses course and emphasises how the speaker will rise "With thee," or with God. The speaker acknowledges his dependence on God for flight. He will therefore "imp," or support himself, by using the feathers on God's wings. The speaker hopes to overcome the sin that is the foundation of the human race in this way.

The poem does, however, take a more upbeat tone in the second stanza. By saying, "With thee," the speaker alludes to dependence on God's favour while acknowledging the power of Christ's resurrection. By attempting to "imp" his wings with "a feather of thine," he is alluding to the divine for assistance and vigour. This "imping" represents a longing to rise above the constraints of sin and death.

The repeated cry, "LIFT me up," deepens the speaker's longing. Acknowledging his frailty, he says he cannot "rise" without God's help. The concept of "wings" now denotes both metamorphosis and ascent. The speaker aims to transform and obtain the spiritual wings required for flight by taking feathers from God's wings.

The poem ends with a stirring proclamation of hope and trust. The speaker declares, "I shall then praise," implying that he will overcome sin and arrive at a place of adoration and praise with God's assistance. The last words, "I have a hope that thou wilt take pleasure in my flight," reaffirm his faith that his ascent and participation in the everlasting celebration of Easter's victory. "Easter Wings" is essentially a contemplative prayer on how Christ's sacrifice has redeemed humanity. It shows the battle with sin, the desire for spiritual ascent, and the final reliance on God's grace to accomplish real spiritual flight and give thanks to Him in everlasting delight. Despite its short length, the poem leaves a deep impression on the reader with its stirring message of transformation and optimism.

SHORT QUESTIONS AND ANSWERS

1. What is the main idea of the poem's first stanza?

Answer: The main idea of the poem's first stanza is the speaker's desire to be transformed by God's love and to be made new in Christ.

2. What does the speaker mean by "ravish me" in the poem?

Answer: The speaker means that he wants God to overwhelm him with His love and to take control of his life.

3. What is the significance of the image of the "prisoner" in the poem?

Answer: The image of the prisoner represents the speaker's feeling of being trapped in his own sin and imperfection, and his desire to be set free by God's love.

4. What is the main theme of the poem?

Answer: The main theme of the poem is the speaker's desire to be transformed by God's love and to be made new in Christ.

5. How does the speaker describe his current state?

Answer: The speaker describes himself as being in a state of sin and imperfection, and as being trapped in his own desires and fears.

6. What does the speaker ask God to do to him?

Answer: The speaker asks God to break, blow, burn, and make him new, to transform him and to make him into a new creation.

ESSAY QUESTIONS AND ANSWERS

1. Analyze the poem's use of metaphor and imagery. How do these literary devices contribute to the poem's meaning and effect?

Answer: The poem uses metaphor and imagery to convey the speaker's desire to be transformed by God's love. The metaphor of the battering ram, for example, represents the speaker's desire to be broken down and remade by God's love. The use of imagery and metaphor creates a rich and complex texture of meaning that rewards close reading and analysis.

2. Discuss the theme of surrender in the poem. How does the speaker's desire to surrender to God's love relate to the broader themes of the poem?

Answer: The theme of surrender is central to the poem, as the speaker desires to surrender to God's love and to be transformed by it. This desire for surrender is related to the broader themes of the poem, including the speaker's desire to be made new in Christ, and to be set free from his own sin and imperfection.

3. Analyze the poem's use of biblical allusion and imagery. How do these literary devices contribute to the poem's meaning and effect?

Answer: The poem uses biblical allusion and imagery to convey the speaker's desire to be transformed by God's love. The allusion to the Trinity, for example, represents the speaker's desire to be made new in Christ. The use of biblical allusion and imagery creates a sense of depth and complexity, and highlights the speaker's desire to be transformed by God's love.

4. Analyze the poem's use of imagery and symbolism. How do these literary devices contribute to the poem's meaning and effect?

Answer: The poem uses imagery and symbolism to convey the speaker's desire to be transformed by God's love. The image of the battering ram, for example, represents the speaker's desire to be broken down and remade by God's love. The use of imagery and symbolism creates a rich and complex texture of meaning that rewards close reading and analysis.

5. Discuss the theme of transformation in the poem. How does the speaker's desire to be transformed by God's love relate to the broader themes of the poem?

Answer: The theme of transformation is central to the poem, as the speaker desires to be transformed by God's love and to be made new in Christ. This desire for transformation is related to the broader themes of the poem, including the speaker's desire to be set free from his own sin and imperfection, and to be made into a new creation.

6. Analyze the poem's use of metaphor and simile. How do these literary devices contribute to the poem's meaning and effect?

Answer: The poem uses metaphor and simile to convey the speaker's desire to be transformed by God's love. The metaphor of the battering ram, for example, represents the speaker's desire to be broken down and remade by God's love. The use of metaphor and simile creates a rich and complex texture of meaning that rewards close reading and analysis.

A CRITICAL ANALYSIS OF THE POEM

The poem begins with a long address to God beginning with the word "Lord." The speaker then interrupts his plea to God by describing the latter as the creator of "man," meaning both humanity and the first man, Adam. Though human life began in a state of carefree abundance in the Garden of Eden, God ceased his generosity when people began to sin. Contrasting the "wealth" of man's early state to the "poor" post-Paradise situation, the lines of the poem shorten as man's status decreases. Yet once things reach their nadir or lowest point, and the lines of the poem are a mere two syllables, the fortunes of man begin to increase again. The speaker resumes his address by asking to rise with God the same way that larks fly—a rich symbol that stands for rebirth, Christ's ascension during the Resurrection, as well as the poet as a singer of songs. The speaker then asks to sing the victories of God, most specifically the victory of life over death represented by Christ's Easter rising. The first stanza ends with a powerful line that makes us reassess everything that came before. "Shall the fall further flight" means that the fall from God's grace is, paradoxically, the exact thing that will allow humanity to soar. This builds on the theological concept of felix culpa,

Latin for "fortunate fall." The idea is that the Fall was a good thing, because it paved the way for Christ's resurrection, which will redeem mankind. Hebert again plays with the more common meaning of "fall," as describing a movement downward, by ending the poem with images of rising upward.

The second stanza parallels the first in meaning and shape. The long lines represent fullness and spiritual heights while the short lines represent the depths of despair experienced as a punishment for sin. If the first stanza followed humanity's difficult but justified journey from high to low back to high, here the story follows the perspective of the individual speaker. Even at a "tender" or young age, the speaker experienced sorrow. If the first man, Adam started life in joy and abundance, everyone who came after started at a lower point. However, as the lines shorten, the speaker's state gets even worse. He experiences "sickness and shame," which are God's punishment for sin. His low spiritual standing is mirrored by his poor health, most specifically his sickly thinness. After reaching his lowest point, the speaker again addresses God. He asks to join with God and not only to "sing" about the victory of Christ's resurrection but to partake in it; he wants to "feel" it. Using a technical term from the practice of falconry, the speaker asks to "imp" his wing to God's: in other words, the speaker is a feather and wants to be fastened to God's wing so he can rise up. The poem then ends with another reference to the idea of felix culpa. In a parallel formulation to the end of the first stanza, the second stanza end with a declaration that "Affliction shall advance the flight in me." Pain and suffering have taught the speaker how to fly.

This short poem is filled with complex parallel and symmetrical structures. First, the two wings mirror each other in the way they are laid out on the page. Then there is the parallel biography of the speaker and humanity as a whole. Both stanzas have the same structure of moving high-low-high along with the diminishing and increasing length of the lines. Finally, many of the lines parallel each other structurally and grammatically. The lowest point in stanza one describes humanity at its "Most poore" while the equivalent point in stanza two talks about the speaker as "most thinne." Similarly, the first appeal to God is "O let me rise" while the second is "Let me combine." Through all of these parallelisms, the poem suggests that the fate of man as a whole mirrors the fate of the individual man who is speaking. Each individual life mirrors the story of humanity. Similarly, the poem's message is that both humanity and each individual human can use their fallen state to be resurrected—if only they model themselves on Christ and tie themselves to God. The happiest fate for man is to be a feather on God's wing.

CHAPTER FOUR

THE RETREAT

The Retreat
BY HENRY VAUGHAN
Happy those early days! when I
Shined in my angel infancy.
Before I understood this place
Appointed for my second race,
Or taught my soul to fancy aught
But a white, celestial thought;
When yet I had not walked above
A mile or two from my first love,
And looking back, at that short space,
Could see a glimpse of His bright face;
When on some gilded cloud or flower
My gazing soul would dwell an hour,
And in those weaker glories spy
Some shadows of eternity;
Before I taught my tongue to wound
My conscience with a sinful sound,
Or had the black art to dispense
A several sin to every sense,
But felt through all this fleshly dress
Bright shoots of everlastingness.
O, how I long to travel back,
And tread again that ancient track!
That I might once more reach that plain
Where first I left my glorious train,
From whence th' enlightened spirit sees

That shady city of palm trees.
But, ah! my soul with too much stay
Is drunk, and staggers in the way.
Some men a forward motion love;
But I by backward steps would move,
And when this dust falls to the urn,
In that state I came, return.

<u>Word Notes</u>:_Early days_ - childhood. _Angel-infancy_ - divine infancy. _Second race_ - life in this world, our original home is the heaven and the life there is our first race.

Fancy - think. _Aught_ - anything. _Celestial_ - heavenly. _First love_ - God in heaven, our first parent.

Gilded cloud - cloud tinged with the golden light of the rising Sun. Gazing - eager or intent. Dwell - contemplate. Spy - espy or see. Shadows of eternity - reflection of eternal world or heaven.

Conscience - mind. Black art - black magic which was forbidden art. Dispense - distribute. Fleshly dress - our gross body, metaphorically our body is the covering of our soul. Shoots of everlastingness - the glory that shoots from the face of God.

Ancient track - childhood time or path. _Glorious train_ - God and angels. _Enlightened_ - liberated. _City of palm trees_ - city of God , a picture in Bible.

Staggers - falters. _Dust_ - the remaining parts when the body is burnt after death. _Urn_ - vessel for keeping the ashes of the dead persons

CRITICAL SUMMARY:

Henry Vaughan's **'The Retreat'** is a metaphysical devotional poem where the poet expresses the glory of childhood and his earnest desire to step backward to his childhood. The poet wants to look forward to the heavenly bliss and peace which he knows very well that only childhood can confer upon him. So he wants to go backstep to his pollution free childhood where there was no material pleasures and entertainments which can provoke him to do any further wrong.

The poet with broken heart yearns for that divine glorious state of childhood as he becomes very tired of his present profitable life. He feels horrible among this gross pleasures.

He says in this poem that in that time of "angel infancy" no sinful thought could stand in the way to his divine communion with God. But his present life of material pleasure makes a distance with his "**first love**" i.e. God.

When he realises that there is a huge distance with his love, he wants eagerly to go back to heaven from where he came from. He wants to bid good bye to the earthly pleasure and his eagerness is clearly visible in the last four lines of the poem:

"Some men a forward motion love;

But I backward steps would move,

And when this dust falls to the urn,

In the state I came, return."

The word "**retreat**" means 's a period of time when somebody stops his usual activities and goes to a quite place for prayer and thought'. The poet Vaughan appropriately uses the word to express his point of view. Here he wants that kind of retreat where he can again see the "glorious train" of angels in the "shady city of palm trees". After a long painfpainful journey he wants to go back to the original home i.e. Heaven.

The same tone is also found in Wordsworth as he writes,

"From God, who is our home:

Heaven lies about us in our infancy."

In Jonne Donne's "Batter My Heart", we also see that he also wants to purify his soul by the battering of God because his soul becomes sinful and polluted.

Important lines and Explanations

Line 1 - 4 :

" **Happy those early days, when I**

Shined in my Angel-infancy !

Before I understood this place

Appointed for my second race,"

The speaker (poet) candidly confesses that his childhood was full of happiness, touched with celestial bliss. His infancy was redolent with angelic purity and glory. The time mentioned here is that period of time when the poet was already allotted his second existence i.e. the life in this world, but he had no knowledge of this unreal place.

Line 5 - 8 :

" **Or taught my soul to fancy aught**

But a white, celestial thought;

When yet I had not walked above

A mile or two from my first love, "

The childhood is that period when the poet was full of pure divine thought as his soul could not think about anything of this world.The childhood is a very short journey,one or two miles,that is a very short period, from heaven and God.

Line 9 -14 :

" And looking back, at that short space,
Could see a glimpse of His bright face;
When on some gilded cloud or flower
My gazing soul would dwell an hour,
And in those weaker glories spy
Some shadows of eternity; "

As childhood is a very short journey from heaven, he was able to catch some glimpses of that glorious place and the bright face of God. Poet's eager soul would contemplate for an hour on the golden cloud of morning and the golden flowers and through this his memory, though now weaker, could have some reflections of divine types of heavenly life.

Line 15 -20 :

" Before I taught my tongue to wound
My conscience with a sinful sound,
Or had the black art to dispense
A several sin to every sense,
But felt through all this fleshly dress
Bright shoots of everlastingness. "

In childhood the poet had not yet learnt hard language to prick others and had not polluted his mind with sinful thought. Then he knew no black magic or cunningness to distribute sin to his every sense. The glory of God could penetrate the gross body of the poet.

Line 21 -26 :

" O, how I long to travel back,
And tread again that ancient track!
That I might once more reach that plain
Where first I left my glorious train,
From whence th' enlightened spirit sees
That shady city of palm trees."

Being tired in this world the poet earnestly desire to go back and tread on the childhood land where he must get the angels and God as his companion and from that place his liberated spirit could notice the blissful city of God.

Line 27 -32 :

" But, ah! my soul with too much stay

Is drunk, and staggers in the way.

Some men a forward motion love;

But I by backward steps would move,

And when this dust falls to the urn,

In that state I came, return."

The poet has become intoxicated with the enjoyment and experience of this mundane life and he is in a staggering state in the attempt of retreating to childhood. Is it not possible ? Some people like to move forward, but the poet likes to move backward, to the divine infancy. It is possible when the body of the poet would turn to dust and be kept in urn. Actually after death the poet may be gifted another childhood if resurrection is granted by God.

<u>EXPLANATIONS</u>

1.Happy those early days! when I

Shined in my Angel-infancy.

Before I understood this

place Appointed for my second race.

These lines have been taken from the poem entitled "The Retreat" written by Henry Vaughan. Vaughan is one of the foremost poets of the metaphysical school. He is a true disciple of John Donne. He has written this poem in praise of childhood.

The poet believes in the fact that before being born on this earth, the human soul passes a period of life in Heaven. He says that the early days of his childhood were the happiest period of his life. Those were the days when he knew none of the evils of this world, where he had come to cover the second part of his journey in Heaven before birth on this earth. Then his thoughts were pure and innocent. He had not gained the experience of this world and so his soul had not learnt to think about anything else except God. As he thought only of God and Heaven, his thoughts were pure like that of an angel.

These lines are remarkable because they express the sincere feeling of the poet in passionate language.

2.When yet I had not walked above

A mile or two from my first love,

And looking back, at that short space,

Could see a glimpse of His bright face;

When on some gilded cloud, or flower

My gazing soul would dwell an hour,
And in those weaker glories spy
Some shadows of eternity.

These lines have been taken from the poem entitled The Retreat written by Henry Vaughan. Vaughan belongs to the romantic school of poetry. Here, he expresses his idea that in childhood man is nearer to Heaven, and gets occasional glimpses of God.

The view contained in these lines is based on the belief that man's life on this earth is not the first of his existence. He lived in Heaven before birth on this earth and the life on this earth represents a journey from Heaven. The distance from birth to childhood, which is the distance from Heaven to childhood, is not much. While residing in Heaven, human soul has no attraction for anything else except God. Therefore, God is his first love. When human soul comes over to this world, it brings with it the love of God. As the distance from Heaven to childhood is short, man can easily look behind and catch a glimpse of the bright face of God. In support of it the poet says that when at times he looked steadfastly at the golden clouds and beautiful flowers, although they were far less radiant and glorious as compared to Heavenly objects, still he noticed in them some reflections of God.

These lines are representative of Henry Vaughan. They express his inmost desire to recapture the spirit of childhood. The language is metaphysical in the accepted sense of the term.

3.Before I taught my tongue to wound
My conscience with a sinful sound,
Or had the black art to dispense
A several sin to every sense,
But felt through all this fleshly dress
Bright shoots of everlastingness.

These lines have been taken from the poem entitled The Retreat written by Henry Vaughan. Vaughan was a religious poet of the metaphysical school. Here, he points out the difference between childhood and advanced age.

As the poet puts it, a child has no need to tell lies. A child does not indulge in sins. But as man grows up, he learns to deceive his conscience by telling lies and by calling right what is wrong. Gradually, a man learns how to employ his various senses in sinful acts. He utters filthy language and lies with his tongue, looks at lustful sights with his eyes and commits murder, loot, rape etc, with his other limbs. In this way he commits sin with all his limbs. The poet says that before he had learnt this black art he had something divine in him. Although the ordinary body hinders attainment of spiritual ends, in childhood the poet felt some glow of immortality even though possessing a body of flesh and blood.

These lines are important because they reflect the highly imaginative mind of Vaughan. The style is what Coleridge calls "neutral".

4.O, how I long to travel back,

And tread again that ancient track!

That I might once more reach that plain

Where first I left my glorious train,

From whence th' enlightened spirit sees

That shady city of palm trees.

These lines form part of the poem entitled The Retreat written by Henry Vaughan. Vaughan belonged to the metaphysical school of poetry. Here, he expresses his desire to return back to childhood.

The poet has come a long way from childhood passing through youth and manhood. He wants to travel back to the plain of childhood through the same old path. His object in doing so is to regain the company of those guardian angels who kept watch over him during his childhood. The Bible says that the child lies in Abraham's bosom. Vaughan has borrowed this idea from the Bible. His other object is to catch once again the vision of Heaven-the shady city of palm trees. The vision of Heaven can be had only by those who have enlightened spirit. As a child lives near god, it gets something of his divine glow. Hence, a child can easily have a vision of Heaven.

These lines are typical of Vaughan. Though the idea is commonplace. the treatment is quite original.

5.But ah! my soul with too much stay

Is drunk, and staggers in the way.

Or,

Some men a forward motion love,

But I by backward steps would move,

And when this dust falls to the urn,

In that state I came, return.

These are the concluding lines of the poem entitled The Retreat written by Henry Vaughan.-Vaughan is an important poet in the realm of metaphysical poetry. Here, Vaughan expresses his inmost desire to return back to childhood. But he feels difficulty in doing so. He had advanced much in years and picked up many evils of this world. His brain has become intoxicated with the vanities of this world. Now his fancies do not consist of celestial thought. He no longer sees the vision of God. Under the influence of worldly intoxication, he cannot move with firm steps on the path leading to the place of childhood. Yet, unlike other men, he still wants to trace his steps back. While common people want to gain more and more experience of the world, the poet wants to get rid of the experience gained by him and to go back to the angel-infancy. His ardent desire is to return after death in the same state of purity and innocence in which he took birth on this earth. He wants to shed all the grossness of this material world here, before departing for Heaven.

These lines are remarkable because they express the sincere feelings of the poet in simple, sensuous and passionate language.

Short Questions and Answers

1. What is the speaker's main concern in the poem?

Answer: The speaker's main concern is his longing for a lost innocence and his desire to recapture the simplicity and joy of his childhood.

2. How does the speaker describe his childhood?

Answer: The speaker describes his childhood as a time of happiness, simplicity, and innocence, when he was free from the cares and complexities of adulthood.

3. What does the speaker mean by "the world's loud toys"?

Answer: The speaker means the distractions and allurements of the world, which he sees as corrupting and destructive of innocence.

4. What is the speaker's main complaint about the world?

Answer: The speaker's main complaint is that the world is corrupt and distracting, and that it has lost its innocence and simplicity.

5. How does the speaker describe his childhood?

Answer: The speaker describes his childhood as a time of happiness, simplicity, and innocence, when he was free from the cares and complexities of adulthood.

6. What does the speaker mean by "the shades of night"?

Answer: The speaker means the darkness and obscurity of the world, which he sees as a place of sin and corruption.

Essay Questions and answers

1. Analyze the poem's use of imagery and symbolism. How do these literary devices contribute to the poem's meaning and effect?

Answer: The poem uses imagery and symbolism to convey the speaker's longing for a lost innocence and his desire to recapture the simplicity and joy of his childhood. The image of the child, for example, represents innocence and simplicity, while the image of the world represents corruption and complexity. The use of imagery and symbolism creates a rich and complex texture of meaning that rewards close reading and analysis.

2. Discuss the theme of nostalgia in the poem. How does the speaker's nostalgia for his childhood relate to the broader themes of the poem?

Answer: The theme of nostalgia is central to the poem, as the speaker looks back longingly on his childhood and desires to recapture its simplicity and joy. This nostalgia is related to the broader themes of the poem, including the speaker's desire to escape the corruptions and complexities of adulthood and to find a sense of peace and innocence in a world that seems to have lost its way.

3. Analyze the poem's use of metaphor and simile. How do these literary devices contribute to the poem's meaning and effect?

Answer: The poem uses metaphor and simile to convey the speaker's longing for a lost innocence and his desire to recapture the simplicity and joy of his childhood. The metaphor of the child, for example, represents innocence and simplicity, while the simile of the world's loud toys represents the distractions and allurements of adulthood. The use of metaphor and simile creates a rich and complex texture of meaning that rewards close reading and analysis.

4. Analyze the poem's use of contrast. How does the speaker use contrast to convey his ideas and emotions?

Answer: The poem uses contrast to convey the speaker's ideas and emotions, particularly the contrast between the simplicity and innocence of childhood and the complexity and corruption of adulthood. This contrast highlights the speaker's nostalgia for his childhood and his desire to escape the corruptions of the world.

5. Discuss the theme of innocence in the poem. How does the speaker's desire for innocence relate to the broader themes of the poem?

Answer: The theme of innocence is central to the poem, as the speaker desires to recapture the simplicity and innocence of his childhood. This desire for innocence is related to the broader themes of the poem, including the speaker's criticism of the world and his desire to escape its corruptions.

6. Analyze the poem's use of symbolism. How does the speaker use symbols to convey his ideas and emotions?

Answer: The poem uses symbolism to convey the speaker's ideas and emotions, particularly the symbol of the child, which represents innocence and simplicity. The use of symbolism creates a rich and complex texture of meaning that rewards close reading and analysis.

Central idea of the poem 'The Retreat'

'The Retreat' of Henry Vaughan is a religious poem as well as a metaphysical poem, better to say a perfect example of metaphysical religious poetry. That the poem is a religious one is conspicuous in the very form of the title word. The term 'Retreat' conforms with the Military Terminology, as it is the signal for a military force to withdraw the army, going back from threatened position. Such a term of hard reality (of battlefield) is brought to the arena of spiritualism, from pugnacity to religiosity. In simple term 'retreat' means 'going back' and obviously a desire of going back on the part of the poet has formed the subject matter and the theme of this poem. The Poet longs for the retreat.

Glorification of childhood: Covering a long path of this mundane life the poet has come to the realisation that the purity of his soul is somehow diminished to a great extent, divine feelings are declining and mind is being corrupted, sinned rather :"A several sin to every sense". Deep sense of disappointment dawns in him which finds expression in the very opening lines of the poem : "Happy those early days, when I/ Shined in my Angel-infancy !" Really, infancy is angelic as this stage is redolent with innocence, full of simplicity and purity, a perfect state for divinity. According to the Platonic doctrine of immortality and of antenatal existence of the soul the life on this temporal world is not our first state of existence, it is our 'second race'. The idea is that the soul before its birth had its existence in heaven and naturally, when the soul wears the 'fleshly dress' i.e. takes birth in this earth, it comes with full memory of that celestial place. Black art , experience or earthly sins can not corrupt the angelic state of innocence and purity of childhood and for this a child "Could see a glimpse of His bright face" , the face of his 'First Love', the face of God. In the weaker and broken memory of a child "Some shadows of eternity" are reflected and divine rays enter through every pores of the 'fleshly dress'. To much stay in this seemingly delightful and pleasurable world, to much absorption in the money, wealth and worldly relation pose as the hindrance for going back to the celestial state of mind. Poet's dolour of mind is manifested in his candid confession : " O how I long to travel back / And tread again that ancient track !" That the childhood is the best part of human life is acknowledged and acclaimed in the 'The Retreat'.

Religious aspect : Herbert, the saint of the metaphysical school, influenced much on Henry Vaughan and turned him to the field of religious poetry. Religion helps a person to realize his/her present profane position and directs that person the way of deliverance, the way of liberation of the soul from the gross body and the delusion of human life. Only the divine field and feeling can help one to find the outlet of this labyrinthine world. That very religious message is explicitly uttered by Vaughan in this poem. The avidity for the retreat to the 'Angel-infancy' is nothing but the poet's longing for the divinity, his 'total surrender' to God. "Sin has dimmed the eye of the soul" and God's revelation is not felt by the poet. The reminiscence of childhood may lead him to the thought of God and Eden, the garden of paradise . As the poem is replete with the Christian belief , it a religious poem with least doubt. The poem expresses the longing for God, for the lost vision of innocence and the sin-fettered existence of man in his sojourned life in this world. The expressions like 'Angel-infancy', 'second race', 'first love', 'shadows of eternity', 'Bright shoots of everlastingness', 'City of palm trees' etc. confirm the religious ambience of this poem , Biblical touch throughout the verse.

Metaphysical and philosophical ideas: 'The Retreat' of Vaughan is a Metaphysical poem and a philosophical lyric. The poem is metaphysical in the intimate sense of the term as the theme is imbrued and inspired with the philosophical conception of life and the universe. Sudden beginning and the argumentative structure, though not direct, add to the metaphysical quality. There is no dearth of metaphysical conceit, 'Bright shoots of everlastingness' being a very compact and effective example of it.

The philosophical idea lies in the eternal law that governs human life and existence. Human being who is destined to live in this world has no power to recede, a grown-up person can never regain his/her childhood physically. Poet's craving for 'backward steps' is not possible, if he rejects the 'forward motion'. Only the 'forward motion' can take this perishable body to the last moment on this earth. Rebirth may again award a person the 'Angel-infancy', the blissful childhood, and this is comprehended and confirmed by the poet in the concluding lines : " And when this dust falls to the urn, / In that state I came, return."

CHAPTER FIVE

CHRIST CRUCIFIED

Christ Crucified

Richard Crashaw

THY restless feet now cannot go
For us and our eternal good,
As they were ever wont. What though
They swim, alas! in their own flood?
Thy hands to give Thou canst not lift,
Yet will Thy hand still giving be;
It gives, but O, itself's the gift!
It gives tho' bound, tho' bound 'tis free!

Introduction :-

The poem follows a tightly structured quatrain form with irregular rhyme and a lyrical cadence typical of Crashaw's devotional verse, echoing metaphysical conceits through paradox and spiritual intensity.

Religious Imagery: The speaker reflects on Christ's immobilized limbs post-crucifixion, drawing focus to hands and feet as instruments of both suffering and ongoing grace, merging physical limitation with divine agency.

Paradox and Devotion: Crashaw emphasizes that though Christ's hands are bound, they remain freely giving—highlighting a metaphysical reversal where limitation amplifies generosity rather than diminishes it.

Contrast with Contemporary Works: Unlike Herbert's restrained introspection or Donne's intellectual argumentation, this poem leans into

Baroque emotionalism, aligning more with continental Catholic aesthetic traditions than with mainstream English Protestant poetry of the time.

Linguistic Features: Archaic diction ("Thou canst not," "'tis") and contraction ("thro'") create a liturgical tone, reinforcing ritualistic reverence and situating the speaker within a sacred, timeless encounter.

Historical Context: Written amid the religious upheavals of mid-17th-century England, the poem's Catholic sympathies mark Crashaw as an outlier, with its emphasis on bodily sacrifice reflecting Counter-Reformation theology.

Less-Discussed Angle: Rather than focusing on redemption through pain, the poem centers on divine continuity—God's active presence persisting beyond the moment of death, suggesting grace is not an event but a perpetual condition.

Place in Author's Oeuvre: Among Crashaw's lesser-known shorter devotional pieces, this stands out for compressing theological complexity into minimal space, lacking the extended imagery of his longer works but achieving similar density.

Tone and Address: The direct apostrophe to Christ personalizes theological doctrine, turning dogma into intimate lament, a mode consistent with Crashaw's mystical inclinations.

Innovation within Convention: While adhering to the era's religious lyric norms—meditation on the Passion, use of paradox—it diverges by assigning agency to Christ's body after death, implying ongoing sacramental activity.

Reference to Context

"Thy restless feet now cannot go
For us and our eternal good,
As they were ever wont. What though
They swim, alas! in their own flood?"

Context:
These lines are addressed to Christ during His Crucifixion. The poet meditates on Christ's suffering on the cross and reflects upon the physical limitations imposed upon Him.

Explanation:
The "restless feet" refer to Christ's active life of preaching, healing, and helping humanity. Earlier, His feet moved constantly for the welfare of

mankind ("our eternal good"). Now, nailed to the cross, they "cannot go." The phrase "swim... in their own flood" is a vivid metaphor referring to Christ's blood flowing from His wounds. Though physically immobilized and bleeding, His sacrifice continues to work for human salvation.

The imagery combines tenderness and intensity. The physical suffering is transformed into a symbol of divine love and redemption.

Significance:

These lines highlight the contrast between Christ's active ministry and His present suffering. They emphasize the idea that even in apparent helplessness, Christ is working for humanity's salvation.

"Thy hands to give Thou canst not lift,
Yet will Thy hand still giving be;
It gives, but O, itself's the gift!
It gives tho' bound, tho' bound 'tis free!"

Context:

The poet continues his meditation, focusing now on Christ's hands nailed to the cross.

Explanation:

Christ's hands, once raised in blessing and charity, are now nailed and unable to move. Yet Crashaw paradoxically says they are "still giving." The greatest gift is not something from His hand but His very self—His life and sacrifice. The line "itself's the gift" conveys the central Christian doctrine of redemption: Christ gives Himself for humanity.

The paradox "bound 'tis free" is characteristic of metaphysical poetry. Though physically bound to the cross, Christ is spiritually free, and through His bondage, He grants spiritual freedom to mankind.

Significance:

The passage powerfully expresses the idea of sacrificial love. It reflects Crashaw's metaphysical style—using paradox, intense emotion, and devotional imagery to express deep theological truths.

Critical Analysis

The given lines are taken from "Christ Crucified" by Richard Crashaw, a prominent Metaphysical poet known for his intense religious devotion and vivid imagery. In this passage, the poet meditates upon Christ's suffering during the Crucifixion and reflects on the spiritual significance of His sacrifice.

The phrase "Thy restless feet now cannot go" refers to Christ's active life before the Crucifixion. His feet once moved constantly to preach, heal, and guide humanity toward salvation. Now, nailed to the cross, they are motionless. The expression "swim... in their own flood" is a powerful metaphor describing Christ's bleeding wounds. Crashaw transforms this painful image into a symbol of divine love. Though physically immobilized, Christ continues to work for "our eternal good." Thus, apparent weakness becomes a source of spiritual strength.

The second stanza shifts attention to Christ's hands. These hands once blessed the poor, healed the sick, and performed miracles. Now they are nailed to the cross and "cannot lift." Yet the poet paradoxically declares that the hands are "still giving." The greatest gift is not material blessing but Christ Himself—"itself's the gift." This line expresses the core Christian doctrine of redemption: Christ offers His own life for humanity's salvation.

The paradox "bound 'tis free" is central to the poem's meaning. Though Christ is physically bound to the cross, His sacrifice brings spiritual freedom to mankind. This contrast between physical limitation and spiritual power is typical of Metaphysical poetry. Crashaw uses paradox, emotional intensity, and religious symbolism to elevate suffering into a divine act of love.

Overall, the passage presents the Crucifixion not as defeat but as the highest expression of generosity and sacrifice. Physical pain is transformed into eternal grace, highlighting the themes of redemption, devotion, and divine love.

CHAPTER SIX

THE EPICURE

THE EPICURE
BY ABRAHAM COWLEY
FILL the bowl with rosy wine,
Around our temples roses twine.
And let us cheerfully awhile,
Like the wine and roses smile.
Crown'd with roses we contemn
Gyge's wealthy diadem.
Today is ours; what do we fear?
Today is ours; we have it here.
Let's treat it kindly, that it may
Wish, at least, with us to stay.
Let's banish business, banish sorrow;
To the Gods belongs tomorrow.

<u>**About the Poet:**</u>

Abraham Cowley (1618 – 28 July 1667) was an English poet and essayist born in the <u>City of London</u> late in 1618. He was one of the leading English poets of the 17th century, with 14 printings of his *Works* published between 1668 and 1721.

He is a transitional figure, a poet who tended to relinquish the emotional values of John Donne and George Herbert and grasp the edges of reason and wit.He was more versatile than the early Metaphysicals: He embraced the influence of Donne and Ben Jonson, relied on the Pindaric form that would take hold in the eighteenth century, conceived of an experimental biblical epic in English (*Davideis*) well in advance of John Milton's major project, and demonstrated an open-mindedness that allowed him to <u>write</u> in support of Francis Bacon, Thomas Hobbes, and the Royal Society. Cowley's elegies on the deaths of William Hervey and Richard Crashaw are extremely frank poems of natural pain and loss, while at the same time the poet recognized the need for the human intellect to be aware of "Things Divine"—the dullness of the earthly as opposed to the reality of the heavenly.

Critical Summary

The poem explores the theme of Epicureanism, which emphasizes the pursuit of pleasure and the avoidance of pain.It employs various poetic devices, including metaphor, simile, and personification, to convey the speaker's message.The speaker's attitude is one of detachment and acceptance, as he acknowledges the fleeting nature of life and the inevitability of death.

The poem features vivid imagery, including the comparison of life to a "short and hasty spark" and the description of death as a "dark and silent grave".The central argument of the poem is that one should live life to the fullest and not worry about the future or the past, as these are beyond one's control.The tone of the poem is contemplative and melancholic, with a sense of resignation and acceptance.The poem is written in a formal, lyrical style, with a consistent rhyme scheme and meter.

Overall, "The Epicure" is a thought-provoking poem that encourages the reader to live in the present moment and to make the most of the time they have.

Questions and Answers:

Question 1: Analyze the theme of Epicureanism in the poem "The Epicure". How does the speaker convey this theme, and what message do you think he is trying to convey?

Answer: The theme of Epicureanism is central to the poem "The Epicure". The speaker conveys this theme through the use of imagery and metaphor, such as the comparison of life to a "short and hasty spark" and the description of death as a "dark and silent grave". The speaker's message is that one should live life to the fullest and not worry about the future or the past, as these are beyond one's control. He encourages the reader to focus on the present moment and to pursue pleasure and happiness.

Question 2: Discuss the speaker's attitude towards death in the poem "The Epicure". How does he view death, and what does this reveal about his philosophy of life?

Answer: The speaker's attitude towards death in the poem "The Epicure" is one of acceptance and detachment. He views death as a natural part of life, and does not seem to fear it. This reveals that the speaker has a stoic philosophy of life, and believes that one should accept the things that are beyond their control. He also believes that one should focus on living in the present moment, rather than worrying about the future or the past.

Question 3: Analyze the use of imagery and metaphor in the poem "The Epicure". How do these literary devices contribute to the poem's meaning and effect?

Answer: The use of imagery and metaphor in the poem "The Epicure" is a key feature of its literary style. The speaker uses imagery and metaphor to convey the theme of Epicureanism, and to create a sense of urgency and impermanence. For example, the comparison of life to a "short and hasty spark" creates a vivid image of the brief and fleeting nature of human existence. The use of imagery and metaphor also adds to the poem's emotional impact, and helps to convey the speaker's message in a powerful and memorable way.

Question 4: Discuss the speaker's philosophy of life in the poem "The Epicure". What values does he seem to hold dear, and how does he think one should live their life?

Answer: The speaker's philosophy of life in the poem "The Epicure" is one of Epicureanism, which emphasizes the pursuit of pleasure and the avoidance of pain. The speaker values simplicity, moderation, and the pursuit of intellectual and aesthetic pleasures. He believes that one should live their life in accordance with reason and nature, and that one should strive to be free from excessive desires and fears.

Question 5: Analyze the tone of the poem "The Epicure". How does the speaker's tone contribute to the poem's meaning and effect?

Answer: The tone of the poem "The Epicure" is contemplative, reflective, and melancholic. The speaker's tone is also detached and accepting, as he acknowledges the fleeting nature of life and the inevitability of death. The tone contributes to the poem's meaning and effect by creating a sense of intimacy and immediacy, and by drawing the reader into the speaker's contemplative and reflective world.

Question 6: Discuss the use of paradox in the poem "The Epicure". How does the speaker use paradox to convey his message?

Answer: The speaker uses paradox to convey his message of living life to the fullest while also acknowledging the inevitability of death. For example, he says "Let us live, my Lesbia, and let us love" while also acknowledging that "our brief and hasty spark of life" will soon be extinguished. This paradox highlights the tension between the desire to live life to the fullest and the reality of mortality.

Question 7: Analyze the speaker's use of classical allusions in the poem "The Epicure". How do these allusions contribute to the poem's meaning and effect?

Answer: The speaker uses classical allusions, such as the reference to Lesbia, to create a sense of cultural and historical depth. These allusions also serve to underscore the speaker's message of living life to the fullest and pursuing pleasure. By invoking the classical tradition, the speaker is able to tap into a rich cultural heritage and add layers of meaning to his poem.

Question 8: Discuss the poem's exploration of the human condition. How does the speaker portray human existence, and what insights does he offer into the human experience?

Answer: The poem portrays human existence as fleeting and ephemeral, subject to the whims of fate and the inevitability of death. The speaker offers insights into the human experience by highlighting the importance of living in the present moment and pursuing pleasure and happiness. He also acknowledges the reality of mortality and the need to accept and make peace with one's own death.

Question 9: Analyze the poem's use of rhetorical devices, such as metaphor and simile. How do these devices contribute to the poem's meaning and effect?

Answer: The poem uses rhetorical devices, such as metaphor and simile, to create vivid and memorable images. For example, the comparison of life to a "short and hasty spark" creates a powerful and evocative image. These devices contribute to the poem's meaning and effect by adding layers of depth and complexity to the speaker's message.

Question 10: Discuss the poem's relevance to contemporary society. How does the speaker's message of living life to the fullest and pursuing pleasure continue to resonate with readers today?

Answer: The poem's message of living life to the fullest and pursuing pleasure continues to resonate with readers today because it speaks to fundamental human desires and aspirations. In a society that often values productivity and achievement over pleasure and enjoyment, the speaker's message serves as a reminder of the importance of living in the present moment and pursuing happiness.

The Rape of the Lock: Canto 1

The Rape of the Lock: Canto 1
By Alexander Pope
Nolueram, Belinda, tuos violare capillos;
Sedjuvat, hoc precibus me tribuisse tuis.
(Martial, Epigrams 12.84)
What dire offence from am'rous causes springs,
What mighty contests rise from trivial things,
I sing—This verse to Caryl, Muse! is due:
This, ev'n Belinda may vouchsafe to view:
Slight is the subject, but not so the praise,
If she inspire, and he approve my lays.
Say what strange motive, Goddess! could compel
A well-bred lord t' assault a gentle belle?
O say what stranger cause, yet unexplor'd,
Could make a gentle belle reject a lord?
In tasks so bold, can little men engage,
And in soft bosoms dwells such mighty rage?
Sol thro' white curtains shot a tim'rous ray,
And op'd those eyes that must eclipse the day;
Now lap-dogs give themselves the rousing shake,
And sleepless lovers, just at twelve, awake:
Thrice rung the bell, the slipper knock'd the ground,
And the press'd watch return'd a silver sound.
Belinda still her downy pillow press'd,
Her guardian sylph prolong'd the balmy rest:

'Twas he had summon'd to her silent bed
The morning dream that hover'd o'er her head;
A youth more glitt'ring than a birthnight beau,
(That ev'n in slumber caus'd her cheek to glow)
Seem'd to her ear his winning lips to lay,
And thus in whispers said, or seem'd to say.
"Fairest of mortals, thou distinguish'd care
Of thousand bright inhabitants of air!
If e'er one vision touch'd thy infant thought,
Of all the nurse and all the priest have taught,
Of airy elves by moonlight shadows seen,
The silver token, and the circled green,
Or virgins visited by angel pow'rs,
With golden crowns and wreaths of heav'nly flow'rs,
Hear and believe! thy own importance know,
Nor bound thy narrow views to things below.
Some secret truths from learned pride conceal'd,
To maids alone and children are reveal'd:
What tho' no credit doubting wits may give?
The fair and innocent shall still believe.
Know then, unnumber'd spirits round thee fly,
The light militia of the lower sky;
These, though unseen, are ever on the wing,
Hang o'er the box, and hover round the Ring.
Think what an equipage thou hast in air,
And view with scorn two pages and a chair.
As now your own, our beings were of old,
And once inclos'd in woman's beauteous mould;
Thence, by a soft transition, we repair
From earthly vehicles to these of air.
Think not, when woman's transient breath is fled,
That all her vanities at once are dead;
Succeeding vanities she still regards,
And tho' she plays no more, o'erlooks the cards.
Her joy in gilded chariots, when alive,
And love of ombre, after death survive.
For when the fair in all their pride expire,
To their first elements their souls retire:

The sprites of fiery termagants in flame
Mount up, and take a Salamander's name.
Soft yielding minds to water glide away,
And sip with Nymphs, their elemental tea.
The graver prude sinks downward to a Gnome,
In search of mischief still on earth to roam.
The light coquettes in Sylphs aloft repair,
And sport and flutter in the fields of air.
Know further yet; whoever fair and chaste
Rejects mankind, is by some sylph embrac'd:
For spirits, freed from mortal laws, with ease
Assume what sexes and what shapes they please.
What guards the purity of melting maids,
In courtly balls, and midnight masquerades,
Safe from the treach'rous friend, the daring spark,
The glance by day, the whisper in the dark,
When kind occasion prompts their warm desires,
When music softens, and when dancing fires?
'Tis but their sylph, the wise celestials know,
Though honour is the word with men below.
Some nymphs there are, too conscious of their face,
For life predestin'd to the gnomes' embrace.
These swell their prospects and exalt their pride,
When offers are disdain'd, and love denied:
Then gay ideas crowd the vacant brain,
While peers, and dukes, and all their sweeping train,
And garters, stars, and coronets appear,
And in soft sounds 'Your Grace' salutes their ear.
'Tis these that early taint the female soul,
Instruct the eyes of young coquettes to roll,
Teach infant cheeks a bidden blush to know,
And little hearts to flutter at a beau.
Oft, when the world imagine women stray,
The Sylphs through mystic mazes guide their way,
Thro' all the giddy circle they pursue,
And old impertinence expel by new.
What tender maid but must a victim fall
To one man's treat, but for another's ball?

When Florio speaks, what virgin could withstand,
If gentle Damon did not squeeze her hand?
With varying vanities, from ev'ry part,
They shift the moving toyshop of their heart;
Where wigs with wigs, with sword-knots sword-knots strive,
Beaux banish beaux, and coaches coaches drive.
This erring mortals levity may call,
Oh blind to truth! the Sylphs contrive it all.
Of these am I, who thy protection claim,
A watchful sprite, and Ariel is my name.
Late, as I rang'd the crystal wilds of air,
In the clear mirror of thy ruling star
I saw, alas! some dread event impend,
Ere to the main this morning sun descend,
But Heav'n reveals not what, or how, or where:
Warn'd by the Sylph, oh pious maid, beware!
This to disclose is all thy guardian can.
Beware of all, but most beware of man!"
He said; when Shock, who thought she slept too long,
Leap'd up, and wak'd his mistress with his tongue.
'Twas then, Belinda, if report say true,
Thy eyes first open'd on a billet-doux;
Wounds, charms, and ardors were no sooner read,
But all the vision vanish'd from thy head.
And now, unveil'd, the toilet stands display'd,
Each silver vase in mystic order laid.
First, rob'd in white, the nymph intent adores
With head uncover'd, the cosmetic pow'rs.
A heav'nly image in the glass appears,
To that she bends, to that her eyes she rears;
Th' inferior priestess, at her altar's side,
Trembling, begins the sacred rites of pride.
Unnumber'd treasures ope at once, and here
The various off'rings of the world appear;
From each she nicely culls with curious toil,
And decks the goddess with the glitt'ring spoil.
This casket India's glowing gems unlocks,
And all Arabia breathes from yonder box.

The tortoise here and elephant unite,
Transform'd to combs, the speckled and the white.
Here files of pins extend their shining rows,
Puffs, powders, patches, bibles, billet-doux.
Now awful beauty puts on all its arms;
The fair each moment rises in her charms,
Repairs her smiles, awakens ev'ry grace,
And calls forth all the wonders of her face;
Sees by degrees a purer blush arise,
And keener lightnings quicken in her eyes.
The busy Sylphs surround their darling care;
These set the head, and those divide the hair,
Some fold the sleeve, whilst others plait the gown;
And Betty's prais'd for labours not her own.

<u>An Introduction to the Poet</u>

Alexander Pope (1688-1744)

Alexander Pope was born in London in 1688. As a Roman Catholic living during a time of Protestant consolidation in England, he was largely excluded from the university system and from political life, and suffered certain social and economic disadvantages because of his religion as well. He was self-taught to a great extent, and was an assiduous scholar from a very early age. He learned several languages on his own, and his early verses were often imitations of poets he admired. His obvious talent found encouragement from his father, a linen-draper, as well as from literary-minded friends. At the age of twelve, Pope contracted a form of tuberculosis that settled in his spine, leaving him stunted and misshapen and causing him great pain for much of his life. He never married, though he formed a number of lifelong friendships in London's literary circles, most notably with Jonathan Swift.

Pope wrote during what is often called the Augustan Age of English literature (indeed, it is Pope's career that defines the age). During this time, the nation had recovered from the English Civil Wars and the Glorious Revolution, and the regained sense of political stability led to a resurgence of support for the arts. For this reason, many compared the period to the reign of Augustus in Rome, under whom both Virgil and Horace had found support for their work. The prevailing taste of the day was neoclassical, and 18th-century English writers tended to value poetry that was learned and allusive, setting less value on originality than the Romantics would in the next century. This literature also tended to be morally and often politically engaged, privileging satire as its dominant mode.

After the publication of The Rape of the Lock, Pope spent many years translating the works of Homer. During the ten years he devoted to this arduous project, he produced very few new poems of his own but refined his taste in literature (and his moral, social, and political opinions) to an incredible degree. When he later recommenced to write original poetry, Pope struck a more serious tone than the one he gave to The Rape of the Lock. These later poems are more severe in their moral judgments and more acid in their satire: Pope's Essay on Man is a philosophical poem on metaphysics, ethics, and human nature, while in the Dunciad, Pope writes a scathing exposé of the bad writers and pseudo-intellectuals of his day. Pope's translations of Homer were successful enough to allow him to move to a comfortable villa in Twickenham in Middlesex, England, where he died at the age of 56 in 1744.

The Features of 18th Century English Literature

The 18th Century English Literature has a unique place in European literary space. Mathew Arnold, the great poet and critic of the Victorian Age sums up the 18th century in English Literature as "The Age of Prose and Reason, our excellent and indispensable 18th century".

In this way, Arnold asserts two significant points about the 18th century: one, it is predominantly the age of prose & reasons and the other, it is exceptionally rich and noticeable period in the literary productions. A close examination of this period substantiates these observations of Mathew Arnold.

Important Features of 18th Century English Literature

Rationality and Reason

One of the defining characteristics of 18th-century English literature was its emphasis on rationality and reason. Influenced by the Enlightenment movement, writers of this era sought to apply logic and critical thinking to various aspects of life. They believed in the power of reason to understand and improve the world, leading to a shift away from the supernatural and the fantastical.

Classical Age of Literature

The 18th century is sum total of Age of Pope or the Augustan Age (1700-1750) AND the Neo-classical age (1660 and 1798). Literature of this period was greatly influenced by the works of the writers of classical antiquity. The literary figures of this era believed classical writers to be the models and the ultimate standards of literary taste.

The poets of the 18th century tried their best to copy the classical writers of Latin Literature. That is why the 18th century is sometimes also called the Classical Age, simply too.

Epoch of Peace and Prosperity of the 18th Century

The 18th century was an era of stable government in England. Queen Anne ensured a stable government which resulted into an epoch of peace and prosperity. This period saw no crisis except in the field of trade and commerce. The upper aristocratic class had great influence on all the socio-political events of the time.

In fact, they were the virtual rulers of the country. They fought the elections of the Parliament and sometimes bought the seats. This upper class became the custodians of the nation's culture and exercised great influence at the court.

The Age of Reason

The 18th century was essentially an Age of Reason. It opposed the individual initiatives in the fields of art, science and social progress. It was a period of false appearances of assured self interest. The Age emphasized rationalism, intellect, logic and wit. It was opposed to excessive emotionalism, sentimentalism, enthusiasm and even imagination.

Human Nature

The principle which got the highest widest recognition during the 18th century was the Pope's 'Nature'. It was not the 'nature' of Romantics but it was 'human nature'. It meant a rational and intelligible moral order in the universe.

However, it also meant the normal course of the world or the ideal truth by which art should be guided. This Age also emphasized the need to adhere to the rules of the literature. It emphasized on correctness and was averse to enthusiasm and emotion.

The Age of Prose

The excellent and indispensable 18th century was essentially an Age of Prose and not of poetry. The poetry of the period developed the qualities of prose. That is why, Mathew Arnold said that "Dryden and Pope are the classics of not our poetry but Prose ". Among the great prose writers of the age are Addison, Steele and Swift.

Swift was in fact, the master of English prose. As a master of simple and direct prose style, he had few rivals and no superior. Addison and Steele contributed significantly to the development of periodical essays. Sheridan and Goldsmith contributed significantly to drama. Pope is the poet par excellence of the time.

On the whole the 18th century had with some distinctive characteristics of its own. It was an Age of enlightenment and understanding.

Conclusion

The features of 18th century English literature set it apart from previous literary periods. The emphasis on reason, satire, neoclassicism, moral instruction, and the rise of the novel all contributed to a distinct literary landscape.

This era witnessed a shift towards rationality, social criticism, and a focus on the human experience. The works of 18th century writers continue to be studied and appreciated for their intellectual depth, social commentary, and enduring literary value.

Background story of The Rape of the Lock

The Rape of the Lock is one of the most famous English-language examples of the mock-epic. Published in its first version in 1712, when Pope was only 23 years old, the poem served to forge his reputation as a poet and remains his most frequently studied work. The inspiration for the poem was an actual incident among Pope's acquaintances in which Robert, Lord Petre, cut off a lock of Arabella Fermor's hair, and the young people's families fell into strife as a result. John Caryll, another member of this same circle of prominent Roman Catholics, asked Pope to write a light poem that would put the episode into a humorous perspective and reconcile the two families. The poem was originally published in a shorter version, which Pope later revised. In this later version he added the "machinery," the retinue of supernaturals who influence the action as well as the moral of the tale.

The Rape of The Lock: Canto 1 - Line by Line Summary

CANTO 1

Lines: 1-6. I shall tell, in this poem, how love affair sometimes cause great offense and trifling incidents lead to serious quarrels. O Muse, this poem is written at the suggestion of Caryll and even Belinda may condescend to go through it. The subject of the poem, no doubt, is a trifling one, but it may justly win great praise if Belinda should inspire my verse and my friend

Caryll speak in approval of it.

Lines: 7-12. Tell me, O goddess (The Muse of Poetry), what strange motive promoted a cultured lord, Lord Petre, to take liberties with a gentle lady to the extent of offending her, and what was the strange reason, not yet found, that a gentle and fashionable lady rejected a nobleman. It is a really surprising that small men can be so bold (as to cut off a lock of a noble lady's hair) and charming young ladies so furious and indignant (as Miss Arabella).

Lines: 13-26. The timid sun threw a beam of light through the white curtains of Belinda's bedroom and opened those eyes, whose brightness was sure to throw even the brightness of the sun into the shade. The lap-dogs awake at that hour and move their limbs to shake off sleep and drowsiness. Lovers, who cannot have sleep till late in the night, awake at mid-day. Belinda rang her bell thrice but getting no response from her maid, knocked the ground with her slipper. She pressed the spring of her repeating watch to know what the last hour was that had struck. Belinda still rested her head on a soft pillow, and a sylph, the guardian spirit in attendance upon her, lengthened the refreshing sleep. It was this sylph who had called silently by the side of her bed the morning dream that was hovering over her head. This sylph had assumed the form of a youngman, looking more handsome than a fashionable courtier, who puts on his best dress in the evening when a king's or a queen's birthday is celebrated. Even in her sleep, he caused a blush on her cheeks. He seemed to lay his charming lips to ear and whispered thus:

Lines: 27-35. O loveliest of all the ladies on earth, you are an object of the special care of thousands of bright spirits of the air, i.e., the Sylphs. If ever any of the stories of fairies, whose presence is detected by the shadows formed by the moonlight, as they dance, or by the silver penny left by them in the shoes of maids or by the discolored circles or rings formed on grassy plots after dewy nights told in your infancy by your nurses: or if ever any of the stories of virgins who are visited by angels, wearing golden crowns and garlands of the flowers of paradise, told by your priest, ever impressed your mind, then listen to me and believe what I say.

Lines: 35-40. Know your own importance and do not confine your thoughts to the things of this world. There are some truths which are kept secret from proud scholars and philosophers but are revealed to young maidens and children. It does not matter if sceptically inclined people do not give them any credit; beautiful girls and innocent children shall always have faith in them.

Lines: 41-50. You should know, therefore, that innumerable spirits fly around you. These are the airy bands that inhabit the lower regions of the sky; i.e., the air. Though they remain invisible, they are always hovering in the air. They hand over your box in the theatre and fly round you as you drive for pleasure in the Hyde Park or sit in your chair to witness a race. They are always in attendance upon you. Realize what a splendid body of attendants you have in the air in the form of these spirits; and look down with contempt, therefore, on the two pages and the sedan chair (that you have got on earth). We also were once beautiful women like yourself now; but, by a gentle change, leaving the earthly frame, we have come to possess these arial forms.

Lines: 51-66. Do not think that when the short period of a woman's life comes to an end, all her vanities also end. She watches with interest the vanities of the succeeding generation of women. Though she can no longer play herself, she enjoys watching others play. Her love of fashionable chariots, and of Ombre, when alive, continue even after her death. When beautiful ladies die in the prime of their beauty and youth, their souls return to the original elements of which they were composed. The souls of fierce and unruly women go back to their element of fire, and they are called Salamanders,

The souls of the women of gentle, and submissive nature pass into water, and instead of the tea which they drank on earth i.e., when alive, they now sip water, the element of which they are composed, with the sea-nymphs i.e., they become water spirits or sea-nymphs. The soul of a woman who pretends to be very modest, takes the inferior form of a gnome and wanders about on earth always in search of some new mischief. The souls of flirts go up the air and take the forms of sylphs, and play and fly about in the fields of air.

Lines: 67-78. You should know further still that a beautiful and chaste lady who rejects all human lovers is embraced by some sylphs, (Spirit of the air), because spirits are free from all those laws which govern human beings, and they can, very easily, assume any shape and sex they please. What is the power which protects the chastity of maidens who are likely to yield to their passion when they attend courtly balls and masked dances at midnight? What saves them from their false friends and daring young gallants, from the sinister glances of people in the day time and their whispering conspiracy in the night? What helps them to preserve their virginity when favorable opportunities excite their amorous feelings, soft music inclines them towards love, and dancing fires their passions? People here, down on earth, in their ignorance think that it is the sense of honor in these ladies that saves them from all those dangers. But the heavenly beings know better. They know that it is their guardian sylphs who guard and protect them.

Lines: 79-90. There are some ladies who are too conscious of their beauty. The fate of such ones are under the charge of the gnomes all their lives through. And they (gnomes) so influence them that they begin to imagine that they have bright matrimonial prospects, and become puffed up and conceited. The result is that they refuse good offers of marriage and reject love suits. Under the influence of these gnomes, their foolish and idle heads are filled with vain, and glittering visions. They think of nothing but great lords and dukes, and their large retinues; they think only of various glittering orders of knight-hood that that Lords wear and of their coronets. They imagine themselves to be duchesses already addressed by people in very gentle and respectful tones: "Your Grace." It is these gnomes who spoil girls when they are still quite young and make flirts of them by teaching them to cast languishing looks, to affect to be modest by getting up insincere, and artificial blushes and by making their youthful hearts throb with pleasurable excitement at the idea of a smart, and fashion lover.

Lines: 91-104. Often when people think that young ladies are deserting the path of virtue and going astray, the truth is that the sylphs lead them with safety through the many intricate paths of a world of pleasure and fashion. They prevent lovers from taking undue liberties with them by getting for them new lovers. A young lady would have certainly been conquered by the entertainment given to her by her first lover, had its effect not been neutralized by a ball given by another lover. A maiden would not be able to resist the offers of Florio, had Damon not been there to press his own love-suit. Thus, these flirts, with their ever-changing frivolities, i.e., by diverting their affections constantly to new, and frivolous objects of desire, which these lovers offer them, transfer their attention from one lover to another. Thus, their hearts are like a moving toy-shop. Fashionable youths, wearing wigs and carrying swords, compete with one another to win their hearts. One gallant displaces another; and the attraction felt for one lover's coach-and-six drives out another; and so it goes on. People, who mistake things and do not know the truth, ignorantly attribute all this to frivolity and inconstancy in the young ladies; but, in fact, it is all the doing of sylphs, who thus, manage to save young ladies from falling victims to the passion of their lovers.

Lines: 105-110. "I am one of these sylphs and I claim the honor of being your protector and guardian. I am a vigilant spirit and my name is Ariel. Lately, as I was flying through the transparent limitless expense of the air, I read with pain, in the star that governs your destiny; that some calamity was to befall you before sunset today.

Lines: 111-114. But, what exactly this misfortune is, how it would happen and where, has not been revealed. Thus, warned by me, O virtuous lady, be on your guard. All that I can tell you is that you should beware of everything; but most particularly, you should guard yourself against man."

Lines: 115-120. Thus, Ariel concluded his talk. Then Shock, Belinda's lap-dog, who thought that his mistress had slept for quite a long time, jumped up and waked her by licking (her hand probably). It was then that Belinda got up, and if the rumor is correct, the first thing that she saw on waking up was a love letter. It contained the conventional love phraseology of such a letter, i.e., the lover's protestation of how Cupid had inflicted wounds on his tender heart, how her exquisite beauty had cast a spell on him and how he burned with the fire of love, and so on. No sooner had she finished the letter than she forgot all about her dream.

Lines: 121-148. The dressing table was then uncovered and it lay exposed to the view. The various silver boxes of paints and powders were arranged in an order, not intelligible to a layman. First of all, dressed in a white garment and with her head uncovered, the lady very earnestly worshipped the divinities that preside over female adornment, i.e., paints, powders, etc. She saw the image of a goddess in the mirror. She bends her eyes in order to see the lower portion of her body and then she raises her eyes in order to see the upper portion of her body. The inferior priestess, Belinda's maid, Betty, stood by the side of the altar. Trembling, she began the sacred ceremony of dressing up her proud mistress. Caskets containing treasures, sent as tributes to the goddess by various countries of the world, opened before the altar. She selected from each of these articles of adornment, with fastidious taste and great care and skill, and with these bright cosmetics, she adorned the goddess.

In one of these caskets, there were bright jewels, imported from India, and in another, all the best perfumes from Arabia. In a third box, the spotted combs made of tortoise shell and white ones made of ivory lay together. Another box contained shining pins of different sizes, arranged in glittering rows. There were also seen puffs, powders, black patches, Bible and love letters. The awe-inspiring lady put all her weapons. She grew more and more beautiful every moment. She mended her smiles and made them more effective, assumed every grace and made her face charming in every possible way. She gave to her cheeks a glowing rosy hue with the help of rouge and painted her eyelashes to make her glances brighter. The watchful sylphs surrounded the dear object of their protection. Some of them adjusted her head to give it the right pose and some others attended to her hair, combing and putting them in proper order. Some folded the sleeves of her garment and some others plaited her gown.

The credit for this fine toilet went to the maid Betty, though the sylphs had contributed a lot to it.

Mock epic elements in this Canto

1.The invocation to the Muse in the opening lines follows the epic manner of the Iliad. Cowley observes that the custom of beginning all poems with a proposition of the whole work and an invocation of some god for his assistance to go through with it was solemnly and religiously observed by all the ancient poets.

2.Poetic diction. During the eighteenth century, poets in general. and epic poets, in particular, formed their language very largely on the style of Milton who frequently uses a periphrasis for the sake of elevation. In Pope's poems, the use of poetic diction is Part of the mock-heroic scheme. "Fol" (for the sun) in line 13 is an example of this poetic diction.

3.The machinery. The machinery in the poem consists of sylphs and grains who play an active part in the story. Ariel, Belinda's guardian sylph, is introduced as early as line 19. It is Ariel who gives warning to Belinda in her morning dream that misfortune will befall her in the day Ariel also describes the different categories of spirits- salamanders, nymphs, gnomes, and sylphs. The function of the sylphs is to protect the purity and virtue of young maidens.

Satirical elements

There are several passages in this Canto in which Pope satirised some of the features of aristocratic life in the eighteenth century. For instance, he refers to sleepless lovers waking at noon. Ariel in his speech to Belinda in her dream speaks of the vanities of women; women's vanities continue even when women themselves die and change into spirits. Again. Ariel speaks of conceited ladies who entertain extravagant notions of their matrimonial prospects. Ariel speaks also of the moving toy shop of the heart of a woman who transfers her affections from one lover to another and then to another.

Next, he poet speaks ironically of the conventional love letters with ner mention of "wounds, charins, and ardours". Finally, there is the celebrated passage describing Belinda at the dressing table. Here the poet is making fun of the excessive attention that women paid (and even today pay) to their toilets. However, this passage is not all satire. It contains a genuine homage to the beauty and charm of Belinda. This is one of the most poetic passages in the story. The most amusing line in the field of satire here is the one in which the poet speaks of "puffs, powders, patches, bibles, billets-doux" lying in confusion about Belinda's dressing table.

Explanations

1.**What dire offence from am'rous causes springs,**

What mighty contests rise from trivial things,

These are the opening lines of the poem The Rape of the Lock written by Alexander Pope. It is written in the voice of the narrator, and addressed to, or overheard, as it were, by the reader of the poem. It refers to the central incident in the poem, the seizing of Belinda's lock of hair (the "rape" referred to in the title of the poem) by Lord Petre, that constitutes the main action of the poem. The seizing of Belinda's lock of hair is a "trivial" event which nonetheless will inspire "mighty contests," which the poem will record in true Homeric fashion. Its significance is that it sets the tone of the poem as a mock epic, dealing with a contest not over great kingdoms and deeds, as in serious epic, but over trivia.

These lines indicate that very serious quarrels may often rise from love affairs and mighty struggles may ensue from trifling incidents.

2.**Slight is the subject, but not so the praise,**

If she inspire, and he approve my lays.

Say what strange motive, Goddess! could compel

A well-bred lord t' assault a gentle belle?

In these lines of The Rape of the Lock, Alexander Pope is invoking the Muse in the true epic manner. He says that although the subject of his mock- heroic poem is trivial and unimportant yet its execution is grand and dignified. Pope being conscious of the trifling subject, justly says that the poem can command praise only if the subject is treated in an effective manner. He is sure that inspired by the beauty and charm of Belinda, he will be able to compose an exquisite verse. But at the same time he also seeks the approval of his friend, Carlyle, who suggested the subject to him and entreated him to write a humourous poem to bring about reconciliation between the two families-Miss Fermor's and Lord Petre's. Having invoked the Muse, the poet comes to introduce his immediate subject-matter. He says that it is strange that a well-bred lord, renowned for his urdainity, should offend a highborn lady. Here Pope refers to the rape of a beautiful lock of Miss Arabella Fermor an aristocratic lady, committed by Lord Petre, a distant relation of Belinda.

3.As now your own, our beings were of old,

And once inclos'd in woman's beauteous mould;

Thence, by a soft transition, we repair

From earthly vehicles to these of air.

In these lines of The Rape of the Lock Pope begins the work of the 'machinery', Aerial, the guardians sylph of Belinda, informed her in a dream that innumerable spirits of air look after her. Now he says that the incorporeal spirits were once beautiful women of fashion like her. They have existed since very old times; death affected a transition and they passed from women's lovely bodies to serial existence.

4.The busy Sylphs surround their darling care;

These set the head, and those divide the hair,

Some fold the sleeve, whilst others plait the gown;

And Betty's prais'd for labours not her own.

These concluding lines of Canto I, of Pope's the Rape of the Lock complete the toilet of Belinda. As stated in the earlier part of the poem by Aerial, the guardian sylph of Belinda, she is the object of care of innumerable spirits of air, the sylphs do the whole work of toilet. Although Betty. her maid-servant, decorated her, the real work is done by the unseen sylphs. Some adjust her hair to give her a fine and attractive pose. Some fold her sleeves over her hands and some set the folds of her gown in order. Thus decorated by the sylphs Belinda attains bewitching beauty, the credit for which goes to Betty although in reality the sylphs deserve all praise.

5.In tasks so bold can little men engage,

And in soft Bosoms dwells such Mighty Raye?

These lines are taken from Canto I of The Rape of the Lock by Alexander Pope. In these lines Pope juxtaposes grand emotions with unheroic character-types, specially "little men" and "women". It is strange to think that men of short stature (Like Lord Peter) can become too bold as it cut off a young beautiful lady's lock of hair and that the gentle heart of a lady (Like Belinda) should be filled with violent anger.

The irony of pairing epic characteristics with lowly human characters contributes to Pope's mock heroic style. Pope uses the mock-heroic genre to elevate and ridicule his subjects simultaneously, creating a satire that chides society for its misplaced values and emphasis on trivial matters.

6.Where wigs with wigs,

With sword-knots sword-knots strive,

Beaux banish beaux, and coaches coaches drive.

These lines are taken from Canto I line-101-102 of The Rape of the Lock by Alexander Pope. Once Belinda saw a dream in which she saw a gallant young man. He said the following words to Belinda. He said that often when wordly people think that women are going astray from the path of morality, the sylphs, the attending spirits, safely guide them through the intricate paths which may make them giddy if the sylphs do not come to their help. Further he said that fashionable lovers who put up wigs and the knots of love round about their swords, fight and banish one another. The people of the world who have a wrong view of the whole show may call it moral depravity or coquetry on the part of women but they do not know the truth. In fact the sylphs, the guardian spirits of the ladies organise and arrange all this show of coquetry in women. These lines show Pope invoking the muse in the true epic manner.

7.But heav'n reveals not what or how, or where;

Warn'd by the sylph, oh, pions maid, beware!

These lines are taken from Canto-I of The Rape of the Lock by Alexander Pope. Once Belinda saw a dream in which she sees a gallant young man named Ariel. He informed Belinda that he is one of the spirits that guards her. He said to Belinda that some dreadful event was to happen in her life that day before sunset. But he does not know where and when this calamity befall her. Being her guardian spirit he feels its his duty to inform her about the calamity and warns her that she should be cautious all the time and keep herself away from the company of man. These lines show Pope invoking the muse in the true epic manner.

8.But since, alas! frail beauty must decay,

Curl'd or uncurl'd, since locks will turn to grey,

Since painted, or not painted, all shall fade,

And she who scorns a man, must die a maid;

The following lines appear in "The Rape of the Lock" Canto Five, lines 25-28. In Canto Five, the action of the poem turns to the consideration regarding the beauty of women and how society looks at the beauty of women.

This being said, at the end of the poem and Canto Five, the recognition regarding one's ability to sustain immortality comes into question. The lines above refer to the fact that only in Heaven can a person and or more importantly, the locks sustain their glory. The lines, therefore, refer to the fact that on earth beauty diminishes (including the golden colour of the locks changing to grey). Only in Heaven, in the stars, can Belinda and her locks remain beautiful and admired for their beauty in a timeless way. But since beauty is weak and hence it must decay sooner or later and lock whether curled or uncurled, will become grey one day and since faces whether painted or not. It will fade and then no man will think of marrying her.

9.Her lively looks a sprightly mind disclose,
Quick as her eyes, and as unfix'd as those:
Favours to none, to all she smiles extends;
Oft she rejects, but never once offends.
Bright as the sun, her eyes the gazers strike,
And, like the sun, they shine on all alike.

The lines have been taken from Canto-2 of The Rape of the Lock by Alexander Pope. Pope was a satirist and moralist.

Belinda, whose beauty excelled the glory of The rays of the sun when it rises in the east and brightens the water of the ocean, embarked on a pleasant boat trip on the transparent water of the river Thames.

Her lively, ever-vivacious eyes disclosed her keen and intelligent brain which was as restless and wandering as her eyes. She bestowed her smiling looks on all the young men in her company without showing any special favour to anyone. She often declined the advances of ardent lovers but she did so with such charming tact and grace that none of them felt offended. Her eyes, bright as the dazzling sun, charmed all who looked at her face. Just as the sun bestows his light and warmth impartially on all. Similarly she directed her bright looks with equal favour to all her admirers without any discrimination. If it is at all possible that beautiful and fashionable ladies have any faults and if Belinda had any, they were left unobserved by anyone because of her natural graceful manners and her freedom from pride.

10.There Affectation, with a sickly mien,

Shows in her cheek the roses of eighteen,

Practis'd to lisp, and hang the head aside,

Faints into airs, and languishes with pride,

These lines have been taken from Canto-IV of The Rape of the Lock by Alexander Pope.

Two maid-servants waited upon throne i.e. her bed. They were equal in rank but they differed widely in their body and shapes. One of the two was ill natured who stood one side like an old maid. Her wrinkled body was clothed in black and white dress. She offered so many prayers in the morning, noon and night, yet her heart was full of abuses and satires.

She seemed to conceal her wicked thoughts by outward platy. The other was affectation. Although she looked an elderly lady with pale and repulsive appearance. It tried to produce on her cheeks the rosy freshness that can be seen on the cheeks of a healthy youthful girl of eighteen. She was skillful in pronouncing words in a broken and indistinct manner like children and bent her head on one side as if out of great modesty so that she might look like a copy of an innocent maiden. She would fall into pretended fits of swooning to attain charming attitudes or pretend to fall suddenly ill like a delicate girl to show her pride. In her pretended illness she, wrapped in her new gown would slowly stretch herself on her artistic bed-cover with a charming posture which showed her suffering and at the same time gave her a graceful appearance. Whenever she got a new fashionable gown she pretends illness to her lovers.

11.The adventurous baron the bright locks admired,

He saw, he wish'd and to the prize aspired,

Resolved to win, he meditates the way,

By force to ravish, or by fraud betray;

The line has been taken from Canto-2 of The Rape of the Lock by Alexander Pope. The lines have been spoken by Baron for Belinda's beauty.

The beautiful lady Belinda had carefully reared two locks for the ruin of the male sex. These beautiful locks of hair collaborated with the glittering ringlets, gracefully hung on her white and smooth neck making it more beautiful. The locks of Belinda were intricate mazes of hair and attracted the hearts of her lovers and imprisoned the hearts of even the mightiest of men kings and warriors. Just as birds are deceived and entrapped by the snares of hair, and the fishes are caught with the fishing lines made of hair, similarly locks of hair on the head of beautiful women entrap the hearts of the haughty and domineering men. A beautiful lady attracts and captivates the hearts of men with nothing more than a single her head.

The bold Baron, Lord Petre, admired the beautiful locks of Belinda. As soon as he saw them, a strong desire to possess them arose in his heart. He determined to get them and thought of the way to get success in his aim. He determined to possess them either by violence or by some treacherous trick because when a lover gets success in winning his prize, none asks whether he achieved his end by fraud or by foul trick.

12.How vain are all these Glories, all our Pains,

Unless good Sense preserve what Beauty gains:

The following lines appear in "The Rape of the Lock", Canto Five, lines 15-16. The lines refer to the fact that beauty is questioned in regards to its being honored by the "wise Man's passion" and the "vain Man's Toast." This is compounded when the question arises about women being compared to angels in regards to their beauty alone- men do not compare women to angels because of their minds or morality.

The lines above refer to the fact that vanity, above all else, seems to be on the minds of men. The women find it insensible that beauty alone holds men and that good sense does not factor into the equation at all. These sad words had been said by Belinda to Baron.

13..Think not, when woman's transient breath is fled,

That all her vanities at once are dead;

Succeeding vanities she still regards,

And tho' she plays no more, o' erlooks the cards.

Having given an account of the origin of these spirits to her, he tells her that when a woman dies, her fondness for earthly foolish frivolities does not die with her. She retains all her vanities and pursuits of fashionable follies even in her airy existence. In other words, the trivialities of fashion and the frivolities of which she was fond on the earth, still occupy her mind even in her airy existence. The only difference is in her position. Just as when fashionable women plays a game of cards, some old and infirm women sit and watch the game, similarly, the disembodied spirit of a dead woman who is no longer in a position to play her part, watches and takes interest with the same fondness in the fashionable follies and frivolities in which the living ones indulge themselves. Thus her old vanities and frivolities continue even in her airy existence.

14.Oft, when the world imagine women stray,

The Sylphs through mystic mazes guide their way,

Thro' all the giddy circle they pursue,

And old impertinence expel by new.

Having informed Belinda in a dream that it is the duty of the sylph to protect the honour of fashionable ladies like her, Aerial, the guardian sylph of Belinda, now describes how the airy spirits accomplish this task. Aerial says that often it so happens that when people think that women are deviating from the path of virtue and are indulging themselves in frivolities, the sylphs lead them safely away from the intricate ways of a feeling pleasure-seeking life. When the sylphs-see the young girls feeling giddy at the advances of young lovers, they protect them from their loss of virtue and conduct them out of danger by diverting them from old extravagance and of foolery to new ones, from one presumptuous lover to one less forward in his address.

15.Th' inferior priestess, at her altar's side,

Trembling begins the sacred rites of pride.

Unnumber'd treasures ope at once, and here

The various off'rings of the world appear;

From each she nicely culls with curious toil,

And decks the goddess with the glitt'ring spoil.

When Belinda began her toilet, Betty, her maid servant, stood beside her. The image of Belinda in the mirror appeared like that of a goddess. Betty. the inferior priestess at the altar of female vanity, began to tremble with reverence as she proceeds to perform the solemn work of beautifying her mistress. Belinda. the chief priestess. There lay on the dressing table innumerable treasures brought from various countries of the world to be offered to the Goddess of Beauty. Out of these varied articles of luxury Betty carefully selected the best specimens and decorated her mistress in a lovely manner with the glittering trifles.

16.Love in these labyrinths his slaves detains,

And mighty hearts are held in slender chains

With hairy springes we the birds betray,

Slight lines of hair surprise the finney prey,

Fair tresses man's imperial race ensnare,

And beauty draws us with a single hair.

In these lines Pope has described the awful charm of the two beautiful locks of hair which Belinda had nourished for the destruction of man folk. They were her most dreadful weapons to captivate young dandies. These locks were so beautiful that the hearts or her lovers were entangled hopelessly in the labyrinths of her tresses. These slender chains of hair captivated the hearts of the mightiest of men. Just as bird are entrapped by nets made of horse hair and fishes are captured by slender strands of hair smiley proud at domineering men, who call themselves rulers of empires and women, are ensnared by the graceful tresses of a beautiful maiden. A beautiful woman captures a bean with nothing more than a single hair of her head.

17.Of twelve vast French romances, neatly gilt.
There lay three garters, half a pair of gloves:
And all the trophies of his former loves:
With tender billet-doux he lights the pyre.
And breathes three am'rous sighs to raise the fire.

When the Baron saw the beautiful locks of Belinda he aspired to possess one by fair or foul means. He implored the gods, especially the god of love, to grant him the possession of Belinda's lock of hair. He built an altar consisting of twelve voluminous French romances which were beautifully gilt at the backs, for the worship of the god of love. Then he placed on the altar three garters, half a pair of gloves and other trophies of love which he had received from his former beloved. He offered all these trophies to Cupid to propitiate him for his help in securing the prized lock of Belinda. Then he lighted the pyre with love-letters which were so full of tender and fiery passions that they served the purpose of match-sticks and heaved three sighs so that the fire (of love) might burst into flames.

18.Whether the nymph shall break Diana's law,
Or some frail china jar receive a flaw:
Or stain her honour, or her new brocade,
Forget her pray'rs, or miss a masquerade:
Or lose her heart, or necklace, at a ball;
Or whether Heav'n has doom'd that Shock must fall.

When Belinda went out in the company of her fashionable admirers, Ariel, her guardian Sylph, foresaw some imminent calamity to befall Belinda Here he mentions a few possible dangers. He did not know whether Belinda would break her vow of chastity or suffer pain caused by the breakage of her ornamental China jar. He could not foresee whether she would blot her fair name by submitting to some scandalous love-affair or stain her new silk dress. He was not aware whether the reason for her suffering would be the forgetting of her usual prayers or her inability to attend a ball dance of masquerade. Probably she might lose her heart or her necklace at a ball.

He also felt that perhaps she might have been doomed by heaven to suffer the death of Shock. her lap-dog, which would be the greatest imaginable calamity for her.

19.One speaks the glory of the British queen,

And one describes a charming Indian screen;

A third interprets motions, looks, and eyes;

At ev'ry word a reputation dies.

Snuff, or the fan, supply each pause of chat,

With singing, laughing, ogling, and all that.

When Belinda and her companions reached the Hampton Court where ministers held meetings and where Queen Anne met her ministers, all the lords and ladies indulged in idle gossip. Some praised the grandeur of the British Queen while others praised one or the other object. Another began to interpret the looks and motions of women in a malicious way. The fashionable ladies and gentlemen often engaged themselves in scandals.

In these lines, Pope presents a true picture of the life in his age. One of the youths gathered there eloquently spoke of Queen Anne's greatness, another talked about the picturesquely painted Indian screen, while a third interpreted the motions, looks and eyes of the ladies in such a way that every word spoken about her brought infamy to her. At every word of such a scandalous talk the reputation of a celebrity was sacrificed. To employ the interval between the conversation fruitfully the fops took snuff and the ladies moved their fans. Some sang, laughed and exchanged amorous glances.

20.Meanwhile, declining from the noon of day,

The sun obliquely shoots his burning ray;

The hungry judges soon the sentence sign,

And wretches hang that jury-men may dine;

When Belinda and her friends, reached the Hampton Court, they engaged themselves in social and political chats and scandals. While they were gossiping the sun having passed the midday was descending towards the west and was casting slanting rays. The hour of dinner was near and all feel hungry. Yielding. to the natural pressure of hunger, the judges finished off the trial hand and signed the sentence hastily. The jury men too gave the verdict of guilty without any scruple in order to be away from the law court and go to dinner.

21.Now move to war her sable Matadores,

In show like leaders of the swarthy Moors.

Spadillio first, unconquerable lord!
Led off two captive trumps, and swept the board.
As many more Manillio fore'd to yield,
And march 'd a victor from the verdant field.

Having spent the day in gossip. Belinda wished to defeat the Baron and his partner single handed in the game of Ombre. The cards were dealt. After scrutinising her hand carefully Belinda declared spades to be the trump. Now the game begins. Pope maintaining the mock-heroic tone describes the game as a war. The green velvet covered surface of the table is the battle-field and the various cards are warriors. Belinda begins the game with her black Matadors who in appearance resemble the chieftains of the black Moors of Africa. The first card that comes forward is Spadillio... the ace of spades. Since spades is the trump, it is the highest card and hence it is unconquerable. It captures two trumps and the board is swept clean. Then she moves Manillio. the second or deuce of spades. It being the second highest card. it also captures two trumps and returns victoriously from the green velvet covered field.

22.Ev'n mighty Pam, that kings and queens o'erthrew
And mow'd down armies in the fights of loo,
Sad chance of war! now destitute of aid,
Falls undistinguish'd by the victor Spade!

Belinda has decided to defeat the Baron and his partner single handed in the game of Ombre. She has declared spades to be the trump and the game is in progress. Belinda now moves the king of spades which is the third highest card The Baron plays the knave of spades and his partner discards the knave of clubs as he has played all his cards or spades. The knave of clubs is the highest card in the game of Lu and can capture even the kings and queens (not to mention other ordinary cards) but in the game of ombre it has no power and suffers a disgraceful defeat at the hands of Belinda's king of spades. It is the sad uncertainty of war that even the mightiest is shorn of power and is left helpless to suffer defeat and humiliation.

23.Thus when dispers'd a routed army runs,
Of Asia's troops, and Afric's sable sons,
With like confusion diff'rent nations fly,
Of various habit, and of various dye,
The pierc'd battalions disunited fall.
In heaps on heaps; one fate o'crwhelms them all.

When Belinda had won the first few tricks in the game of Ombre, Pate smiled on the Baron. After winning his queen of spades, he played with his suit of diamonds. Belinda and the third player, the Baron's partner discarded cards of other suits they lay on the table in a disorderly manner. Pope says that the forces of Belinda and the third player could not stand erect before the attack launched by the army of the Baron. They lay on the verdant field in wild confusion. The condition of the worsted battalions of diamonds, hearts and clubs was like that of the defeated and retreating black troops of Asia and Africa belonging to different nations and wearing different uniforms of different colours. Just as when their battle formation is broken the soldiers run helter-skelter and get killed in large numbers. Similarly, the vanquished battalions of diamonds, hearts and clubs were completely disorganized and fell dead on the verdant field, the same fate overtook them all.

> **24.Oh thoughtless mortals! ever blind to fate,**
> **Too soon dejected, and too soon elate!**
> **Sudden, these honours shall be snatch'd away,**
> **And curs'd forever this victorious day.**

When Belinda got victory over the Baron and his partner in the game of Ombre she was overjoyed. She was puffed up with pride and filled the sky with her joyous shouts. The whole atmosphere echoed them. Here Pope laments human nature. He says that human beings do not have the power to know what their fate would be in future. They never have the slightest knowledge of the mysterious destiny. They are unthinking and foolish. They gave way to despair at the slightest adversity and are muffed up with joy and pride when they achieve some trifling success & prosperity. They little realise that their success and hence joy is short-lived. The poet means to say that when Belinda got victory over the Baron in the game of Ombre, she became extremely hilarious and not know that very soon all her exultation would be converted into sorrow and she would have to curse the victorious day.

> **25.Ah cease, rash youth! desist ere 'tis too late,**
> **Fear the just gods, and think of Seylla's fate!**
> **Chang'd to a bird, and sent to flit in air,**
> **She dearly pays for Nisus' injur'd hair!**

The Baron ardently wished to possess the beautiful lock of Belinda's hair. As he was sipping coffee in the Hampton Court in the company of Belinda and other fashionable gentlemen and ladies, the fume of coffee filled his brain with new stratagems to own the prize lock and he decided to cut it off. The poet says that the Baron should refrain from cutting the lock of Belinda's hair because once he had done it, it would not be possible for him to undo it. He should think that by attempting to do so he will provoke the wrath of good who are just and who never let a wrong go unpunished. He should also think of the fate of Scylla who was changed into a bird and sent to wander in the air for stealing the purple hair of her father Nisus' head and giving it to Minos for the sake of her love. Just as she was doomed forever by gods like-wise he might also be subjected to similar fate.

26.Here living teapots stand, one arm held out,
One bent; the handle this, and that the spout:
A pipkin there, like Homer's tripod, walks;
Here sighs a jar, and there a goose pie talks;
Men prove with child, as powerful fancy works,
And maids, turned bottles, call aloud for corks.

In these lines Pope has described the Cave of Spleen. So many human bodies had been changed into various shapes like bottles, teapots, etc. by Spleen. He means to say that persons suffering from Spleen fancied themselves as being transformed into fantastic forms. Some sickly women who imagined themselves to have been changed into tea-pots stood there with one arm outstretched representing the spout through which tea is poured out and the other arm curved so as to represent the handle. There was a lady who imagined herself to be an earthen vessel and walked about like the three-legged stools made by Vulcan (Mulcible) as mentioned by Homer in the loud, XVIII. Another lady who imagined herself to be a China-jar stood sighing in another corner. while another lady who thought herself to be changed into a goose-pye talked incessantly. (According to Pope this alludes to a real-fact; a lady of distinction imagined herself in this condition). Yet most strange spectacle was that of some men who believed themselves to be pregnant and of some women who thought themselves to have been transformed into bottles and called aloud for corks.

27.Not half so fix'd the Trojan could remain,
While Anna begg'd and Dido rag'd in vain.

Belinda wept bitterly when the Baron refused to return the lock of hair. Thalestris reproached him but in vain. He turned a deaf ear to Belinda's importunities and passionate appeals and Thalestris' reproaches. He was adamant to keep it. In these lines Pope says that the Baron was more firm than Aeneas, the Trojan prince who was bent upon leaving Carthage and paid heed to the importunities of Dicks, his c dear wife and the solicitations of Anna, her sister. In other words even Aeneas did not show half such obstinacy before the plaintive appeals of Anna and the dignified wrath of her sister Queen Dido when he deserted the latter as the Baron was showing so Belinda

28.What dire offence from am'rous causes springs,
What mighty contests rise from trivial things.

These are the opening lines of The Rape of the Lock written by Alexander Pope. These lines. Pope suggests that people are taking a trivial incident too seriously, displaying an exaggerated sense of their own importance. Very serious quarrels may often rise from love affairs and mighty struggles may ensue from trifling incidents. Throughout the poem Pope continues to make this point through his use of the mock-epic style, which itself takes a trivial incident too seriously, and uses disproportionately grand language to describe an unworthy subject

29..Hear and believe! thy own Importance know,
Nor bound thy narrow views to things below.
Some secret Truths, from Learned pride concealed,
To Maids, alone and children are reveal'd
Or,
What tho' no Credit doubting Wits may give?
The Fair and Innocent shall still believe.

These lines have been taken from The Rape of the Lock by Alexander Pope. The gallant young man of Belinda's dream told her that she was the most beautiful of all the creatures living on the earth. She should listen to and believe whatever he told her. She should know her importance. She should not allow herself to be tied to the narrow views of men of this world. There were certain truths which were kept concealed from men who took pride in their learning. Those truths were revealed only to maids and children because learned men doubted the existence of fairies and angels whereas children and maids being Innocent and credulous believed in the existence of fairies and angels and in their association with men and women of the earth.

30.What guards the purity of melting maid,
In Courtly Balls, and Midnight Masquerades.
Or,
Safe from the treach'rous Friend the daring Spark,
The Glance by day, the Whisper in the Dark,

When kind occassion prompts their warm Desires,
When Musick softens and when Dancing fires?
'Tis but their Sylph, the wise celestials know,
Tho' Honour is the Word with Men below.

These lines have been taken from The Rape of the Lock by Alexander Pope. In these lines Pope says that what guards the chastity of minds who are inclined to yield to the advance of lovers in stately dances and masked dances which continue till midnight and how they are saved from deceitful friends? What protects them from gay and fashionable young men and from the evil looks which are cast at them in the day and from the whisper that is spread against them in the night? When a favourable opportunity excites their passions, how are able to check themselves? What saves them from moral degradation when tilting notes of music soften the hearts and when dancing fires up their passions? All the heavenly beings know that it is sylph, the attending spirit, that protects their chastity from the amorous nets on the above stated occasions although worldly people believe that the lady rejects the amorous advances of a lover because of her sense of honour and modesty.

31. Resolved to win, he mediates the way,
By force to ravish, or by fraud betray.

These lines are taken from Canto-II of The Rape of the Lock by Alexander Pope. in these lines Baron admired the beautiful locks of Belinda. As soon as he saw them, a strong desire to possess them arose in his heart. He determined to get them and thought of the way to get success in his aim. He determined to possess them either by violence or by some treacherous trick because when a lover gets success in winning his prize, none asks whether he achieved his end by fraud or by foul trick. Though these lines are trivial and unimportant yet their execution is grand and dignified.

32. Not fierce Othello in so loud a strain,
Roared for the handkerchief that caused his pain.

These lines have been taken from Canto-V of The Rape of the Lock by Alexander Pope. Belinda loudly asks Baron to restore the lock but the lock itself has gone missing. The vaulted roofs of the Hampton court echoed and re-echoed with her cries. Pope makes an allusion to his fellow Brit, William Shakespeare where he gives references of Othello and his wife's infamous handkerchief. He equates Belinda's lock of hair with the handkerchief that causes Othello's jealousy and his eventual murder of Desdemona. Othello itself did not cry when he demanded the handkerchief from Desdemona, as

Belinda did.

This time Pope got more juxtaposition here with a high tragedy to the comedy of this scene.

The Rape of the Lock Short Questions and Answers

1.What is the central theme of 'The Rape of the Lock'?

Answer: The poem explores themes of vanity, gender roles, and the triviality of social conflicts, illustrating how a seemingly minor incident—such as the cutting of a lock of hair—can spiral into significant consequences and reveal deeper societal issues.

2.How does Pope use satire in the poem?

Answer: Pope employs satire by exaggerating the importance of the events surrounding the cutting of Belinda's hair. He compares this trivial matter to epic battles and serious affairs, thereby mocking the frivolity of high society's concerns.

3. What role do the Sylphs play in the poem?

Answer: The Sylphs serve as guardians and represent the feminine virtues of chastity and beauty. They embody the delicate nature of women's social standing and are tied to the supernatural, emphasizing the poem's blend of the mundane and the fantastical.

4. Why is Belinda's hair significant in the poem?

Answer: Belinda's hair symbolizes her beauty and social status. The act of cutting it represents not only the loss of her beauty but also a violation of her integrity and the trivialization of female identity.

5. What can we learn from Belinda's character regarding societal expectations?

Answer: Belinda embodies the struggle between personal identity and societal expectations. Her obsession with beauty and social acceptance reflects the pressure women face to conform to beauty standards and the consequences of failing to meet these expectations.

6. Discuss the significance of the duel between Belinda and the Baron.

Answer: The duel symbolizes the conflict between male aggression and female virtue. It also highlights the absurdity of social norms, where a battle for a lock of hair is elevated to the status of epic conflict, illustrating both the triviality and the seriousness with which such matters were treated in society.

7. How does Pope's portrayal of women challenge or reinforce societal norms of his time?

Answer: While Pope's portrayal of women can be seen as reinforcing the idea of women's beauty as their primary virtue, it simultaneously critiques the absurdity of the societal norms that place such importance on superficial qualities, inviting readers to question the status quo.

8. What is the poem's commentary on the nature of honor and reputation?

Answer: The poem suggests that honor and reputation are fragile and can be easily tarnished by gossip and social scrutiny. It highlights how women, in particular, are subject to the whims of public opinion, making their societal standing precarious.

9.In what ways does 'The Rape of the Lock' continue to resonate in contemporary discussions of gender and society?

Answer: The poem's exploration of beauty, vanity, and social conflict remains relevant today as issues surrounding body image, gender roles, and societal expectations continue to impact individuals, particularly women, in contemporary society.

10.How does Pope's use of epic conventions affect the reading of 'The Rape of the Lock'?

Answer: By employing epic conventions—such as grandiose language, elaborate similes, and supernatural elements—Pope elevates a petty social squabble to the level of epic significance, enriching the irony and humor of the poem.

<u>Some more questions to look at</u>

(i) What does the title of 'The Rape of the Lock' refer to?

Ans. The poem's title might seem confusing until we do a little digging into the etymology of the word "rape". In the 18th century, in Pope's day, "rape" also meant to carry away or take something from someone by force. The word "lock" here means the tress, curl, or ringlet of a woman's hair.

(ii) What is the setting of 'The Rape of the Lock'?

Ans. The action takes place in London and its environs in the early 1700's on a single day. The story begins at the London residence of Belinda. The scene then shifts to the Thames. The rest of the story takes place at Hampton Court Palace, except for a brief scene in the cave of the Queen of Spleen.

(iii) 'The Rape of the Lock' is called a mock epic poem. Why?

Ans. Like typical epics, there is a statement of purpose and invocation to the Muse in "The Rape of the Lock". It is divided into Cantos and written in heroic couplets. Moreover, there is use of supernatural machinery.

However, there is a satirical twist in this epic. It satirizes the absurdities and frivolities of the aristocratic ladies and gentlemen. This makes this poem a 'mock epic'.

(iv) Define allegory.

Ans. An allegory is an extended metaphor in which abstract ideas, concepts and principles are described in terms of characters, figures and events in ways that are comprehensible to its viewers, readers, or listeners. For example, George Orwell's novel "Animal Farm" is a political allegory.

(v) What is a heroic couplet?

Ans. A heroic couplet is a traditional form for English poetry, commonly used in epic and narrative poetry. It refers to poems constructed from a sequence of rhyming pairs of lines in iambic pentameter. For example: "Know then thyself, presume not God to scan/ The proper study of Mankind is Man".

(vi) What are the satirical targets of 'The Rape of the Lock'?

Ans. The principal satirical targets of "The Rape of the Lock" are the absurdities and frivolities of the fashionable circle - aristocratic ladies and gentlemen - of the 18th century England.

(vii) What are some of the images that recur through the poem 'The Rape of the Lock'?

Ans. The first recurring image is the sun. It marks the passing of time in the poem and emphasizes the dramatic unity of the story. Another image that recurs is that of china. Delicate dishes that are beautiful, fragile, and purely luxurious form a fitting counterpart to a world that is ornamental. The images of gold and silver signify the real value of underlying glittery and mesmerizing surfaces.

(viii) Write the names of the women in the poem 'The Rape of the Lock'?

Ans. There are five major women in the poem. Belinda is the heroine of the poem. Thalestris is Belinda's friend. Betty is Belinda's maid. Clarissa is an attendant at the Hampton Court Party. Spleen is the queen of bad tempers and the source of detestable qualities in human beings.

(ix) What is Belinda's full name in 'The Rape of the Lock'?

Ans. Belinda is the heroine of the poem "The Rape of the Lock" by Alexander Pope. She is named for a real person: Arabella Fermor; a member of Pope's circle of prominent Roman Catholics.

(x) Who was the guardian spirit of Belinda?

Ans. The guardian spirit of Belinda is Ariel. He is a sylph. He warns her that something dreadful may happen and sets a guard of sylphs to protect his charge, but he is unsuccessful in preventing the loss of the lock of hair.

(xi) What spirit does Pope call upon to help him write his poem?

Ans. Usually a poet calls upon one the the 'nine daughter of Zeus' to sanctify his poetry. However, in 'The Rape of the Lock", Alexander Pope invokes his catholic friend John Caryll instead, as a muse to provide him with blessings to narrate a story of not a great hero but a rich, vain woman called Belinda.

(xii) To whom does Pope dedicate the poem 'The Rape of the Lock'?

Ans. Pope dedicates this poem to John Caryll. He was the friend of Arabella Fermor (Belinda) and Pope. He was who originally asked Pope to write this poem.

(xiii) Who adores the 'sparkling cross' Belinda has on her neck?

Ans. Infidels adore this cross. Pope is highlighting the fact that the cross has as much meaning to Belinda as it would to a person without any religious beliefs. The cross is adored by the Infidels, kissed by the Jews, but no mention of Priests or Gallants is made in reference to the cross.

(xiv) According to Pope, when women die, their spirits live on. What are the four possible forms these spirits will take?

Ans. When quarrelsome women die, their souls go to fire and they become Salamanders. When polite and submissive women die, their souls return to water and they become Nymphs. The souls of proud and serious minded women go to earth and they become Gnomes. The souls of flirt and coquette women go to air and they become Sylphs.

(xv) What everyday feminine ritual is Pope connecting with the ancient Greco-Roman sacrifice?

Ans. Sacrifice was the essential element of Greek and Roman religious rituals. Pope is connecting the feminine ritual of dressing with the ancient Greco-Roman sacrifice. Belinda's morning routine can be connected with a hero's ritualized preparation before battle. Belinda's reflection in the mirror becomes the image of goddess while her maid is the 'inferior priestess', worshiping at the altar.

<u>**Long Questions and Answers**</u>

1.Alexander Pope as a Satirist

Posterity has remembered Alexander Pope for his satires. Undoubtedly, while shaping his growth in the direction demanded by classicism, the feeling for which he strengthened more and more within himself. Pope developed his talent for satire and argument in verse.

It is in this province of literature that he has written his strongest works. It is not pure, poetry which benefited, but the vigor of temperament that reveals itself produced its most characteristic fruits.

In fact Pope's satire is inspired not by any large view of human its vices and weaknesses; no such dark misanthropy as glares at and horrifies us, and flashes of which are seen in Byron, no such moral sincerity as we find in Juvenal. His satires do not blend anger and pure fun the kind of which we find in Burns. "Personal animosity is the feather with which Pope's satiric arrows are fledged." Thus to do full justice to The Dunciad, Moral Essays and Imitation of Horace the reader must be fully familiar with the social background of the age. As, for example, in 1725 he published an edition of Shakespeare which was vehemently criticized by Lewis Theobald in his Shakespeare Restored (1726). Theobald suggested many valuable restorations and emendations and exposed Pope's inefficiency as a critic. As retaliation, Pope made him the hero of his Dunciad, a violent satire of which three books were published anonymously in 1728. For a poet of Pope's stature the Dunciad is a movement of misapplied power.

The Rape of the Lock which is, a mock-heroic poem is, however, Pope's greatest satiric poem. As such the characters are to a large extent, mocking versions of epic characters. The portraits are not realistic; they are not meant to mock at the follies and foibles of the aristocratic society of Pope's times. The objective being to expose human follies, especially the feminine, characterization is naturally from the general rather than the individual point of view.

Exaggeration is one mode through which a portrait assumes ironic or satiric light. The excessive praise bestowed on Belinda's charms, for Instance, Belinda shedding her gaiety on all and sundry like the sun sheds its light, suggests flippancy and inconstancy in character.

Another mode of satiric portraiture adopted by Pope is through describing these very ordinary human beings in epic terms, thus achieving the desired comic effect through ironic juxtaposition. Comparison of Belinda's toilet ritual to "sacred rites" does not elevate her to the position of a goddess, but satirizes her as a human being for the excessive vanity. The Baron is constantly spoken in terms of the knight-errant of the Middle

Ages. All his actions, from his aspiration to "the prize", his ritual prayer at the altar of love, to his "heroic" gestures after cutting the lock and finally his defeat are a mockery of higher characters. In the process, his vacuity, superficiality, foppishness and vapidity are revealed—for the prize he aspires to is a lock of hair, his altar is made of ridiculous items, he is inspired by coffee, and is defeated by a pinch of snuff. The "heroism" is superbly punctured to reveal the conceited fop of the eighteenth century. For the sake of variety, Pope does not have merely mock-heroic portraitures: Sir Plume is a minor figure, but he is a directly satiric portrait of an ineffectual, ridiculously vapid fop. Pope builds up his picture with the aid of a few traits typical of the dandy of that age—the snuff box, the cane, meaningless oaths. We are directly told of his "earnest eyes" and "round unthinking face." There is no subtlety here, but straightforward satire.

Pope does not indulge in satirizing particular individuals in The Rape of the Lock. Through the satiric portraits, he presents a satirical picture of the age. Belinda, Thalestris, the Baron and Sir Plume are typical of that society. The characteristics they are given are those common to the "high" society of eighteenth century London.

To conclude, Pope's method of satiric portraiture varies, not only from portrait to portrait, but within the characterization of a single person itself. He uses the mode most fitting to the situation concerned. He appears to praise, but the result is quite the opposite—one is all the more clearly aware of the essential smallness and ridiculousness of the character involved. This is Pope's mastery of ironic portraiture.

2.The Rape of the Lock as a Mock Heroic or Mock Epic Poem

The epic is a narrative poem, of supposed divine inspiration, treating of a subject of great and momentous importance for mankind, the characters of the story being partly human and partly divine, and the language and style in which the incidents are related being full of elevation and dignity.

If a long narrative poem should satisfy all the tests of epic poetry, but if the subject which is celebrated be of a trivial nature, like the cutting off a lock of a woman's hair, which is the story that is related in Pope's The Rape of the Lock, then such a poem is called a mock-epic poem. A mock-epic poem is supposed to be the inspiration of a Muse, the characters are partly human and partly divine, and the language is stilted and grandiose, but the subject is of a very frivolous and commonplace nature. Pope called

The Rape of the Lock a "heroi-comical poem", which is another name for a mock-epic. It belongs to the class of literature called "burlesque". A burlesque is a parody on a large scale, in which not a single poem, but a whole type of style of literature is parodied, the language and thought proper to a serious theme reproduced in setting forth something ridiculous or trivial.

Instead of grand passions and great fights between heroes in which the immortals take part, we have as the theme of The Rape of the Lock a petty amorous quarrel assisted by the spirits of the air. The epic portrays an age round the personality of a god or a semi-god, and its characters are heroes. The Rape of the Lock, on the other hand, gives us a picture of a fashionable society. The central figure in that picture is a pretty society girl, and the other characters are a rash youth, a foolish dandy and a few frivolous women. Instead of deep and genuine passions as found in ancient epics, we come across a succession of mock passions in The Rape of the Lock.

The action of The Rape of the Lock turns on a trivial incident—the cutting off a lock of hair from a lady's head. Such a thing had taken place in reality. One lord Petre cut off a lock of hair from the head of Lady Arabella Fermor. There was a quarrel between the two families, and Pope was requested to make a jest of the incident, and 'laugh them together'. This was the occasion of the composition of the poem. Pope did give to the world a fine work of wit—the best mock-heroic poem in the English language, but we do not know whether the families were reconciled.

The theme of the poem is suggested in the invocation, as in an epic poem, but the theme is ridiculously trivial, in comparison with the grand theme of an epic. The action opens with a mock-heroic manner with the awakening of Belinda, the heroine of the poem. Belinda is the very goddess of beauty, and the luster of her eyes surpasses that of the sun, who peeped timorously through the white curtains in Belinda's room: "Sol through white curtains shot a timorous ray, / And opened those eyes that must eclipse the day."

The whole structure of The Rape of the Lock is cast in the epic mood, but it could not be a serious epic because the incident is trivial—so we have the mock-heroic or heroi-comical poem. The poem is divided into Cantos like an epic poem, and there are ironic parallels to the main Incidents of the epic. The poem begins with an invocation in epic tradition: "Say, what strange motive, Goddness! could compel / A well-bred lord to assault a gentle belle?" As in epics, in The Rape of the Lock, too, divine beings are portrayed. Belinda is in the divine care of the sylphs: "Fairest of mortals, thou distinguished 'care, / Of thousand bright inhabitants of air". But then the sylphs are fragile, airy beings and they are helpless before the caprices of men. Despite all their concern for Belinda, her beautiful lock of hair is raped by the naughty Baron. There is the mischievous gnome who, like Milton's Satan, is intent upon making Belinda miserable and thereby all her admirers. The gnome, addresses the wayward Queen who rules the sex from fifteen to fifty, thus: "Hear me, and touch Belinda with chagrin, / That single act gives half the world the spleen."

The epic always uses the supernatural element. In The Iliad there are gods and goddesses; in The Rape of the Lock, there are the sylphs and gnomes. These aerial spirits are small and insignificant things, and are, therefore, exactly in keeping with the triviality of the theme. They guard the person of the heroine and when there is a fight between the followers of Belinda and those of the Baron; they take part in the fight, like the gods and goddesses in the Trojan War: "Propped on their bodkin spears, the spirits survey, / The growing combat or assist the fray."

An epic poem must contain some episodes also. In keeping with this practice Pope has introduced the episode of the game of Ombre which is described in great detail. There is also the hazardous journey of Umbriel to the Cave of Spleen. Then there is the battle between the lords and ladies just like the battles in epic poetry. But in the true mock-heroic style this battle is fought with fans and snuff instead of with swords and spears.

There are single combats also between Belinda and the Baron and between Clarissa and Sir Plume. Belinda's toilet is another engaging account in which Pope has attributed in a perfect mock-heroic manner, the solemnity of a religious observance to the luxurious toilet of a lady of fashion and frivolity. Puffs, powders, patches, bibles, billet-doux, are all brought to the same table and the slight and the series are all strangely synthesized.

The Rape of the Lock is a rare instance in which the slight theme is given an exalted treatment for satirical purposes. All through the poem, a pose of importance is given to all that is thoroughly unimportant and insignificant and practically meaningless and farcical. The very conception of writing an epic on the rape of a lock of hair is funny and bears testimony to the poet's effort to make the little great and the great little.

In The Rape of the Lock the balance between the concealed irony and the assumed gravity is nicely trimmed: the little is made great and the great made little. It is the triumph of insignificance, the apotheosis of foppery and folly.

3.Use of Machinery in The Rape of the Lock

In the dedication to the poem, Pope explains that machinery is a term invented by the critics to signify the part which deities, angels, or demons play in a poem. He goes on to say that the machinery in his poem is based on the Rosicrucian doctrine of spirits.

According to this doctrine the four elements are inhabited by sylphs, nymphs, gnomes, and salamanders. The sylphs, whose habitation is in the air, are supposed to be the best-conditioned creatures imaginable. In The Rape of the Lock, Pope tells us that beautiful women return, after their death, to the elements from which they were derived. Termagants, or violent tempered women become salamanders or spirits of the fire. Women of gentle and pleasing disposition pass into nymphs or water-spirits. Prudish women become gnomes or earth-spirits. Light-hearted coquettes are changed into sylphs or spirits of the air. Pope attributes to the mischievous influence of the gnomes, many unguarded follies of the female sex which he holds up to ridicule.

The first and perhaps the foremost occupation of the sylphs is the protection of fair and chaste ladies who reject the male sex. It is they who guard and save the chastity of maidens who are on the point of yielding to their lovers. They save the chastity of maidens from falling victims to the allurements of "treacherous friends" and dashing young men whose music softens their minds and dancing inflames their passions. The gnomes or earth-spirits fill the minds of proud maidens with foolish ideas which make them indulge in vain dreams of being married to lords and peers. These gnomes teach young coquettes to ogle and pretend blushing at the sight of fashionable young men who cause their hearts to flutter. It is the sylphs, however, who safely guide the maidens through all dangers. It is most amusing to note how these sylphs do this. Whenever a maiden is about to yield to the seduction of a particular young man, another who is more attractive and tempting appears on the scene and the fashionable maiden at once transfers her favor to the newcomer. This may be called levity of fickleness in women, but it is all contrived by the sylphs. The sylphs are led by Ariel (named after Shakespeare's immortal creation in The Tempest). Ariel tells us in the poem that to him and his followers have been assigned the humble but pleasant duty of serving fashionable young ladies. The functions of these sylphs are described humorously and include saving the powder from being blown off from the cheeks of ladies, preventing scents from evaporating, preparing cosmetics, teaching the ladies to blush and to put on enchanting airs, suggesting new ideas about dress. The sylphs show a delightful down-scaling of the epic machines. They are "light" by any heroic standards. They feel scared when a crisis approaches. Yet they are in every detail Belinda's intimates and counselors. They explain the various complicated conventions and anxieties that make up Belinda's day.

The sylphs in this poem are both a mirror and mock-apotheosis of the customs and conventions of the society of the time. Belinda is told in a dream that sylphs guide and protect her through the dangers of life. Ariel's account of the predicament of the "tender mind" in a circle of rakes reduces his use of noble words such as "innocent", "honour", and "purity" to the level of a muddle and a sham. He is there, he tells her, to protect her purity according to sylphic theology. Defended by sylphs, the "melting maids" are safe, for what we call "honour" is really no more than Providence. Reassuring Belinda in this way, Ariel is in effect undermining her moral position, taking away with one hand the credit he gives with the other. What we call "levity" in women, says Ariel, is the effect of the same driving guidance as determined their "honour". The concealed implication, that the two qualities are roughly on a par, is very cruel. But Ariel merrily goes on to warn Belinda in the epic style of the danger that threatens her. He concludes with a plea for caution, and the words of caution come from the lips that have just encouraged flirtatiousness.

Thus Pope has provided the myth of the sylphs in order to symbolize the polite conventions which govern the conduct of maidens. We miss the whole point if we regard the sylphs as merely supernatural machinery. In general, we may say that Pope's use of this myth represents his attempt to do justice or the intricacies of the feminine mind. His treatment of the sylphs allows him to develop his whole attitude toward Belinda and the special world which she graces.

4.Character of Belinda

Introduction

Belinda is the central character in Alexander Pope's "The Rape of the Lock." She is a young woman who embodies beauty, charm, and social status within the aristocratic society depicted in the poem. Here is an analysis of Belinda's character:

Physical Beauty:

Belinda is described as a stunningly beautiful young woman with captivating features. Her most significant physical attribute is her luxuriant lock of hair, which becomes the narrative's focal point. Her physical beauty symbolizes her desirability and the admiration she receives from others.

Vanity and Social Status:

Belinda is conscious of her beauty and the attention it garners. She takes pride in her appearance and actively participates in the social scene of the elite society. Belinda's preoccupation with her external image reflects the values of the society she inhabits, which places a high emphasis on superficiality and outward appearances.

Vulnerability and Innocence:

Belinda's character also portrays vulnerability and innocence. Despite her beauty and social standing, she is depicted as naive and easily swayed by the flattery and attention of others, particularly men. Her innocence is highlighted by her obliviousness to the theft of her lock of hair, which serves as an exaggeration of her detachment from the consequences of her vanity.

The object of Desire:

Belinda's lock of hair becomes a coveted object of desire for the Baron. It is through this incident that the poem explores the power dynamics and objectification of women in the society of the time. Belinda's character represents the object of male desire, and her loss of the lock symbolizes the violation of her boundaries.

Resilience and Resurgence:

Despite the violation of her personal space and the loss of her lock, Belinda exhibits resilience and a determination to regain her agency. She seeks solace from her female companions and relies on the support of the sylphs to retrieve her stolen hair. Belinda's character demonstrates a spirit of resilience and an ability to overcome adversity.

Belinda's character in "The Rape of the Lock" embodies the contradictions and complexities of the society in which she exists. She represents the ideals of beauty, vanity, vulnerability, and resilience, serving as a vehicle through which Pope satirizes the superficiality and social dynamics of the aristocratic world.

Belinda as a Main Character:

Belinda is an ambiguous character and plays the role of ambivalent in "The Rape of the Lock". This paradox in the character of Belinda is explained by the fact that Pope looks upon her as a charming butterfly, an embodiment of physical beauty and laudable qualities of head and heart and at the same time he presents her as the type of figure of the coquettes of the time and the butt of his social satire.

There are times when even the praise of Belinda's attractions seems to be a mere mask for Pope's satiric attack on her, as the representative of her degenerate, unscrupulous class. One of Pope's contemporaries John Denies tried to undermine Belinda's character by saying that she is a 'chimera and not a character.

Belinda represents Miss Arabella Fermor of real life whom Lord Petre offended by stealing a lock of her hair. Pope wrote this poem to patch up the quarrel between the Fermors and Petres on a trivial matter. To achieve his objective he has to present Belinda as a good individual. He treats her satirically only when she represents the type of the pleasure-loving, unscrupulous and spineless aristocracy.

The moralist in Pope was aware of the decadence of values in the fashionable society and so he is critical of Belinda to the extent that she tries to follow all the decadent values of the society despite her natural beauty, youth and charm. So the portrayal of Belinda is at once despicable and endearing.

"The Rape of the Lock" is a mock epic poem depicting a social drama of the 18th century fashionable society. Belinda is the main target of satire in the poem. She embodies all the vanities, follies, and lack of moral scruples typical of upper-class ladies at the time. She is a late riser, wakes up at twelve falls asleep again and is roused from her sleep by the licking tongue of her pet dog, Shock.

When Belinda is engaged in her toilet, her beauty and charm are laid and stressed open. She is assisted by her servant Betty, in decorating and embellishing herself with cosmetics and jewellery. She is here compared to a warrior as she dresses herself:

"Now awful beauty puts all its arms; The fair each moment rises in her charms."

(line-149-140, Canto-1)

She wears a sparkling cross, her looks are lively and she smiles at everyone, but does not show any special favour towards anyone:

"Bright as the sun, her eyes the gazers strike And, like the sun, they shine on all alike."

(line-149-140, Canto-1)

Her faults, if any are hidden by her graceful ease and sweetness. She has a thirst for fame which leads to her encounter with two "adventurous knights" at the game of cards known as Ombre. She is jubilant and shouts exultantly when she is victorious in the game of Ombre. Her jubilation and exultation at her victory show that she is vain and is rather superficial in her mind.

In the dedicatory epistle, Pope mentions the unscrupulous beauty of Belinda. There is ample evidence to suggest that Belinda did indeed possess an ineffable beauty and charm, because of which she is the cynosure of her fashionable society. She has exquisite charm, Belinda is not only exceptionally beautiful but also the cause of joy and brightness in the world where she figures, Pope describes her as the "fair nymph", "virgin" and even a "Goddess".

Belinda is not only beautiful, but she is also keen to display her beauty. Her pleasure ride in a boat on the Thames is a part of this programme. With her repaired smiles and artistically heightened and purified blush, Belinda is playing a role most of the time. Her role is that of an amiable beautiful maid who rejects without causing any offence and scatters her smiles on all, even at her grief after the snipping off the Lock of her hair, which is a studied art. As Pope puts it:

"Then seen the nymph in beauteous grief appears, Her eyes half-langu, half-drawned in tears."

These lines evoke the picture of a highly self-conscious actress who knows the kind of histrionics the particular roles as the moment demands. Court is the very place she can kill with her eyes and for which she dresses herself so deliberately. She knows in her heart of heart that the cutting of her Lock is a compliment to her beauty. But she knows that the event will make her a 'degraded toast'. Privately she has enjoyed the adoration of the Baron but publicly she must condemn his action:

"On hadst thou cruel! Been content to seize Hairs less in sight, or any hairs but these!"

As a representative of the 18th century, English aristocratic ladies, Belinda has all the vanities, frivolities and fashions of her social type. Pope stresses Belinda's divinity, he also stresses her spiritual shallowness.

Conclusion

To conclude, it can be said that Belinda in "The Rape of the Lock" is seen in many different lights- as coquette, injured, innocent, sweet-charmer, society belle, rival of the sun ad murderer of millions. This Cleopatra lie variety indicates simultaneously her charm and lack of character. At one point the praise of her attraction may be a mere mark for Pope's satiric attack on the type figure of the coquette; at another point it is praise no irony can fully undermine. The part that Belinda plays in the elaborate social drama is at once despicable, ridiculous, endearing, precarious, poignant and petty.

5.Supernatural Machinery in The Rape of The Lock Or

Q. What is the significance of supernatural machinery in "The Rape of the Lock"?Or

Q. Alexander Pope's use of supernatural machinery heightens the mock-heroic effect of the poem The Rape of the Lock. Discuss.

Supernatural machinery is a term that refers to the involvement of gods or other supernatural entities in the unfolding of a story, a common device in ancient epic poems like Homer's "The Iliad" and Virgil's "Aeneid."

Pope borrows this device but modifies it according to his poem's lighter and satirical spirit. Instead of gods and goddesses, Pope introduces a society of spirits or "sylphs" that watch over the poem's protagonist, Belinda, and other high-born ladies.

Belinda's world is controlled not by gods but by these trivial sylphs and gnomes, a metaphor for the frivolity of the society Pope is satirizing. Ariel, the chief of these sylphs, is no Zeus or Athena but a light and somewhat ineffectual sprite whose primary concern is preserving Belinda's chastity and, more importantly, her beauty.

The sylphs' attempts to prevent the lock's "rape" (or cutting) and their failure to do so mimic the epic battles and divine interventions of classical epics but in a faraway heroic context, creating a mock-heroic effect.

Influence of Rosicrucian Doctrine

Pope's use of supernatural machinery in "The Rape of the Lock" heightens the poem's mock-heroic effect by juxtaposing the epic and the trivial, the grandiose and the petty, the divine and the vain.

The result is a rich satire that exposes and ridicules the pretensions of its time while also providing a delightful reading experience filled with wit and humour.

Alexander Pope introduces several supernatural beings that form part of the Rosicrucian cosmology. Here's a list of these beings with some details:

1- Sylphs (Air): These are spirits of the air, led by Ariel. In the poem, they are portrayed as light and ethereal beings. They have the task of protecting Belinda, the poem's protagonist. Sylphs hover around her, guarding her beauty and virtue. They also attempt to prevent the Baron from cutting off a lock of Belinda's hair but fail in their endeavour.

2- Gnomes (Earth): Gnomes are spirits associated with the earth element. They are not central to the action in "The Rape of the Lock." In the Rosicrucian tradition, gnomes are often associated with hidden treasures and secrets beneath the earth. It fits Pope's subtext about society's hidden desires and vanity.

3- Nymphs (Water): Nymphs are water spirits. They don't play a significant role in the narrative. However, they, along with the sylphs, gnomes, and salamanders, contribute to the mock-epic tone of the poem. Traditionally, nymphs are linked to emotions and romantic pursuits.

4- Salamanders (Fire): Salamanders are spirits associated with the fire element. Like the gnomes and nymphs, salamanders do not play a prominent role in the poem. Traditionally, they symbolize passion and transformation.

The Sylphs' Role in the Toilet Scene

Pope uses the Sylphs to magnify the triviality and exaggerated importance placed on outward beauty by society. Pope presents the Sylphs' dedication to safeguarding Belinda's cosmetic rituals and beauty products in a mock-heroic style. He uses epic language to describe their actions, which raises ordinary activities to epic proportions.

To fifty chosen Sylphs, of special note,
We trust th' important charge, the Petticoat:
Oft have we known that seven-fold fence to fail,
Tho' stiff with hoops, and arm'd with ribs of whale;
Form a strong line about the silver bound,
And guard the wide circumference around.

This description humorously emphasizes the extreme measures taken to protect the sacred realm of Belinda's toilette. The Sylphs' involvement in the toilet scene highlights the ridiculousness of the societal values that prioritize physical appearance over more important matters.

Militia of the Lower Sky

In 'The Rape of the Lock', Pope uses the phrase 'militia of the lower sky' to describe the sylphs. These supernatural beings act as Belinda's protectors and guardians.

Know then, unnumber'd spirits round thee fly,
The light militia of the lower sky
The Cave of Spleen
The "Cave of Spleen" is an essential supernatural element in Alexander Pope's mock-epic poem, "The Rape of the Lock."

It also personifies the psychological condition of "spleen," a term in Pope's time associated with various forms of melancholy, irritability, or capricious mood.

The description portrays the Cave of Spleen as a dark and gloomy place where discontent, ill humour, and weak spirits reside. Pope creates an atmospheric image of the cave:

Here living Teapots stand, one arm held out,
One bent; the handle this, and that the spout:
A Pipkin there like Homer's Tripod walks;
Here sighs a Jar, and there a Goose-pie talks;

These lines depict the cave as a surreal place filled with anthropomorphic household objects, emphasizing the triviality of the issues causing spleen.

The Cave of Spleen plays a significant role in escalating the poem's conflict. The allegorical figure of ill-humour offers a 'spleen' and a 'vapour' to Belinda. She is in distress and upset after the Baron cuts off her lock of hair.

These items symbolize emotional distress and exaggerated sentimentality, further inflating Belinda's reaction to her loss.

The Cave of Spleen is a brilliant example of Pope's use of supernatural machinery to heighten the mock-heroic effect. Alexander Pope gives physical form to the emotional state of the spleen. He depicts it as a place of dark and absurd melancholy.

Pope satirizes the irrational mood swings and disproportionate emotional reactions of the aristocratic society he's portraying. Thus The Cave of Spleen satirizes upper-class society's petty concerns and exaggerated emotions.

Conclusion

In conclusion, using supernatural machinery in Alexander Pope's "The Rape of the Lock" is integral to the poem's satirical effect and overall meaning. The sylphs, the dream, the Cave of Spleen, and the celestial judgment of the lock all serve to transform a trivial social incident into an epic event. It reveals Pope's mastery of the mock-heroic style.

The inclusion of supernatural elements elevates the trivialities of the social elite to the level of divine importance. This is consistent with Pope's objective to satirize the petty squabbles and shallow concerns of the aristocracy in the 18th century.

Pope demonstrates the absurdity of his society's disproportionate reactions to trivial matters by applying epic conventions to a trivial subject matter.

Furthermore, the supernatural machinery underscores the importance of appearance, reputation, and social conventions in the society Pope depicts. The sylphs' efforts to preserve Belinda's beauty, the ill omen of the dream, the melancholy and petulance represented by the Cave of Spleen, and the transformation of the lock into a star all reflect the social obsessions of the time.

Although invisible and ethereal, the sylphs, gnomes, nymphs, and salamanders mirror the human characters' vanity, superficiality, and pretensions. Thus, these supernatural entities are not just decorative elements but also instrumental in the poem's beauty.

6.Belinda in The Rape of the Lock : Pope's Critique of Feminine Follies

The Rape of the Lock, a mock heroic epic by <u>Alexander Pope</u>, is both a careful exploration of the contemporary social follies and a representation of the inner fabrics of the feminine mind. However, it would be wrong to say that Pope was entirely engrossed in the question of his heroine's divine beauty. He rather shows a remarkably delightful treatment of the epic manner though rich satire rendering a roundness to his creative imagination. However, he makes Belinda the axis of his aesthetic presentation, thereby necessitating a more careful study of her stature.

Being primarily an epic, and at the same time a mockery of the form, The Rape of the Lock is characterized by a unique use of the dual device of amplification followed by immediate deflation. The words of Ariel, the guardian angel of Belinda in Canto I make the readers subconsciously form religious associations:

Virgins visited by angel pow'rs.

What begins to operate in the reader's mind is a trigger to produce a vision, of perhaps Virgin Mary or Joan of Arc. The poet does not bind the free flow of imagination by specifying any one virgin or angel. Consequently, the arena is widened and the reader is automatically prepared for the elevation of Belinda to divinity. It, therefore, becomes easier to accept her importance as stated by Ariel triumphantly:

...thy own importance know

At this point, Pope's purpose is served, and his work gains the initial momentum it requires. However, what takes place immediately after this is the hilarious arrival of Shock, the lapdog, which puts an end to the ethereal speech of Ariel, quite anticlimactically.

This is the undercurrent of irony that pervades the whole of the poem. The theme itself is a mockery, against the frailty of social conventions—of the distorted perception of social beings; yet the presentation is truly artistic. There is no conflict between Pope, the artist and Pope, the satirist—they work in unison creating harmony of aesthetic experience in the reader's mind. Nowhere is this harmony perceived more distinctly than in the Second part of the First Canto where Belinda is seen at her Dressing Table. Pope goes on describing her actions with ritualistic fervor:

A heavenly image in the glass appears
To that she bends, to that her eyes she

Belinda is definitely a goddess but she puts her divinity on her dressing mirror. Such is the paradox of beauty-worship that Belinda is both, the sincere devotee and the worshiped deity herself. The poet observes the gradual enhancement of Belinda's made-up beauty through witty satire:

Sees by degrees a purer blush arise

It would be, however, a great mistake to laugh too easily at the expression: "purer blush", which actually appears as being contrary to what it pretends to mean. At least, at this point, Belinda's concentration correlates to the actual commitment of an artist. Her process of self beautification is seen both as an ornamentation governed by pride as well as the realization of a true artistic merit. In her essay, "The case of Miss Arabella Fermor", Cleanth Brooks rightly observes that, "...regardless of whatever we make of the 'purer blush', Belinda's dressing table does glow with a radiance." Indeed, despite being scornful of the "beauty regime", Pope is nonetheless conscious of the actual beauty which it genuinely possesses.

However, the true artist in Pope can be detected by the various images which run throughout the poem. Had Pope been confined to the dictates of the satiric form, he could have satisfied himself by laughing away the divinity of Belinda. On the contrary, the artist in him looks at her beauty and compares her to the brightest celestial body, the glowing sun. In Canto I, the sun is placed as a rival to Belinda's glory:

Sol through white curtains shot a timorous ray,
And oped those eyes that must eclipse the day:

The rivalry continues to Canto II where he directly calls her the "rival of his Beams".

It is interesting to note the way Pope applies the sun metaphor to describe Belinda's generous gaze on "all alike." Is she a flirtatious maiden, (then pope is a satirist); or is she a generous impartial recipient of admiration (then Pope is more than a satirist). The sun comparison contains all these implications and goes beyond the level of momentary jest.

However, the height of Pope's Imagination is seen vis-à-vis Belinda's interaction with the sylphs. The machinery of the sylphs is a unique representation of Pope's wholly naturalistic interpretation of the feminine mind. As a satirist he adds the element of absurdity to them, and yet as an artist he sees them as the manifestations of Belinda's self-consciousness.

The Sylphs are actually honor, as Ariel points out—and such a definition at once satirizes the social perception of chastity. The equivalence of lost virginity and broken china jar at once directs at the root cause of such a distorted perception—the spiritual blindness.This blindness makes the cross worn by Belinda an ornament that "Jews kiss and infidels adore." Such is the force of Pope's satire that it wrings the heart of the readers yet never descends from the artistic plane of poetry.

The late waking of "sleepless lovers", the equal adoration for lapdogs and husbands, the snuffbox, the ritualistic dressing procedure, the lack of judgement, "altar of love", the game of Ombre and the violent reaction of Belinda at the loss of her lock are not merely diverse social satire—they are artistically woven into a tapestry—in the form of a climax to lead to the miraculous disappearance of the lock only to immortalize the name of Belinda.

7. *Comment on Belinda's Dressing Table.*

The uncovering of the dressing table reveals silver vases containing cosmetics and jewellery arranged in a particular way, particular to fashionable ladies, described here as 'mystic order laid". A Nymph dressed in white and with her head uncovered, first offers prayers intensely to the "cosmetic powers". She then looks reverentially at the heavenly reflection of Belinda that appears in the mirror and offers respects. The Nymph is inferior to Belinda as she is only a priestess to Belinda, the heavenly figure. She then stands by the dressing table, which is equated with alter, the place of worship, and begins "the sacred rites of Pride" with all fear and respect. The making-up of Belinda is elevated here to the level of sacred rites, but ridiculed as those of Pride. Caskets containing innumerable precious objects like jewels, perfumes etc., offerings from several parts of the world, are opened. The Nymph picks their contents with scrupulous care and decorates Belinda with sparkling things. The poet now goes on to mention the contents of different caskets laid on the table. One casket contains glittering gems from India; another has the perfumes brought from Arabia. Combs made of tortoise shell and ivory, presented here as transformations of tortoise and elephant, are seen lying together on the table. The combs made of tortoise shell are speckled or spotted while those of ivory are white in colour. Several kinds of pins are arranged in rows, Puffs, patches, powders, bible, and love letters are also there. Now Belinda has put on all beautifying things, which are likened to arms of a warrior in an epic and her charm increases as beautifying process progress. In addition, she improves her smiles, 'awakens every grace' and displays all the wonderful attractive features of her face. Gradually, even her blushing improves and the brightness in her eyes increases. The poet introduces the machinery of spirits with the description of sylphs getting busy in assisting Belinda's dressing-up. Some of them divide her hair into braids and set them properly, while some others fold the sleeve of her dress, and some plait her gown, Betty, the servant maid of Belinda is given credit for the make-up even though she does not deserve it, as the whole beautification is done by the Nymph and the Sylphs.

CHAPTER EIGHT

THE SPECTATOR CLUB

The Spectator Club
Addison and Steele

Ast alii sex

Et plures uno conclamant ore.

—Juvenal, "Satires," vii. 166.

THE FIRST of our society is a gentleman of Worcestershire, of an ancient descent, a baronet, his name Sir Roger de Coverley. His great-grandfather was inventor of that famous country-dance which is called after him. All who know that shire are very well acquainted with the parts and merits of Sir Roger. He is a gentleman that is very singular in his behavior, but his singularities proceed from his good sense, and are contradictions to the manners of the world, only as he thinks the world is in the wrong. However, this humor creates him no enemies, for he does nothing with sourness or obstinacy; and his being unconfined to modes and forms makes him but the readier and more capable to please and oblige all who know him. When he is in town he lives in Soho Square. It is said he keeps himself a bachelor by reason he was crossed in love by a perverse beautiful widow of the next county to him. Before this disappointment, Sir Roger was what you call a fine gentleman, had often supped with my Lord Rochester and Sir George Etherege, fought a duel upon his first coming to town, and kicked bully Dawson in a public coffee-house for calling him youngster. But being ill-used by the above-mentioned widow, he was very serious for a year and a half; and though, his temper being naturally jovial, he at last got over it, he grew careless of himself and never dressed afterwards. He continues to wear a coat and doublet of the same cut that were in fashion at the time of his repulse, which, in his merry humors, he tells us, has been in and out twelve times since he first wore it. It is said Sir Roger grew humble in his desires after he had forgot his cruel beauty, insomuch that it is reported he has frequently offended with beggars and gypsies; but this is looked upon, by his friends, rather as matter of raillery than truth. He is now in his fifty-sixth year, cheerful, gay, and hearty; keeps a good house both in town and country; a great lover of mankind; but there is such a mirthful cast in his behavior, that he is rather beloved than esteemed. His tenants grow rich, his servants look satisfied, all the young women profess love to him, and the young men are glad of his company. When he comes into a house, he calls the servants by their names, and talks all the way upstairs to a visit. I must not omit that Sir Roger is a justice of the quorum; that he fills the chair at a quarter-session with great abilities, and three months ago gained universal applause, by explaining a passage in the Game Act.

The gentleman next in esteem and authority among us is another bachelor, who is a member of the Inner Temple, a man of great probity, wit, and understanding; but he has chosen his place of residence rather to obey the direction of an old humorsome father than in pursuit of his own inclinations. He was placed there to study the laws of the land, and is the most learned of any of the house in those of the stage. Aristotle and Longinus are much better understood by him than Littleton or Coke. The father sends up every post questions relating to marriage-articles, leases, and tenures, in the neighborhood; all which questions he agrees with an attorney to answer and take care of in the lump. He is studying the passions themselves, when he should be inquiring into the debates among men which arise from them. He knows the argument of each of the orations of Demosthenes and Tully, but not one case in the reports of our own courts. No one ever took him for a fool; but none, except his intimate friends, know he has a great deal of wit. This turn makes him at once both disinterested and agreeable. As few of his thoughts are drawn from business, they are most of them fit for conversation. His taste for books is a little too just for the age he lives in; he has read all, but approves of very few. His familiarity with the customs, manners, actions, and writings of the ancients, makes him a very delicate observer of what occurs to him in the present world. He is an excellent critic, and the time of the play is his hour of business; exactly at five he passes through New-inn, crosses through Russell-court, and takes a turn at Will's till the play begins; he has his shoes rubbed and his periwig powdered at the barber's as you go into the Rose. It is for the good of the audience when he is at the play, for the actors have an ambition to please him.

The person of next consideration is Sir Andrew Freeport, a merchant of great eminence in the city of London; a person of indefatigable industry, strong reason, and great experience. His notions of trade are noble and generous, and (as every rich man has usually some sly way of jesting, which would make no great figure were he not a rich man) he calls the sea the British Common. He is acquainted with commerce in all its parts, and will tell you that it is a stupid and barbarous way to extend dominion by arms; for true power is to be got by arts and industry. He will often argue that, if this part of our trade were well cultivated, we should gain from one nation; and if another, from another. I have heard him prove that diligence makes more lasting acquisitions than valor, and that sloth has ruined more nations than the sword. He abounds in several frugal maxims, amongst which the greatest favorite is, "A penny saved is a penny got." A general trader of good sense is pleasanter company than a general scholar; and Sir Andrew having a natural unaffected eloquence, the perspicuity of his discourse gives the same pleasure that wit would in another man. He has made his fortune himself; and says that England may be richer than other kingdoms by as plain methods as he himself is richer than other men; though at the same time I can say this of him, that there is not a point in the compass but blows home a ship in which he is an owner.

Next to Sir Andrew in the clubroom sits Captain Sentry, a gentleman of great courage, good understanding, but invincible modesty. He is one of those that deserve very well, but are very awkward at putting their talents within the observation of such as should take notice of them. He was some years a captain, and behaved himself with great gallantry in several engagements and at several sieges; but having a small estate of his own, and being next heir to Sir Roger, he has quitted a way of life in which no man can rise suitably to his merit, who is not something of a courtier as well as a soldier. I have heard him often lament that, in a profession where merit is placed in so conspicuous a view, impudence should get the better of modesty. When he has talked to this purpose, I never heard him make a sour expression, but frankly confess that he left the world because he was not fit for it. A strict honesty and an even regular behavior are in themselves obstacles to him that must press through crowds, who endeavor at the same end with himself, the favor of a commander. He will, however, in his way of talk excuse generals for not disposing according to men's dessert, or inquiring into it; for, says he, that great man who has a mind to help me has as many to break through to come to me as I have to come at him:

therefore he will conclude that the man who would make a figure, especially in a military way, must get over all false modesty, and assist his patron against the importunity of other pretenders, by a proper assurance in his own vindication. He says it is a civil cowardice to be backward in asserting what you ought to expect, as it is a military fear to be slow in attacking when it is your duty. With this candor does the gentleman speak of himself and others. The same frankness runs through all his conversation. The military part of his life has furnished him with many adventures, in the relation of which he is very agreeable to the company; for he is never overbearing, though accustomed to command men in the utmost degree below him; nor ever too obsequious, from an habit of obeying men highly above him.

But that our society may not appear a set of humorists, unacquainted with the gallantries and pleasures of the age, we have amongst us the gallant Will Honeycomb, a gentleman who, according to his years, should be in the decline of his life; but having ever been very careful of his person, and always had a very easy fortune, time has made but a very little impression either by wrinkles on his forehead, or traces on his brain. His person is well turned, and of a good height. He is very ready at that sort of discourse with which men usually entertain women. He has all his life dressed very well, and remembers habits as others do men. He can smile when one speaks to him, and laughs easily. He knows the history of every mode, and can inform you from which of the French king's wenches our wives and daughters had this manner of curling their hair, that way of placing their hoods; whose frailty was covered by such a sort of a petticoat, and whose vanity to show her foot made that part of the dress so short in such a year. In a word, all his conversation and knowledge have been in the female world. As other men of his age will take notice to you what such a minister said upon such and such an occasion, he will tell you when the Duke of Monmouth danced at court, such a woman was then smitten, another was taken with him at the head of his troop in the park. In all these important relations, he has ever about the same time received a kind glance, or a blow of a fan from some celebrated beauty, mother of the present Lord Such-a-one. If you speak of a young commoner that said a lively thing in the House, he starts up, "He has good blood in his veins; Tom Mirable begot him; the rogue cheated me in that affair; that young fellow's mother used me more like a dog than any woman I ever made advances to." This way of talking of his very much enlivens the conversation among us of a more sedate turn, and I find there is not one of the company, but myself, who rarely speak at all, but speaks of him as of that sort of a man who is usually called a well-bred fine gentleman. To conclude his character, where women are not concerned, he is an honest worthy man.

I cannot tell whether I am to account him, whom I am next to speak of, as one of our company; for he visits us but seldom, but when he does, it adds to every man else a new enjoyment of himself. He is a clergyman, a very philosophic man, of general learning, great sanctity of life, and the most exact good breeding. He has the misfortune to be of a very weak constitution, and consequently cannot accept of such cares and business as preferments in his function would oblige him to; he is therefore among divines what a chamber-counsellor is among lawyers. The probity of his mind, and the integrity of his life, create him followers, as being eloquent or loud advances others. He seldom introduces the subject he speaks upon; but we are so far gone in years that he observes, when he is among us, an earnestness to have him fall on some divine topic, which he always treats with much authority, as one who has no interest in this world, as one who is hastening to the object of all his wishes, and conceives hope from his decays and infirmities. These are my ordinary companions.

An introduction to the essay

"The Spectator Club" is an essay introducing readers to the members of the Spectator Club, a fictional group representing different facets of society. Each character embodies specific social traits and values, serving as a satirical commentary on 18th-century English society. Sir Roger de Coverley, the kind and eccentric country gentleman, Captain Sentry, the sensible soldier, and Will Honeycomb, the fashionable bachelor, are among the club's memorable characters. Through these personas, Addison and Steele explore various themes, including class differences, manners, and personal quirks, presenting a humorous yet insightful portrait of the time. "The Spectator Club" emphasizes the importance of observing and understanding people from diverse backgrounds, encouraging readers to appreciate both the strengths and flaws of society.

The essay "The Spectator Club" is the second essay in the 'The Spectator'. Steele conceived a club with members drawn from different stages of life, society and profession. Each of them has own individual qualities. Thus the club is the miniature version of the society of the day. Yet there is no representative of the lower classes. The club was meant to be of intellectuals. In this essay Steele gives an account of the six gentle men. They were members of the Spectator Club in addition to Mr. Spectator. This essay reveals Steele's keen power of observation, skill in characterization and his delicate mockery which is easy and informal style.

The Good Natured Sir Roger de Coverley:

Sir Roger de Coverley is a gentleman of an ancient family. His great-grand-father was the inventor of the Coverley dance. His eccentricities proceed from his good sense. He is free from the bondage of custom and fashion. When he is in town, he lives in Soho-Square. Once he fell in love with beautiful widow. She was a perverse (wicked) lady of the next country. She rejected his love after this disappointment he remained very serious for a year and a half. Then he gradually got over it. So he keeps himself a bachelor. Before this incident, he was a fine gentleman and had relation with many important persons of the age. This incident made him careless of his dress and appearance. Now he is fifty six years old. He possesses a cheerful and gay personality. He has two houses, one in the town and the other in the country. He is good natured. So everyone loves him. He is justice of quorum and carries out his duties with great abilities. Sometime ago he won universal applause by explaining a passage in the Game-Act.

The Shrewd Critic of Drama: The Member of the Inner-Temple:

Next important person is The Templar. He is another bachelor. He is a member of the Inner-Temple. He is an honest and wise man. He took to the study of law to obey his old father, against his willingness. But his favourite subject of study was the arts and the stage. He was a well-read man in the classics. He had read the customs, manners, actions and writings of the ancients. This made him a shrewd observer of men and things. He was a good critic of drama (stage). If he was present in any performance, every actor would do the best to please him. The bachelor visits the theatre often; his scholarship enables him to be a keen judge of dramatic performance

The Successful Merchant Sir Andrew Freeport:

Sir Andrew Freeport is a merchant of great importance in London. He is a man of industry, strong reason and great experience. He has his own noble and generous ideas of trade. He calls the sea the British common. He thinks that is a stupid way to extend dominion by arms. He considers the real strength of a nation consists in its arts and industry. He approves diligence and labour. He is known for a few maxims "a penny saved is a penny got" and "sloth is a great destroyer than the sword". He has a natural unaffected eloquence. It makes his discourse very pleasing. He has become rich by plain labour and honest methods. He thinks that England may become richer than other nations by the same methods. He has business contacts throughout the world.

The Courageous Captain Sentry:

Captain Sentry is the next important person. He is a man of great courage, good understanding, but invincible modesty. He possesses great merits. He does not want to show them. He was in the army for several years and served as captain. He behaved himself with great gallantry in several engagements. He has a small estate of his own. Being next heir to Sri Roger, he left the army. This does not make him feel unpleasant. He asserts that in the army those who are assertive and pushing and those who do no possess any false sense of modesty can rise. It was unsuitable to his shy temperament. Therefore he has left the army. His military life has furnished him with many adventures. He relates them to others in a pleasing manner.

The Gallant Will Honeycomb:

The next member of the club, Will Honeycomb, is the next in importance. He is a gallant. According to his years, he should be in the decline of his life. He has been very careful of his person. So, age has not made any impression either on his body or mind. He is tall. He dresses himself very well. He is good at that type of conversation with which men usually entertain women. He knows the history of every fashion. His entire knowledge is confined to the female world. He can tell when the Duke of Monmouth danced at court, and which woman fell in love with him at that time. He has been given a tender attention and kind treatment by beautiful ladies of the day. His conversation is pleasing. Everyone calls him a well-bred fine gentleman.

The Pious Clergyman:

The Clergyman is the last member of the club. He comes to attend the meetings rarely. He is a learned and pious man. He is very weak in health. He cannot take heavy responsibilities of his profession. Therefore he is among divines, what a chamber-counsellor is among lawyers. He speaks any divine topic with authority. He seems to have no interest in this world. So he is hastening to the object of his soul's desire. Thus, in the description of the members of the Spectator club, Steele depicts the cross-section of the Contemporary society and the interaction of the social classes.

<u>Two-Mark Questions with Answers</u>

1.What is "The Spectator Club"?

"The Spectator Club" is a fictional club introduced by Addison and Steele, featuring characters who represent different aspects of 18th-century English society.

2.Who is Sir Roger de Coverley?

Sir Roger de Coverley is a kind but eccentric country gentleman and one of the central characters in "The Spectator Club," symbolizing traditional values and simplicity.

3.What trait does Captain Sentry represent in the club?

Captain Sentry represents sensibility and discipline, embodying the values of a respectable soldier within the club.

4.Who is Will Honeycomb in "The Spectator Club"?

Will Honeycomb is a fashionable, charming bachelor, representing the social and flirtatious aspects of urban life in the club.

5.What is the purpose of "The Spectator Club"?

The purpose of "The Spectator Club" is to present a satirical commentary on English society by introducing characters who embody various social traits and values.

6.What is Sir Roger de Coverley's role in the essay?

Sir Roger de Coverley serves as a symbol of rural wisdom and simplicity, providing a contrast to the more modern, urban values of other club members.

7.How does Captain Sentry contribute to the club?

Captain Sentry brings a sense of discipline, honor, and sensibility, representing the respectable qualities of military service within the club.

8.Why is Will Honeycomb's character significant?

Will Honeycomb's character is significant as he represents the fashion, charm, and social dynamics of city life, adding humor and diversity to the club's portrayal.

9.What does "The Spectator Club" reveal about society?

"The Spectator Club" reveals society's diversity, highlighting various social classes and personalities and encouraging an understanding of different perspectives.

10.What message do Addison and Steele convey through "The Spectator Club"?

Addison and Steele convey a message of tolerance and understanding, encouraging readers to appreciate the unique qualities and quirks of individuals from different walks of life.

<u>**Five-Mark Questions with Answers**</u>

1.Explain the purpose of "The Spectator Club" as a satirical commentary on society.

"The Spectator Club" serves as a satirical commentary on English society, introducing characters who represent different social classes, values, and personalities. Through the club's members, Addison and Steele explore themes of manners, eccentricities, and societal norms. Each character embodies unique traits that highlight both the strengths and flaws of society, from Sir Roger's traditionalism to Will Honeycomb's urban charm. The essay encourages readers to reflect on the diversity of society, promoting tolerance and understanding of various perspectives. By using humor and satire, Addison and Steele offer insights into human nature and social dynamics.

2.Describe the character of Sir Roger de Coverley and his role in "The Spectator Club."

Sir Roger de Coverley is portrayed as a kind-hearted, eccentric country gentleman, representing the values of rural England. His character embodies simplicity, kindness, and traditional values, contrasting with the more modern, urban attitudes of other club members. Sir Roger often provides humorous, unconventional insights, which endear him to readers and reveal the charm of rural wisdom. His role in "The Spectator Club" is to highlight the virtues of simplicity and authenticity, offering a nostalgic view of rural life in contrast to the sophistication of city life. Sir Roger's character brings warmth and balance to the club's portrayal.

3.How does Captain Sentry represent the values of discipline and sensibility in the club?

Captain Sentry embodies the values of discipline, honor, and sensibility, representing the military's respectable qualities. His character brings a sense of order and responsibility to the club, providing a contrast to the more playful and eccentric members. Captain Sentry's level-headed nature reflects the importance of duty and integrity, offering a steady perspective within the group. Through his disciplined outlook, Captain Sentry serves as a model of respectability and dedication, reminding readers of the value of self-discipline and service to society. His presence in the club underscores the diversity of personalities and values.

4.What role does Will Honeycomb play in "The Spectator Club"?

Will Honeycomb is a charming bachelor known for his fashionable appearance and social skills, representing the lively, flirtatious side of city life. His character adds humor and a touch of sophistication to the club, as he is well-versed in the latest trends and social customs. Will's charm and wit provide a contrast to Sir Roger's simplicity and Captain Sentry's discipline, highlighting the diversity of the club's members. Through Will Honeycomb, Addison and Steele satirize the superficial aspects of urban society, while also acknowledging its appeal. His role brings balance and variety to the club's portrayal.

5.What is the significance of using diverse characters in "The Spectator Club"?

The diverse characters in "The Spectator Club" allow Addison and Steele to present a comprehensive view of English society, capturing a range of social classes, values, and personalities. By including characters like Sir Roger, Captain Sentry, and Will Honeycomb, the essay explores themes of tradition, discipline, and urban sophistication. Each character embodies distinct traits that reflect different aspects of society, creating a satirical commentary on social dynamics. The diversity of characters emphasizes the importance of understanding and accepting others' quirks, encouraging readers to appreciate the richness of human nature.

<u>**Essay Questions with Detailed Answers**</u>

1.Analyze how Addison and Steele use the characters in "The Spectator Club" to provide social commentary, discussing the traits each character represents and the broader message conveyed.

• Introduction:

o "The Spectator Club" by Joseph Addison and Sir Richard Steele introduces a group of fictional characters who represent various aspects of 18th-century English society. Through these characters, Addison and Steele provide a humorous yet insightful social commentary, highlighting the diversity of values and personalities that make up society. Each member of the club embodies specific traits, allowing the authors to explore themes of tradition, discipline, and social sophistication. This essay analyzes how the characters in "The Spectator Club" serve as a reflection of society, illustrating the importance of tolerance and understanding.

• Subtitles and Explanations:

1. Sir Roger de Coverley: Tradition and Rural Wisdom:

Sir Roger de Coverley represents traditional values and the simplicity of rural life. His kind-hearted and eccentric nature provides a nostalgic view of English country life, contrasting with the more modern, urban attitudes of the club's other members. Through Sir Roger, Addison and Steele emphasize the virtues of authenticity, kindness, and the charm of rural wisdom.

2. Captain Sentry: Discipline and Responsibility:

Captain Sentry is a sensible and disciplined character, embodying the values of duty and respectability. His character represents the military's honorable qualities, providing a steady presence within the club. Captain Sentry's outlook reflects the importance of self-discipline and responsibility, highlighting the value of integrity in society.

3. Will Honeycomb: Fashion and Urban Sophistication:

Will Honeycomb, a fashionable and charming bachelor, represents the lively, sophisticated side of city life. Known for his social skills and knowledge of trends, Will adds humor and style to the club. His character satirizes the superficial aspects of urban society, while also acknowledging its allure, showcasing the diversity within the club.

4. The Templar: Law and Intellectualism:

The Templar, another club member, represents the legal profession and the intellectual pursuits of the time. His character adds depth to the club, offering insights into the educated and professional classes. Through the Templar, Addison and Steele highlight the importance of intellectual growth and the role of law in society.

5. The Clergyman: Morality and Spirituality:

The Clergyman represents the moral and spiritual side of society, embodying values of piety and ethics. His presence in the club brings a perspective of faith and moral guidance, emphasizing the role of religion in everyday life. The Clergyman's character underscores the importance of moral integrity and spiritual values.

6. Satirical Commentary on Social Dynamics:

Through these diverse characters, Addison and Steele create a satirical commentary on social dynamics, using humor to reflect the quirks and eccentricities of each class. The club's members showcase different aspects of society, encouraging readers to understand and appreciate diverse perspectives.

7. Humor and Tolerance in Observing Society:

Addison and Steele use humor to present the club's members in an endearing light, making their quirks and flaws relatable. This humorous portrayal fosters tolerance, as readers are invited to see the positive traits of each character, despite their differences.

8. Reflection of 18th-Century English Society:

"The Spectator Club" provides a reflection of 18th-century English society, capturing the values, manners, and personalities that define the era. Each character serves as a microcosm of the broader social structure, allowing readers to gain insight into the diverse fabric of society.

9. Encouraging Appreciation of Diversity:

The diverse characters in the club encourage readers to appreciate the uniqueness of each individual, promoting a message of inclusivity. Addison and Steele suggest that society benefits from the diversity of personalities and values, emphasizing the importance of mutual respect.

10. Conclusion:

"The Spectator Club" by Addison and Steele uses a cast of diverse characters to present a humorous and insightful social commentary. Through Sir Roger, Captain Sentry, Will Honeycomb, and others, the authors capture the complexity of 18th-century society, highlighting both its strengths and weaknesses. The essay promotes tolerance, encouraging readers to appreciate the unique qualities of each character, and by extension, the richness of human nature.

2.Comment on Steele as an Essayist

Introduction: Steele earned an everlasting renown as an essayist. His contribution to The Tatler and The Spectator is very significant. They are the hallmarks of periodical essay writing. He wrote with an aim to bring moral reforms, order and decorum in the society. The Tatler and The Spectator became effective mediums in his hands.

Expression of Social Life: Steele worked with Addison and established the essay as a very important form of literature. His essays appeared as the expression of the social life of the nation. Thus he is known as a great social critic in the history of English literature. In his essays he beautifully satirized the vices of the society of his time. He exposed the false arts of life. He pulled of the disguises of cunning, vanity and affectations. He inculcated good morals among the people of his age. He recommended general simplicity in our dress, discourse and behavior.He recommended truth, innocence, honour and virtue as the chief ornaments of life. He treated of everything that was going on in the town. As a social humourist he painted his whole age – the political and literary disputes, the fine gentlemen and ladies, the new books, the new plays etc. Thus he is called the moral monitor of his age.

Steele's Creativity: Steele was more original and inventive. Without Addison he framed the plan of The Tater. He has initially outlined the character of Sir Roger. It was he who suggested the idea of the Spectator and his club. All the members of the Spectator club were the product of Steele's creative imagination. They were drawn from the different stages of the life, society and profession. They all were developed by Steele.

Versatility and Originality: Addison and Steele both wrote with a common aim to bring moral reforms, order and decorum in the society. Both share the same literary background but not the same temperament. Steele's essays have sincerity, frankness and genuine autobiographical touches. He brought to his work a wide experience of life, generous sympathies and a sunny humour. His genius was like his life – unequal, generous and impulsive. He was passionate and full of animal spirits. He had a vein of romanticism in him. He was impulsive and given to sensual pleasures. Addison, no doubt, was superior to Steele. He was a more consummate artist. But some critics assert that Steele is not less worthy than Addison. In versatility and in originality he is at least Addison's equal.

Humour: Steele belongs to the great race of English humourists. He was influenced by Pope, Addison and others who laid stress on the value of humour.He used humour in a very effective manner. His humour is broader and less restrained than Addison with a naïve, pathetic touch about it that is reminiscent of Goldsmith. His pathos is more attractive and more humane. In Addison the head is dominant, in Steele the heart. Steele's appeal is emotional and Addison's intellectual. He is incapable of irony. He lacks penetration and power.

Prose Style: The hallmark of Steele's essay is his naturalness and spontaneity. He never tries to mystify his readers. He has a friendly and amiable tone. It produces a friendly relationship between the readers and the author. Steele's prose style is highly communicative. He wrote in a conventional style. He chose the language of the common man.

And thus he was able to popularize philosophy among common men. Steele chose his words with great care. He was not verbose. According to Thackeray, 'Steele's style was like his life, full of faults and careless blunders.' He remained free from any kind of pedantry. His language is never obscure or even complex. It is often lucid, powerful and straightforward. In this context he can be compared with Dickens, Thackeray, Lamb, Hazlitt and Stevenson. If Addison excelled Steele in correctness, elegance and command of language, Steele surpassed him in passion, warmth, forcefulness and sympathy.

Conclusion: Thus Steele is one of the greatest essayists in the history of English literature. He is one of the forerunners of English novelists. His art of characterization is a valuable gift to English literature.

CHAPTER NINE

Sir Roger At Church

Sir Roger At Church
Joseph Addison
Addison's Essays edited by J H Fowler Spectator No. 112, 9/7/1711
ancient greek
(First, in obedience to thy country's rites, Worship the immortal Gods. — Pythagoras)

I AM always very well pleased with a country Sunday; and think, if keeping holy the seventh day were only a human institution, it would be the best method that could have been thought of for the polishing and civilizing of mankind. It is certain the country-people would soon degenerate into a kind of savages and barbarians, were there not such frequent returns of a stated time, in which the whole village meet together with their best faces, and in their cleanliest habits, to converse with one another upon indifferent subjects, hear their duties explained to them, and join together in adoration of the Supreme Being. Sunday clears away the rust of the whole week, not only as it refreshes in their minds the notions of religion, but as it puts both the sexes upon appearing in their most agreeable forms, and exerting all such qualities as are apt to give them a figure in the eye of the village. A country-fellow distinguishes himself as much in the churchyard as a citizen does upon the Change, the whole parish politics being generally discussed in that place either after sermon or before the bell rings.

My friend Sir Roger, being a good church-man, has beautified the inside of his church with several texts of his own choosing: he has likewise given a handsome pulpit-cloth, and railed in the communion-table at his own expense. He has often told me, that at his coming to his estate he found his parishioners very irregular; and that in order to make them kneel and join in the responses, he gave every one of them a hassoc and a Common Prayer

Book; and at the same time employed an itinerant singing-master, who goes about the country for that purpose, to instruct them rightly in the tunes of the psalms; upon which they now very much value themselves, and indeed out-do most of the country churches that I have ever heard.

As Sir Roger is landlord to the whole congregation, he keeps them in very good order, and will suffer nobody to sleep in it besides himself; for if by chance he has been surprised into a short nap at sermon, upon recovering out of it he stands up and looks about him, and if he sees anybody else nodding, either wakes them himself, or sends his servant to them. Several other of the old knight's particularities break out upon these occasions: sometimes he will be lengthening out a verse in the singing-psalms, half a minute after the rest of the congregation have done with it; sometimes, when he is pleased with the matter of his devotion, he pronounces Amen three or four times to the same prayer; and sometimes stands up when everybody else is upon their knees, to count the congregation, or see if any of his tenants are missing.

I was yesterday very much surprised to hear my old friend, in the midst of the service, calling out to one John Matthews to mind what he was about, and not disturb the congregation. This John Matthews, it seems, is remarkable for being an idle fellow, and at that time was kicking his heels for his diversion. This authority of the knight, though exerted in that odd manner which accompanies him in all circumstances of life, has a very good effect upon the parish, who are not polite enough to see anything ridiculous in his behaviour; besides that the general good sense and worthiness of his character, make his friends observe these little singularities as foils that rather set off than blemish his good qualities.

As soon as the sermon is finished, nobody presumes to stir till Sir Roger is gone out of the church. The knight walks down from his seat in the chancel between a double row of his tenants, that stand bowing to him on each side; and every now and then he inquires how such an one's wife, or mother, or son, or father do, whom he does not see at church; which is understood as a secret reprimand to the person that is absent.

The chaplain has often told me, that upon a catechising-day, when Sir Roger has been pleased with a boy that answers well, he has ordered a Bible to be given him next day for his encouragement; and sometimes accompanies it with a flitch of bacon to his mother. Sir Roger has likewise added five pounds a year to the clerk's place; and that he may encourage the young fellows to make themselves perfect in the church-service, has promised, upon the death of the present incumbent, who is very old, to bestow it according to merit.

The fair understanding between Sir Roger and his chaplain, and their mutual concurrence in doing good, is the more remarkable, because the very next village is famous for the differences and contentions that rise between the parson and the 'squire, who live in a perpetual state of war. The parson is always at the 'squire, and the 'squire, to be revenged on the parson, never comes to church. The 'squire has made all his tenants atheists and tithe-stealers; while the parson instructs them every Sunday in the dignity of his order, and insinuates to them, almost in every sermon, that he is a better man than his patron. In short, matters are come to such an extremity, that the 'squire has not said his prayers either in public or private this half year; and that the parson threatens him, if he does not mend his manners, to pray for him in the face of the whole congregation.

Feuds of this nature, though too frequent in the country, are very fatal to the ordinary people; who are so used to be dazzled with riches, that they pay as much deference to the understanding of a man of an estate, as of a man of learning; and are very hardly brought to regard any truth, how important so ever it may be, that is preached to them, when they know there are several men of five hundred a year who do not believe it.

A brief understanding of what is in this essay

Joseph Addison's essay Sir Roger at Church is about a unique individual named Roger. Addison begins the essay by saying that the observance of Sunday as a holy day keeps mankind civilised and polished. On Sundays people are at their very best. They appear clean and talk to other people on boring topics. Just like a merchant discusses exchange rates, the Parish people discuss the affairs of the parish.

Sir Roger has spent a lot of money on the church and continues to do so. Most of the parishioners are his tenants and he has a degree of control over them. Sir Roger employs a singer to help them sing their hymns in church properly. This has dramatically improved the services at the church.

However Roger has many peculiarities. He often falls asleep during the service, but would not allow anyone else to sleep while the service is going on. Another habit of his is to continue singing even when everyone else has stopped. He also continues saying Amen multiple times if he is satisfied with his piety. While everybody else kneels in the church, he stands to count the number of people to find out who is absent. The chaplain of the church has no issues with Sir Roger as he provides money for the improvement of the church.

However in the nearby village, things are not that smooth. The parson (priest) and the squire (similar to a landlord like Sir Roger) have many differences of opinion and hence the squire does not come to church. He also prevents his tenants from going to church or contributing any money to it. Neither the parson, nor the squire are ready to settle their issues. Addison says that these kinds of feuds affect the ordinary people in parishes in the countryside.

LINE BY LINE PARAPHRASE

Line. 12-20. Sunday clears away......the bell rings: Sunday has a double beneficial effect on people of the countryside. Firstly it has a good effect on their minds and, secondly, it makes them put on their best appearances. It removes the deadening effect of the routine work of the weekdays from their minds. It refreshes their minds which are bored though working at the dull routine and renovates their belief in religion. It is a fresh change from the worldly business of making money and being clever through six whole days. The mind which has rusted under such conditions gets renewed with the thought of religion on Sunday. Further, Sunday bringing an opportunity for the villagers to gather at the church makes them all put on cheerful faces and their best dresses, so as to cut a good figure in the eyes of fellow villagers. Church-going serves the purpose of a social function in villages. The villager has an opportunity to distinguish himself and become popular with his fellow villagers at church gatherings just as his counterpart in the cities has a similar chance at the exchange. It is an opportunity to discuss local issues of the parish. After the sermon, the villagers can exchange their views on all matters and especially the village politics. The passage shows Addison's felicity of expression. The essay is didactic in tone and here Addison as the Spectator explains the importance of Sunday. The passage also presents evidence of Addison s power of observation as when he remarks that villagers find an opportunity to discuss local politics at church gatherings.

Line. 33-38. As Sir Roger......servants to them: In this essay Addison's description of Sir Roger's behavior in church vindicates Steel's appraisal of the old knight's character. At church, he gives ample evidence of his oddities. One such peculiarity is described in this passage. Sir Roger is the squire of the village and hence most of the villagers are his tenants and he their landlord. As such, he takes it upon himself to see that there is discipline kept up in the church during the service. He will see to it that no one in the congregation sleeps during the service, though he seems to exclude himself from the rule! He falls asleep by chance during the sermon at times. When he wakes up, however, he stands up and looks all over the congregation to see if anyone else had fallen asleep. If he sees anyone dozing or about to fall asleep, he wakes him up or he sends his servants to do so. This is most amusing and Addison has used irony most effectively in this humorous passage.

Line. 51-59. This authority......good qualities: The oddities of Sir Roger's character come to the surface in his behavior at church. Being the squire of the village and the landlord of most of the villagers, he exerts his authority to keep them disciplined. This authority is exerted in that peculiar manner that is typical of the knight. But it has a good effect upon the villagers and keeps them from behaving badly. The villagers are too simple and unrefined and unsophisticated to see anything odd in Sir Roger's eccentric behavior. They do not find his conduct ridiculous. Indeed the knight has a number of good qualities. He is sensible and has a worthy character. As a result the eccentricities of behavior that he shows act as foils to show up his good side. The oddities act as a contrast to the good qualities and hence his friends appreciate his good sense all the better.

Line. 79-94. The person is......than his patron: Sir Roger and his chaplain have a perfect relationship and understanding between each other. This is all the more remarkable because in the very next village, there is conflict between the squire and the parson. They do not get on well together and there is a continual state of discord between them. The person in his sermons always seems to hint that he is preaching against vices which are being indulged in by the squire. He seems to imply that the squire indulges in all kinds of vices. The squire to take his revenge against the parson has stopped attending the church. This has a bad effect and villagers, who follow the higher classes in their behavior, have slowly lost faith in religion and are turning atheists. As they see that the squire has no respect for the person, they do not pay the tax that they should do for the upkeep of the clergy. Every Sunday they hear from the parson about how dignified the office of a clergyman is and, at the same time, that he is a better man than the squire who is his patron. Addison is clearly didactic in writing this passage. He deplores discord between squire and clergy and condemns it for the bad effect it has on the parishioners. He conveys his point that such discord may be very harmful to the common people by giving a concrete example which he has invented for the purpose. The example also serves to add vividness to his conclusion.

Line. 90-96. Feuds......believe it: Sir Roger and his chaplain have an amicable relationship but in the very next parish there was an example of discord between squire and parson. This kind of quarrel was only too common in the villages but they were very harmful to the welfare of the common people. These ordinary villagers are simple and are impressed by riches. They consider rich people to be intelligent and wise as well. They give equal respect to a rich man's power of understanding and his wisdom as they do to that of a learned man. In fact, they respect a rich man's judgment more than they do a learned man's. It is very difficult to convince them that what a learned man says is true and useful if they are aware that a rich man does not pay these statements any respect. Such villagers do not have an independent outlook and generally follow the views of the rich. When they find that the rich squire and the parson quarrel, they prefer to follow the squire and lose their faith in religion. Addison is clearly didactic here. He is very much against the squires and their parsons indulging in a war of wits with each other for this invariably causes harm to the poor and simple villagers. He makes the valid observation that the lower classes generally follow the ways of the richer classes and the latter, therefore, should set them a good example. Note also the mild satire of the lines, "when they know there are several men of five hundred a year who do not believe it" a gentle dig at the simplicity of a common villager.

Sir Roger at Church by Joseph Addison - Important points to remember

Introduction:

"Sir Roger at Church" is an essay written by Joseph Addison, first published in "The Spectator" in 1711. In this essay, Addison reflects on the character of Sir Roger de Coverley, a fictional country gentleman, and his behavior and attitudes during church services.

Background of the Essay:

Joseph Addison, along with his friend Richard Steele, founded "The Spectator," a periodical publication that featured essays, social commentary, and satire. "Sir Roger at Church" is part of a series of essays that depict the life and adventures of Sir Roger de Coverley.

Sir Roger's Character:

Sir Roger de Coverley is depicted as a benevolent, traditional English country gentleman. He embodies virtues such as kindness, generosity, and a deep sense of duty to his community. Despite his old-fashioned ways, Sir

Roger is well-respected and admired by those around him.

Sir Roger's Religious Observance:

In the essay, Addison observes Sir Roger's devoutness and reverence towards religious practices. Sir Roger is described as a regular churchgoer who attends services every Sunday without fail. His attendance is not merely out of obligation but stems from a genuine piety and reverence for God.

Sir Roger's Behavior in Church:

Addison highlights Sir Roger's demeanor during church services, noting his earnestness and sincerity in prayer. Despite his occasional eccentricities, such as falling asleep during sermons or humming hymns out of tune, Sir Roger's faith remains steadfast.

Sir Roger's Interactions with Others:

During church services, Sir Roger demonstrates his compassion and concern for his fellow parishioners. He is depicted as a friendly and approachable figure, often engaging in small talk and exchanging pleasantries with those around him.

Sir Roger's Reflections on Religion:

Through Sir Roger, Addison explores themes of faith and spirituality. Despite living in a rapidly changing world, Sir Roger's faith provides him with a sense of stability and comfort. His simple, heartfelt approach to religion serves as a contrast to the more cynical and worldly attitudes prevalent in society.

Conclusion:

"Sir Roger at Church" offers a glimpse into the life and beliefs of Sir Roger de Coverley, a character beloved for his warmth, kindness, and unwavering faith. Through Addison's portrayal, readers are invited to reflect on the enduring values of piety, community, and tradition. Sir Roger serves as a reminder of the timeless virtues that continue to enrich our lives today.

Some crucial points about the essay in details

Sundays in The Countryside

Country Sundays are special occasions and the Spectator considers them of great value. These days see the country folk dressed in their best and putting on a cheerful front. Sunday, says Addison, clears the rust of the whole week. It not only refreshes the notions of religion in minds of the villagers but also makes them all come forth at best because each wants to appear good and become popular and distinguish himself. Church gatherings in the country have the same effect on the country folk as the

Exchange has on the town dwellers.

Sir Roger's Interest in the Village Church

Sir Roger took great interest in the village church and also saw to it that his tenants attended church regularly. He had got the church decorated with quotations from the Bible which he selected himself. He had presented the church with a new pulpit cloth which was beautiful. He had also got the communion table enclosed in a railing. He had gifted parishioners with a Common Prayer book and a hassock to kneel on in church to encourage them to attend church regularly. Further, he had got a traveling musician to come and instruct the parishioners to sing the Psalms in the right tune, as a result, they prided themselves upon the fact that they sang much better than the congregation of any other village church.

Sir Roger's Behaviour in Church

Sir Roger being the landlord of all in the congregation felt personally responsible for their behavior and exerted his authority to keep them disciplined. He allowed no one to sleep in the church except himself. If he fell asleep during the sermon, on waking up he would look around and if he found anyone dozing off he would immediately wake up that person or send his servants to wake him up. Many of his oddities came out in the church. He would still be singing a verse long after it had been sung by the rest of the congregation. If he liked a particular prayer, he would say 'amen' a number of times at the end of that prayer. Often when the rest of the congregation was kneeling, he would stand to the count the number of people present to note anyone's absence. If he felt anyone was disturbing the service, he would not stop from calling that person to order in the middle of the service. The parishioners were too simple and naive to find anything ridiculous in the behavior of the knight. In fact, these oddities merely served to make his virtues seem all the more striking.

Squire-chaplain Relationship

Sir Roger and his chaplain had a perfect understanding between each other and there was an amicable relationship between them. This was all the more remarkable because, in the very next village, this cordial relation between squire and chaplain was absent. There the two were all the time indulging in some dispute. The person seemed to preach at the squire who stayed away from church. The parishioners were encouraged not to pay their dues to the upkeep of the clergyman and they became quite slack about attending church. The squire and the parson ought to have a good relationship with one another. The villagers were usually simple and generally equated richness with good sense and wisdom. They thus followed the squire's viewpoint. This kind of discord led to eroding of faith in the commoners.

Sir Roger at Church Summary

The essay, Sir Roger at Church, was first published in "The Spectator" on 9th July, 1711 AD wherein the author told us about the importance of Sunday for the villagers and Sir Roger acted on the Sundays as a churchman. The Sundays, the author surmised, should be observed absolutely as a holiday by the people, wherever they be. For the villagers, however, the Sundays have greater values because if observed properly, it is the best method for making one courteous and cultured. Not only for the villagers, it is rather the best method for all the people of the world and of all nations. The Christians and the English people observe the Sunday as essentially a holiday.

On such a Sunday, a holiday Addison had been in a village. There he realised what importance a Sunday usually has in a village. A Sunday comes after every six weekdays, the working days, and on this day the villagers go to the church where they meet with other villagers, their neighbours and distant relations. Since the day is a holiday the villagers wear the best dress they have and always remain in cheerful mood. They talk with one another on many topics and on many subjects. The most striking thing is, on this day the subjects which the villagers discuss among themselves have no relation at all with their personal matters. Very patiently they hear the sermon of the clergy. The clergy in his sermon tells them what their duty to the society is. What duties they should perform towards their own family, what obedience they should show and what duties they are to perform towards the religion and above all to God. The sermon impresses the villager and they hear it patiently. After hearing the sermon they sing together to praise and worship God. All these things have a good effect on the villagers. These make them courteous and cultured. Generally the villagers are not very polished or sophisticated. But they become courteous and cultured only by going to the church.

The Sunday is remarkable for other reason also. The whole week's labourious life and work make the people unclean in their hearts. They cannot think right things properly. The Sundays remove this dirt from their thoughts. For the whole week the villagers have to work hard to earn their bare subsistence even. They are surrounded with so much worldly cares that they have very little diversion or amusements in their lives.

Naturally, they cannot think clearly. They become selfish, ill treating, rough mannered, an easy prey for vices. The Sunday helps them to get rid of all these vices. They hear the clergyman's sermon and listen good advices. The clergyman's sermon reminds them of their duties towards their own family, towards the society, to the religion and God. This helps them to refresh their idea of religion in their minds. Thus the Sundays simply brighten their minds and ideas of duty and religion which the week's toil had already made dim.

Apart from these, the Sundays encouraged both men and women at their best. On this day they try to show all their good qualities, that they possess. They try to show their importance to the other fellow villagers. Addison opined that as the Royal Exchange of London is a good place for the merchants likewise the churchyard on Sunday's is a good place for the villagers. Talking lofty things about his success in the market a businessman tries to show his importance to the other businessmen in the Royal Exchange of London. In the same way a villager talks about different subjects while he meets other fellow villagers on the church compound on Sunday and tries to establish his importance within their mind. Within this church compound, the villagers discuss all the politics of their ecclesiastical division which they do either before hearing the clergyman's sermon or after hearing it.

Sir Roger de Coverley was a very good churchman and a strong supporter of the rights, customs and interest of the church as he was a religious man. He took great interest in the village church and carefully looked that his tenants attended the church regularly. He was careful about the beautification of the church and decorated the inner part of the church of his parish with many beautiful and significant lines from the Bible which he himself had carefully selected. He had given a beautiful cloth to cover the pulpit and built a railing in front of the communion table at his own cost. He had often told the author how much indifferent the people of his parish were towards the religion and the church. Sir Roger was a rich man and had inherited a landed property in Worcestershire sometimes back. So he went there to settle permanently. He found that the villagers of that parish were very irregular to go to the church and he took serious note of it. He wanted that every one of that village should go to the church and must kneel down in prayer. In order to attract the villagers in the church and make them to go there, he gave, at his own cost, every one of them a cushion for kneeling on and a common prayer book. He also engaged a singer who went from place to place, to sing religious song in the church. He advised the singer to teach the villagers how to sing the religious songs correctly. The singer was doing his task perfectly and remained busy in doing that. He went about the parish and taught the people how to sing the religious songs properly. He was successful in his work and the people could now sing the songs correctly for which they themselves were proud too. The author Addison had heard their songs too and it appeared to him that the people of that parish sing far better than the people of many other country churches. The credit for this was obviously of Sir Roger de Coverley's.

Sir Roger was the master of all the villagers who attended the Church. He always kept the assembly in the church in strict discipline and good decorum. He never allowed any one to sleep during the sermon. But the moment he was awaken he very cautiously looked to others and if found any one asleep on dozing, he himself waked them up or sent his servants to wake them up Addison told us that besides these Sir Roger had many other peculiarities. These were often exhibited when he was present at the church at the time of prayer. During the prayer psalms were sung by the people present there and Sir Roger too, used to sing with them. But sometimes, though the others had stopped singing, he sang the line continuously. Sometimes again, when the subject matter of the prayer pleased him he said 'Amen' three or four times even after ii. Often when all persons were kneeling, and praying, Sir Roger stood alone to count the number of people present and counting to note if anyone was absent. If he felt that any one man was disturbing the service, he even called that person to order in the middle of the service. Addison told us about an incident which exhibited Sir Roger's great authority over the tenants. Addison saw it himself when one day he went to the church with Sir Roger. Among the tenants of Sir Roger present in the church was a villager, John Matthews. Sir Roger was very much angry with him and scolded Matthews even when the sermon was going on. He asked Matthews to behave properly and never to disturb the people who gather in the church. Matthews was an idle man and everyone knew it. He often misbehaved in the gathering. Idly he was knocking his heels together to amuse himself but that disturbed others. When Sir Roger scolded him Matthews became silent. This trifle incident proved that Sir Roger had tremendous influence over his tenants. He had complete authority over his subjects and he exercised that authority in a typical way. Yet that produced good effect on the villagers who were not at all well behaved and polished mannered people. His subjects the villagers blindly obeyed his order and never thought that he was behaving in a funny way. But his friends saw his behaviour from a different angle. They found peculiarities in him yet they all admired his common sense and goodness of character. They took his peculiarities not as his defects but as the greater brilliance to his good qualities and good character.

The sermon finished and all the people were eagerly awaiting for the departure of Sir Roger. Sir Roger stood up from his seat in the chancel, where he used to seat and walked through two rows of his tenants who were standing up on either side and bowed their heads to show him respect while he was passing. Among these people he could not found a few men and women. He stopped and enquired about their health. But this was not a mere enquiry. Rather, it was a kind of secret reprimand for their absence. Sir Roger was, indeed, deeply interested in religion and church. Out of this interest, he used different methods to encourage the children and the young men and the clerk of the church to do their religious duty properly and with care. On a particular day the children were examined in their knowledge of Bible by means of different questions and answers on the holy Book. When a boy's knowledge of the Bible pleased Sir Roger he used to give the boy a copy of the Bible. Sometimes a slice of roasted pig was also sent along with the Bible to the boy's mother. This act obviously encouraged both the young boy and his mother. He had also increased the salary of the clerk of the church by five pounds a year so that the clerk was encouraged to do his work seriously and sincerely. He wanted that the young men should be fully able to take their service in the church. He, as such, often tried to encourage them by saying that the clerk's office in the church would be given to the ablest man in future.

Sir Roger had quite a friendly relation with his chaplain. Both had recognized the good of the other, and agreed each other in doing good to the villagers. They had, indeed, an appreciable cordial relation between them. This good relation between the landlord and the parson was generally not found in the very next village. They always had differences of opinion and often argued against each other which usually left them in constant rivalry and conflict. The parson always spoke against the landlord and the latter to take revenge, never visited the church, rather made all the subjects non-believers in God and religion. Even due to his instigation the tenants became defaulters in paying the tithes to the parson and never paid him the tenth part of their income. So, the clergyman became very angry to the landlord and on every Sunday, he used to tell the people assembled in the church to hear his sermon that he was a far better man than the landlord, having much of honour and importance in his post. This ill feelings between the landlord and the parson had reached to such an extent that parson always threatened the landlord and the landlord too did not make prayer either in public or private for a long time just to show his negligence to the parson. Eventually the parson threatened the landlord that if the latter failed to show more respect to religion and the church, the parson then would pray to God in presence of all the persons gathered in the church to pronounce the landlord an unrepentant sinner.

Now Addison, the author, gave us his own opinion about the undesirability of such quarrels between the squires or landlords and the parsons in the villages, though such a quarrel was very common in the rural areas. It had an obvious bad effect on the common men.

This is because the common villagers are bewildered by seeing the wealth of the rich men while they equally respect a learned man, the priest. There are many rich men who earn five hundred pounds a year and thus, being rich they believe that the teachings taught by the priests carry no meaning or truth. The common people simply follow what these moneyed men say and hence when they go to the church they hear the priest talking, but never care of what he was speaking, neither believe the truth of his talks. This only degrades the high position of the priesthood.

CRITICAL ANALYSIS

The essay, Sir Roger at Church aims at a reform in the attendance at church. He desires peaceful relations between the squire and the parson in a village to ensure good attendance at church and improvement of the faith of people. In this essay, there is support of Steele's appraisal of the character of Sir Roger as an eccentric man. The oddities of his character come out during the church service. There is much humor in his behavior at church and delicate irony too i.e, he allows no one to sleep during the service except himself; he has engaged a singing master for rest of the congregation but he is oblivious to the fact that he continues to sing for some time after the verse is finished! But the knight's interest in the church and his parishioners is genuine and though his behavior is odd, he has the best of the intentions behind his actions.

Addison is frankly didactic in his aim. This essay is clearly critical of the prevailing habit of the country squire and the country parson being hostile to one another This according to Addison harmed the parishioners who slacked off and finally became atheistic. A harmonious relationship between the squire and the parson helps in the development of morality and steadfast religious faith. He gives the example of Sir Roger as the ideal to be followed. As usual, Addison conveys his point with the help of a concrete example.

Sir Roger at Church Analysis line by line

1.Sunday........... village.

Joseph Addison, the great English essayist in his remarkable piece of work, Sir Roger at Church laid greater stress to the importance of Sunday as a holiday, specially in the villages. He told us that in his opinion the Sunday should be a holy day for all the people of the world. In the above lines the essayist told us the special importance of Sunday to the villagers of England. The Sunday practically removed the dirt from the minds and thoughts of villagers that they pile up throughout the week's hard labour and toil. They have to work hard for the remaining six days of the week to earn their bare subsistence and always have to look for worldly care and self interest. This makes them selfish and rough in their manners. On each Sunday the villagers go to the church and hear the sermons of the clergyman in which they are given good advices about their duties and responsibilities towards their own family, their society, towards the religion, church and God. All these are good advices and since the villagers have no other diversion or amusement these advices speak good on them. Their coating of selfish, narrow mindedness is brushed off with clear ideas and they brighten their minds with fresh ideas of religion and responsibilities. It's a kind of rebirth for them. Moreover, on Sunday both men and women appear in their most pleasant form in the church. They wear their best dress to show them good looking and dignified. Being present in the church they try to show all their best qualities and discussing on many things and topics try to show them will acquainted with everything and also try to make themselves important in the eyes of their fellow villagers. Thus, the Sunday sermons practically refresh the minds of the villagers. They become courteous and cultured.

2.A country fellow........bell rings.

In his essay 'Sir Roger at Church', Joseph Addison, the essayist told as about his belief that Sunday, as holiday, is a blessing for the villagers. This is the day when the villagers go to the church and hear the sermon of the clergyman which speaks them about their duties towards their families, society, religion and God. They hear it patiently and giving up their selfishness and rough manner clean themselves with civilized and cultured manners. The Sunday church is important and significant to the villagers for another reason too. This is the day when all the villagers meet each other in the church compound. They put on their best dresses to make them look beautiful and smart. Both men and women appear fresh and jubilant. They talk on different topics and subjects and try to appear before others as an important great man. Addison, the author, compared a village. Sunday church compound with that of the London Royal Exchange. In the Royal Exchange a merchant shows his greatness or importance by talking about his merchandise or about his ability in business activities and transactions and eulogizes himself in such manner so that the fellow businessmen appreciate his ability and worth. He thus become an important figure to them. Likewise, the villagers show their greatness or importance to the fellow villagers by talking about impersonal matters. The matters they discuss generally are related to the politics to the whole ecclesiastical division. They discuss on the subjects not on their own merit, neither on their own knowledge. Rather they discuss about them either after hearing the sermon delivered by the priest or before hearing it. If they talk before hearing the sermon they stop talking when the bell rung to call them inside the church to hear the sermon of the priest.

3.The general good........good qualities.

Joseph, Addison depicted Sir Roger-de-Coverley, in his essay 'Sir Roger at Church,' as a fine churchman Sir Roger was a religious man and never tolerated any indiscipline in the church. If ever he found any one disturbing the congregation in the church he warned him instantly. In one such occasion, he even warned and scolded John Matthews, a villager, and an idle fellow, who was knocking his hills together to amuse himself but disturbing others during prayer time. Sir Roger warned him to behave properly. This incident shows one of the peculiarities of Sir Roger's behaviour. He had many other peculiarities as well. His friends knew about the peculiarities of his behaviour. But they do not think much on it because they knew that Sir Roger possessed many good qualities and good common senses as well. So they do not consider the peculiarities as his defects. Rather they believed that these peculiarities, on the other hand, have acted as foil that sharpened and brightened many of his good qualities and senses.

4.Sir Roger has.........to merit.

In his essay 'Sir Roger at Church', the author essayist, Joseph Addison told us how much Sir Roger was interested to see the church functioning properly. He adopted different methods to attract the people, especially the children and young man to the religion and church. For this on many occasions he tested the children's knowledge on Bible and the boy who could satisfy him usually received a Bible from him Sometimes he also gave a slice of roasted pig along with the Bible to the boy's mother to give them encouragement. In order to make the clerk of the church discharge his duties more efficiently and properly he had increased his salary by five pounds a year. It encouraged the young clerk no doubt, and by encouraging him Sir Roger practically encouraged the whole younger generation of his tenants. He wanted these young men to join the church service. Since the present working clerk was getting old and would not be able to work long, Sir Roger assured his young tenants that one of them would surely be appointed in his place. Yet he placed one condition that such appointment would be made only on the basis of merit and the post would be given to a really deserving candidate.

5.Feuds of..........believe it.

In his essay "Sir Roger at Church" Joseph Addison, the author, drew a vivid pen-picture of the rift that was very common in the villages between the landlord and the parson of the church. Sir Roger himself was a landlord, yet his relation with his parson was very cordial. But in the village next to Sir Roger's village, the relation between the squire and parson was so strained that they were almost at daggers drawn to each other. Their quarrel never come to an end: But this type of quarrel between the landlord and the priests were so common feature in the country side of England that it virtually had a very bad effect on the common people of the area. These common people respect both the rich man, the landlord, for his money and wealth, as well as the priest for his depth of knowledge which they hear with respect and awe when he delivers his sermons. They can hardly distinguish between a rich man and a learned man. In the event of such unwanted conflict going on before their eyes, the common men will never respect the priest, neither will hear his sermons attentively or attach any importance to it. They believe only the rich men and there are many rich men who earn more than five hundred pounds a year. These people do not believe the sermons of the priests and neither the common people will care to believe it in consequence.

Here are some questions and answers about Sir Roger at Church by Joseph Addison:

1.What does Sir Roger's behavior in church show about his faith?

Sir Roger's behavior in church shows his sincere faith and desire to uphold traditional values and customs.

2.How does Sir Roger's behavior in church set an example for others?

Sir Roger's behavior in church sets a good example for his tenants and servants.

3.How does Sir Roger's behavior in church contrast with others?

Sir Roger's behavior contrasts with the frivolous and often superficial concerns of other people.

4.What does Sir Roger's behavior in church show about his piety?

Sir Roger's behavior in church underscores his piety and his commitment to upholding traditional values.

5.What does Sir Roger's behavior in church show about his devotion?

Sir Roger's behavior in church represents a pure and genuine form of devotion and piety.

6.What does Sir Roger's behavior in church show about his moral guide?

Sir Roger's behavior in church serves as a moral guide for his community.

Sir Roger is a popular and lovable character created by Addison. He is a humourist with a cheerful nature and kind disposition.

7.Who was Sir Roger de Coverley?

a-A character created by Addison and described in the Spectator, Sir Roger wasa member of the Spectator Club, 'a gentleman of Worcestershire, of ancientdescent, a baronet.

8.What is the importance of Sunday for the villagers in Sir Roger at Church?

a. Sunday clears away the rust of the whole week, not only as it refreshes thenotions of religion in the minds of the villagers, but as it encourages bothmen and women to appear as their most agreeable selves.

9.Write about the manner in which Addison spent his days at the country-seat of the Sir Roger

a. Addison was allowed to rise and go to bed at his own pleasure. It was up tohim whether he dined at Sir Roger's table or in his own chamber. He was freeto stay silent and was never asked to be merry by force.

10.What kind of a master was Sir Roger?

a. Sir Roger is the best master in the world, he seldom changes his servants andas he is beloved by all, his servants never care to leave him. As a result, hisdomestics have all grown old with their master.

<u>Long Questions and Answers</u>

1.Comment on Addison's style as found in 'Sir Roger at Church' and 'Sir Roger at Home'

Addison's style as found in 'Sir Roger at Church' and 'Sir Roger at Home'

Comment on Addison's style as found in 'Sir Roger at Church' and 'Sir Roger at Home'

Have you ever heard of Addison? Well, he is considered one of the greatest writers in English literary history when it comes to prose style. He pioneered a style called the "middle style", which was all about simplicity, clarity, and naturalness. No extravagant expressions or complicated obscurities here.

One remarkable feature of Addison's style is how clear and easy to understand it is. Even his longer sentences aren't difficult to grasp. You can easily understand the meaning of his long sentences right from the get-go. And when the situation calls for it, Addison also uses shorter sentences. For example, he once wrote, "As soon as the sermon is finished, nobody presumes to stir till Sir Roger is gone out of the Church."

What sets Addison apart is his use of humor.He carries irony, satire, and on occasion even a hint of funniness into his writing. It's never harsh or bitter, even though. He aims to accurate societal flaws mildly and mildly.

Unlike other writers, Addison's fashion would not heavily depend upon figurative language. He does not use resourceful similes or metaphors until he deems them necessary and effective for his cause. Instead, he fills his writing with allusions, anecdotes, and references. You'll locate that maximum of his essays start with relevant quotations from classical or contemporary authors.

Addison's prose style is much like normal conversations, however, it's no longer as informal as Montaigne's. It creates stability in conversational language and the formal tone of a severe piece of writing.

In precis, Addison's prose fashion had a full-size effect on English literature. He stripped away the excesses and extravagances of writers within the eighteenth century, bringing forth clarity, lucidity, and precision in his writing.

2.Addison's Approach to Society as Revealed within the Essays, "Sir Roger at Church":

Now let's talk approximately Addison's perspective on society, which he expressed through his essays in The Spectator. Alongside his pal Richard Steele, Addison aimed to bring about superb adjustments in people's lives.

He used his essays to critique the manners and morals of society, constantly to reform it. His motto became to mix wit with morality, making it active and tasty.

By observing the man or woman Mr. Spectator, Addison and Steele wanted to subtly remodel English society. One of their first-rate characters became Sir Roger de Coverley, a fictional illustration of a Tory squire. Sir Roger embodied the conventional United States gentleman stereotype, which The Spectator mocked as old and nostalgic. However, this backfired as it made Sir Roger appear sympathetic and commendable. His adherence to old-fashioned country hospitality set him apart from the new generation of heartless aristocrats.

On the other hand, Sir Roger's interactions with the local church were highly satirized. Mr. Spectator couldn't help but find amusement in Sir Roger's authoritative demeanor within the church. As the landlord of the entire congregation, he enforced strict rules, making sure nobody slept during services. The squire often disrupted the sermon to remind people to show respect and avoid fidgeting or making noise. Mr. Spectator recognized the quirks of Sir Roger's behavior but believed they were overshadowed by his overall worthiness. Unfortunately, none of the other parishioners were able to see the ridiculousness of Sir Roger's actions or his control over the church.

These observations of Sir Roger's devotion to the high Anglican church in the countryside played a crucial role in Addison and Steele's goal of ridiculing the seemingly backward rural Tories. At the time of writing The Spectator, strict conformity was gradually giving way to religious toleration. Sir Roger, being a Tory, stubbornly resisted this change and had personal interests tied to the authority of the church.

3.Sir Roger de Coverley: An Analysis of His Character:

Let's dive deeper into the character of Sir Roger de Coverley. Created by Addison and Steele, Sir Roger represents a farcical stereotype of the Tory squire from a bygone era. His character embodies qualities such as hospitality, humanity, love, helpfulness, disappointment, superstition, singularities, kindness, honesty, and goodness. Despite being designed to mock the mannerisms of the Tories, Sir Roger is portrayed in as a substitute agreeable manner, thanks to Addison's moderate satire.

In instances, Sir Roger's conduct can also appear extraordinary, but it constantly stems from his desirable feel. He is truly cherished with the aid of individuals who understand him, instead of honestly esteemed.

While being depicted as a nostalgic relic, Sir Roger's traditional paternalistic approach towards his tenants and servants is at first supposed to be satirized. However, this try honestly made him appear sympathetic and commendable, contrasting with the callousness of the brand-new generation of landed aristocrats. Sir Roger's unwavering commitment to traditional customs of United States hospitality further set him apart.

In the essay "Sir Roger at Church," his eccentricity is highlighted through his workout of authority. Although the healthy residing and paternalistic communal family members confirmed through Sir Roger garner diffused admiration, his conduct within the neighborhood church will become a subject of satire. Mr. Spectator finds entertainment in Sir Roger's entire dominance, noting that, as the owner, he maintains the congregation in proper order and would not allow every person else to sleep in the church. The squire's disruption of the provider, such as lengthening the psalms or standing whilst others kneel, showcases his zeal for maintaining discipline. While those characteristics may appear eccentric to others, Mr. Spectator believes they are extra like foils rather than flaws in Sir Roger's man or woman. Interestingly, no different parishioners own the politeness or training to recognize the absurdity of Sir Roger's conduct or his authority over the church.

In the end, Sir Roger de Coverley is a character of superb honor, humor, and low eccentricities. Despite the eccentricities that make him specific, Addison's final aim became not entirely to entertain us, but also to accurately society's follies and absurdities. The man or woman of Sir Roger serves as a way to reform diverse aspects of existence, as Mr. Spectator set out to achieve through his essays.

CHAPTER TEN

ROBINSON CRUSOE - DANIEL DEFOE

Robinson Crusoe is a <u>realistic novel</u> written by Daniel Defoe and published in 1719. It tells the story of a young Englishman named Robinson Crusoe who becomes a sailor and goes on a series of adventures, eventually becoming shipwrecked on a deserted island where he must learn to survive on his own. The novel is considered the first <u>realistic novel</u> in English literature, and Defoe based the character of Crusoe on the real-life story of Alexander Selkirk, a Scottish sailor who was marooned on an uninhabited island in the Pacific Ocean for four years.

The novel was published during the early 18th century, a period known as <u>the Augustan Age</u> in English literature. This period is characterized by a focus on reason, order, and classical influence, as well as the emergence of the novel as a popular literary form. Some of the notable authors and works of this period include Jonathan Swift, Alexander Pope, John Dryden, Samuel Richardson, and Laurence Sterne.

The full title of Robinson Crusoe appears on the title page as "The Life and Strange Surprizing Adventures of Robinson Crusoe, Of York, Mariner: Who lived Eight and Twenty Years, all alone in an un-inhabited Island on the Coast of America, near the Mouth of the Great River of Oroonoque; Having been cast on Shore by Shipwreck, wherein all the Men perished but himself. With An Account how he was at last as strangely deliver'd by Pyrates." This lengthy title summarizes the entire narrative of the novel, while also providing several factual details such as Crusoe's background, the duration of his experiences on the island, and the location of the island. The title page credits Robinson as the author of the book, which was originally published in 1719. This, along with the inclusion of a foreword by an

"Editor" who claims that the story is a "just history of fact," helped to convince readers that the book was a travelogue, or an authentic first-person account written by a real person. Defoe used these techniques to support the illusion that Robinson Crusoe was a true story.

Robinson Crusoe is structured as a first-person narrative, with Crusoe telling the story of his life and adventures. The original version of the novel, which was published in the monthly magazine "Bentley's Miscellany", contained three books and 63 chapters. Later editions of the novel included more than 50 chapters. The novel follows Crusoe's journey from his early years as a seaman and merchant, through his time as a castaway on the uninhabited island, to his eventual rescue and return to civilization. Along the way, he faces numerous challenges and adventures, including encounters with cannibals, pirates, and wild animals.

The main characters in Robinson Crusoe are Crusoe himself, who is the narrator and main protagonist of the story, and Friday, a native. Friday is saved by Robinson from the cannibals who had brought him to the island to eat him. That's how Friday becomes Robinson's servant and companion. There are also several minor characters in the novel, including pirates and a captain of a mutinied ship who rescues Crusoe at the end of the story.

Robinson Crusoe is set in a number of different locations, including Brazil, the Caribbean, and Europe. The main setting of the novel is the uninhabited island on which Crusoe is stranded for 28 years. The island is located off the coast of South America, near the mouth of the Oroonoque River in what is now modern-day Brazil. The novel also includes scenes set in Europe, including England, Portugal, and Africa.

In terms of setting in time, the novel covers a period of approximately 28 years, starting with Crusoe's early years as a sailor and ending with his rescue and return to civilization. It is important to note that the concept of time here is different from the concept of time expressed in works from the Renaissance. The passing of time was shown through the description of the seasons or human decay. In this novel, instead, time is concrete: it is counted to be used. Robinson keeps a calendar and keeps a diary in which he annotates all of his thoughts and actions.

The action of the novel takes place in the early 18th century, during the Age of Exploration and the period of European colonization. Once again we have to point out the concept of place differs in the Renaissance compared to the same concept in the Augustan Age. In the Renaissance, places mirrored the stability of the social classes. The setting in place is clearly indicated in *Robinson Crusoe*, with geographical and topographical information, longitudes and latitudes, and names of real countries, oceans, and rivers.

There are several themes in Robinson Crusoe, including survival, self-reliance, and the encounter between European and non-European cultures. A further theme is the process of European exploration and colonization, with the island representing the new territories being explored and colonized by Europeans and Crusoe's efforts to impose his own way of life on the island representing the way in which European powers sought to assert their control over these territories and their native populations.

Robinson Crusoe also explores themes of religion and redemption, as Crusoe faces questions of faith and the purpose of his suffering on the island. He ultimately comes to see his time on the island as a test of his faith and a chance to repent for his past sins, and he becomes a more devout Christian as a result of his experiences. The novel also portrays the theme of colonialism and the effects of Westernization on non-Western cultures, as Crusoe's encounter with Friday reveals the ways in which European colonization impacted the lives and cultures of native peoples.

Some symbols in the novel include the island itself, which stands for Crusoe's isolation and the challenges he faces, and Friday, who represents the encounter between European and non-European cultures. He becomes a symbol of the impact of Westernization on non-Western cultures. The tools and weapons that Crusoe uses to survive on the island can also be seen as symbols of the technological superiority of European culture and the way in which it was used to assert control over other parts of the world.

Here are a few quotes from the novel that illustrate these themes and symbols:

- "I had now been...eight and twenty years upon this island, and had never yet seen any human creature" (Crusoe's isolation on the island)
- "I was now an absolute monarch...all the world was my own" (Crusoe's colonization of the island)
- "I had a great mind to kill him, but I had a curiosity to see how he would behave" (Crusoe's encounter with Friday)
- "I was here delivered of all the people I had been so long with" (Crusoe's isolation and survival on the island)
- "I had been so long in this way of living, that I seemed to have been born to it" (Crusoe's self-reliance and adaptation to life on the island)

- "I began to think of making me a canoe, that I might go round the island" (Crusoe's resourcefulness and determination)
- "I began to consider that God Almighty was come down to this place to save my life" (Crusoe's encounter with Friday and the beginning of his spiritual journey)
- "I reflected upon my past life with such horror" (Crusoe's realization of his past sins)
- "I began to be very serious in the main affair of my soul" (Crusoe's growing devotion to Christianity)
- "I was nothing but a poor ignorant, unhappy wretch, a prisoner" (Crusoe's recognition of his need for redemption)
- "I began to consider myself as a human creature, cast upon that dreadful place as surely as if I had been thrown from the drawer of a ship" (Crusoe's colonization of the island)
- "I gave him bread, and tried to make him understand me, that he should go to the boat with me" (Crusoe's efforts to "civilize" Friday)
- "He had been in the boat before, and knew the word boat" (Crusoe's introduction of European words and concepts to Friday)
- "I began to be a little proud of my cave" (Crusoe's use of his skills and resources to create a comfortable home on the island)
- "I had now got all the tools I wanted" (Crusoe's use of European technology to survive on the island)
- "I began to think of making me a canoe" (Crusoe's resourcefulness and determination in using his tools and skills to adapt to life on the island)

This presentation is not exhaustive and only expands on a few of the key aspects of "Robinson Crusoe". There are many other interesting and important elements of the novel that could be further expanded upon, including its themes of religion and redemption, its portrayal of colonialism and the effects of Westernization on non-Western cultures, and its use of symbols such as the island, Friday, and Crusoe's tools and weapons. Additionally, the novel's portrayal of the encounter between European and non-European cultures and its themes of survival, self-reliance, and resourcefulness make it a timeless and thought-provoking work that continues to be widely read and studied today.

Robinson Crusoe Summary Overview

An adventurous young Englishman, despite his family's objections, chooses the sea over studying law. His initial voyage proves successful, but his ambitions lead him to a disastrous second journey. He becomes a captive of Moorish pirates but eventually escapes with a fellow slave, and they sail the African coast until rescued by a Portuguese captain. Sold by the protagonist to the captain, the slave boy offers passage to Brazil, where the Englishman becomes a successful plantation owner. Driven by the desire for cheap labor, he ventures to West Africa for slaves, only to be shipwrecked near Trinidad.

Surviving alone, he salvages anything useful from the wreck and establishes a life on the island, marking each day to keep track of time. He fortifies his shelter, cultivates food, and even trains a pet parrot and goat. His peaceful solitude is broken by the discovery of a human footprint, which he links to regional cannibals. He lives in fear, further fortifying his home until he witnesses a group of cannibals bringing their victims to the island. One victim escapes and runs towards the Englishman's dwelling, who slays the pursuers and takes in the grateful escapee, naming him Friday.

Friday, quick to learn English and the ways of Christianity, reveals that the cannibals are split into nations and only consume their enemies. He also shares that the cannibals had rescued Spaniards from a shipwreck, who are living nearby. As they plan to meet the Spaniards, they thwart a group of cannibals, rescuing a Spaniard and Friday's father. Their tranquil life is disrupted by a mutinying English ship. The islanders manage to turn the tide, capturing the ship and its mutineers. Deeming the island an imperial territory, they offer the men freedom in exchange for their return to England for justice. Overwhelmed, the protagonist faints upon securing the ship.

Back in England, he learns of his family's demise but is pleased to discover the profits from his plantation in Brazil, which the Portuguese captain had honestly managed. Despite his apprehension towards sea travel, his restlessness leads him to the East Indies as a trader. He revisits his island, now a thriving colony under the Spaniards' rule.

Preface

An unidentified narrator shares his motivations for presenting the forthcoming tale. He refrains from directly referencing Robinson Crusoe or his journey, instead, he characterizes the story as a "private man's adventures in the world" and praises its authenticity, calling it a "just history of fact." The narrator declares the story to be humble and solemn, containing valuable lessons that prompt us to appreciate "the wisdom of Providence." In light of this, he believes that by sharing Crusoe's story, he contributes significantly to society.

chapter 1

Robinson Crusoe, born in 1632 in York, England, pens his life journey. His father, of German descent and originally named Kreutznaer, raises him as the youngest of three brothers. His eldest brother is a soldier, while his other brother's whereabouts remain unknown. As the last born, his inheritance is minimal, prompting his father to push him towards studying law. However, Crusoe yearns for a seafaring life, a desire his family rejects. Despite his father's heartfelt advice on the virtues of a moderate lifestyle, Crusoe gives in to his wanderlust. One of his friends sets sail for London and Crusoe, unable to resist, joins him on September 1, 1651. A devastating storm hits near Yarmouth, filling Crusoe with fear and pushing him to plead with God for salvation. The ship survives the storm, and everyone onboard is safe. Crusoe takes this harrowing experience as a clear sign to abandon his dreams of the sea. His friend's father reinforces this idea, echoing the stern warning given by Crusoe's own father.

chapter 2

Leaving his friend, Crusoe ventures to London on foot. Here, he befriends a ship captain who invites him to join a forthcoming trade journey. Crusoe secures a forty-pound investment from his family for trade goods. The journey proves fruitful, yielding a profit of 300 pounds. Believing this to be a good fortune, Crusoe uses hundred pounds for his next trip, entrusting the remaining 200 to a widow he knows.

The subsequent venture sees Crusoe fall victim to Moorish pirates near the Sallee coastline in North Africa. His ship is captured, and Crusoe, the sole Brit in Moorish custody, is forced into slavery. His captors assign him to fishing due to his innate talents. On a foggy day, their fishing boat loses its way, prompting the installation of a compass on board. The master also stashes gunpowder on the boat for an incoming shooting party that never arrives. Meanwhile, Crusoe bides his time.

chapter 3

Robinson embarks on a fishing trip with two fellow slaves, Ismael and a lad named Xury. He takes Ismael by surprise, pushing him overboard. When Ismael pleads to be rescued, Robinson threatens him with a gun and forces him back to shore. He then secures Xury's loyalty, who agrees to accompany him. By dusk, they have navigated 150 miles south from Sallee. They spot lions on land which Robinson successfully hunts and skins with Xury's help. Continuing their journey south, they edge closer to what Robinson suspects are the Cape Verde or Canary Islands. They encounter native Africans who they initially fear, but soon form a friendly rapport with after the natives offer them nourishment. The natives admire Robinson's shooting skills when he kills a leopard, gifting him the animal's hide. Lost, Robinson spots a European vessel on the horizon. The ship rescues the pair, and its friendly Portuguese captain agrees to transport them to Brazil. The captain also purchases Robinson's boat and Xury.

chapter 4

Crusoe's journey to Brazil spans twenty-two days, and he receives numerous parting gifts from the Portuguese captain. He befriends his Anglo-Brazilian neighbor and comes up with the idea of starting a tobacco farm. The initial two years yield only enough for survival, but the third year brings prosperity. He regrets selling his slave, Xury, considering the potential labor loss. The Portuguese captain assists Crusoe by arranging the transfer of half of his 200 pounds left in England to Brazil and sends additional gifts. Feeling relatively affluent, Crusoe is keen to expand his enterprise through slave labor. He consents to a friend's proposal to sail to Guinea in search of Black slaves, promising him a portion of the slaves in return.

chapter 5

Crusoe, having signed a will that leaves half his belongings to the Portuguese captain, embarks on a journey to Guinea on the first of September, 1659. He carries small objects to trade for slaves. His ship sails up the South American coastline and confronts a storm, causing the loss of two crew members. This fills Crusoe with dread for his own safety. Once they reach the Caribbean, another storm hits. The force drives the ship onto the sand, destroys the rudder and leaves the crew no choice but to abandon the ship and head for the shore in small boats. Amidst the chaos, an enormous wave sweeps Crusoe's companions away and he loses sight of them. Crusoe manages to reach the shore, immediately thanking God for his survival. He spots no other surviving crew member. He quenches his thirst with freshwater, finds a tree to rest in, and thus spends his first night on the deserted island.

chapter 6

After a rejuvenating sleep, Crusoe heads to the beach to inspect the ship's wreckage. He swims around it, but climbing aboard proves to be a challenge until he spots a hanging chain he can use. Crusoe then hatches a plan to build a raft from the shattered wood, piling it high with rations like bread, rice, goat meat, cheese, and more. He also discovers clothing, weapons, and fresh water. He navigates his fully-loaded raft to a nearby cove and unloads his trove. He observes wild birds in the area but sees no signs of human life.

In the following thirteen days, Crusoe goes back to the ship a dozen times. During one of these visits, he stumbles upon thirty-six pounds, prompting a sorrowful reflection on the currency's insignificance in his situation. A fierce wind blows one night and when he wakes up the following day, the remnants of the ship have disappeared.

chapter 7

Concerned about potential natives, Crusoe deems it necessary to establish a fortified residence. He selects a location overlooking the ocean, shielded from wildlife and sun, and close to a water source. Constructing walls from wooden stakes driven into the ground, he creates a safe and secure space to sleep. On the following day, he moves all his belongings inside, setting up a hammock for sleeping and constructing an underground storage area. During a storm, he worries about his gunpowder, which he subsequently separates and stores safely underground.

Noticing wild goats on the island, he kills an adult and its young. Around the twelfth day, Crusoe builds a large cross, engraving the date of his landing, September 30, 1659. He decides to mark each day by carving a notch on the cross. Further, he initiates a journal to track the positive and negative experiences, until he exhausts his ink supply. He constantly keeps an eye out for any passing ships, but to his disappointment, none appear.

chapter 8

In this section, Crusoe introduces us to his diary, starting the entries with the date "September 30, 1659," and detailing his experiences on the "Island of Despair," as he names it. He recounts past incidents, including the shipwreck discovery, the scavenging for supplies, the storm that wipes out the ship, and the building of his shelter among other things. Having lost count of the days, Crusoe no longer knows when Sunday is, impeding his ability to observe the Sabbath. The entries also describe his efforts in crafting various items of furniture and tools, and his success in domesticating his first goat.

chapter 9

Crusoe's diary continues with his unsuccessful efforts to domesticate pigeons and his creation of candles using goat fat. He shares the almost magical discovery of barley after discarding some corn husks in a shaded spot, later unearthing fully-grown barley plants. He conscientiously preserves the crop for future planting, eventually enabling him to make his own bread. On the 16th of April, he narrowly escapes death when an earthquake strikes while he's at the entrance of his cellar. Surviving two subsequent tremors, he is grateful that his life and possessions remain unscathed.

chapter 10

Following the earthquake, a storm strikes. Crusoe seeks refuge in his cave, carving out a drain for his abode and enduring the heavy downpour. The possibility of another earthquake causing the cliff above his residence to collapse sets off his worries and prompts him to consider relocating. However, his attention is diverted upon finding barrels of gunpowder and other wreckage from the ship washed ashore by the storm. Crusoe dedicates several days to gather these valuable remains.

chapter 11

Crusoe is struck down by a serious illness, made worse by the continuous rain. He's so weak that he can barely move, even though he needs water. He begs God for help. In his fever, he imagines a man appearing from a dark cloud in a burst of flame. The phantom figure threatens Crusoe, claiming he hasn't yet repented for his past. Shaken, Crusoe contemplates on his many close brushes with death and is moved to tears by his own ungratefulness. He prays sincerely for the first time, pleading for relief.

The following day, he starts to regain some strength, though he is still frail. His mind is consumed by self-pity, which is then replaced by a wave of self-reproach. After consuming some tobacco and rum, his perspective changes. He picks up the Bible and is deeply affected by a verse about seeking God's help in difficult times. He then falls into a deep, day-long sleep, which disrupts his sense of time forever.

In the subsequent days, his health greatly improves. He thanks God and avoids eating wild birds while he's still unwell, opting for turtle eggs instead. Crusoe immerses himself in the New Testament and starts to regret his past. He begins to see his solitude on the island as a form of salvation from his previous sins.

chapter 12

In Crusoe's tenth month stranded, he experiences the unhealthy rainy season of July. He decides to explore the island, acknowledging that only Providence has the power to save him. In his exploration, he finds sugarcane and grapes, greatly appreciating the beauty of a particular valley. Filled with joy, Crusoe sees himself as the ruler of this land. He dries grapes to make raisins and gathers a hefty quantity of limes and grapes. He considers making this valley his new home and spends the rest of the month building a shelter there. He observes some cats have taken up residence in his home. To mark his first year on the island, he fasts for a day. Soon after, his journal comes to a halt when he runs out of ink.

chapter 13

Learning from his error of sowing seeds in the dry period, Crusoe successfully develops a calendar to track the climate for better farming. He is pleasantly surprised to find the wooden stakes he used for his rural dwelling, or "bower," have grown over time into a natural canopy offering soothing shade. In addition, Crusoe hones his skills in basket weaving, drawing inspiration from memories of crafters from his past. Despite these accomplishments, he still yearns for tobacco pipes, glass vessels, and a kettle.

chapter 14

Crusoe finally takes up his earlier desire to thoroughly examine his island, venturing to its western end. He spots land far away, speculating it's part of Spanish America. Fear of cannibals holds him back from investigating further. He befriends a parrot, training it to talk, and uncovers a group of penguins. Crusoe takes in a goat kid which almost dies in his bower from neglect until he remembers to feed it. Two years into his stay on the island, Crusoe's periods of contentment are punctuated by bouts of gloom. He finds solace in reading the Bible, particularly a verse reassuring him that God will never abandon him.

chapter 15

Crusoe dedicates a fair amount of time to constructing a shelf in his dwelling. When the rainy season arrives, he sows his rice and grain seeds but soon becomes frustrated when birds start to ruin his crops. By shooting a few birds and using them as scarecrows, he successfully deters them from coming back. Once his crop is ready, Crusoe begins to master the intricate tasks of grinding flour and baking bread.

In his pursuit of creating pottery, Crusoe initially struggles to mold the clay into usable shapes. Over time, he gets the hang of forming, firing, and glazing his creations. The thought of journeying to the mainland crosses his mind once again, and he decides to pay a visit to the ship's boat that was overturned in a storm. Despite his effort over several weeks, he is unable to flip the boat back over due to his lack of strength.

chapter 16

Crusoe decides to build a large canoe from a massive cedar tree. It takes him several months to remove the branches, shape the outside, and carve out the inside. However, he overlooks the issue of moving the canoe due to its size. He contemplates digging a canal to bring water to the canoe but dismisses it as it would take too much time. Four years have now lapsed since his shipwreck. He realizes he has all he needs to survive on the island and feels thankful for his situation, considering the alternatives. Crusoe notes that certain key events in his life have fallen on the same calendar dates, which he finds striking. He proceeds to create new clothes from animal hides and makes an umbrella. He also constructs a smaller canoe for an exploratory trip around the island. During the expedition, he narrowly escapes a strong current that could have swept him out to sea. Upon his safe return to the island, he is greeted by his parrot Poll who repeatedly calls his name, asking where he had been.

chapter 17

Crusoe spends a peaceful year in his island home, longing only for companionship. He takes pride in his newly learned crafts of basket weaving and pottery. Concerned about his dwindling gunpowder stock and the possibility of not being able to hunt goats, Crusoe explores animal farming. He manages to trap three young goats and in a span of eighteen months, he raises a herd of twelve. He masters the art of milking them and establishes a dairy that yields cheese and butter. He relishes his complete dominion over his island subjects and takes pleasure in feasting like a monarch, in the company of his parrot, his aged dog, and his two cats. He gives a brief summary of his island assets: two separate living areas - his initial dwelling and his secondary residence, a grape vineyard, cultivated lands, and goat enclosures.

chapter 18

Crusoe stumbles upon a single, bare human footprint in the sand, leaving him shocked and fearful. He rushes back to his "castle," contemplating the possibility of a devilish presence on the island. When he concludes that the footprint belongs to a human, not the devil, his fear doesn't ease. He reflects on the paradox of longing for human touch, then finding a man's presence terrifying. Fear pushes him to reinforce his home, setting up guns and maintaining a vigilant watch. Concern for his goats leads him to construct an underground cavern for their nightly shelter and establish another distant pasture for a secondary herd. For the next two years, Crusoe lives in a state of constant fear.

chapter 19

Stumbling upon a portion of the coast littered with human remains, Crusoe grasps he isn't in peril from the cannibals. Initially, he contemplates killing them as retribution for their heinous acts and consequently rescuing their future victims. He spends days armed and ready on a hill, but eventually, he reconsiders his plan. Crusoe understands he lacks the divine right to pass judgement or take lives. He also recognizes the potential backlash of his actions - a full-blown assault from other tribesmen.

chapter 20

Crusoe takes careful steps to elude the cannibals, hardly ever lighting fires, erasing signs of his presence, and even formulating a method to cook underground. On exploring a newfound large cave, he is startled by glowing eyes looking at him. Overcoming his fear, he revisits the cave with a burning stick, only to find out it's an elderly male goat. Crusoe contemplates making this cave his new home. Later, while at his watch post, he spots nine bare savages on the shore, still around the leftovers of their cannibal meal. He heads towards them, gun ready, but they've retreated back to sea by the time he reaches. Crusoe surveys the grisly scene they've left behind, filled with revulsion.

chapter 21

Whilst engaged in reading the Bible, Crusoe hears a couple of gunshots in quick succession. Believing they might be from a ship, he quickly lights a fire to signal his existence. Come morning, he realizes the shots were from a wrecked ship, now deserted or with deceased crew members. In gratitude for his safety, he thanks Providence. After discovering a dead young man on the shore, Crusoe decides to venture to the ship using his canoe. On board, he finds it to be of Spanish origin, filled with wine, clothes, and a significant amount of gold and doubloons. He manages to transport all these valuables back to his home.

chapter 22

Crusoe contemplates his history of poor decisions, including ignoring his father's advice, which he refers to as his "original sin". He has a dream one night of a man being chased by eleven cannibals on his island. About a year and a half later, the dream almost turns into reality. He comes across thirty cannibals preparing two victims for a feast on his island. One escapee rushes towards Crusoe's hideout, chased by two cannibals. Crusoe intervenes and saves him. The escapee, grateful and scared, pledges loyalty to Crusoe. They bury the bodies of the cannibals Crusoe killed to avoid detection later and return to Crusoe's camp where the native rests.

chapter 23

Crusoe gives the local the moniker Friday, in honor of the day he rescued him. Friday reiterates his loyalty to Crusoe. Crusoe imparts basic English terms to Friday and dresses him. They go back together to the carnage site, where Crusoe instructs Friday to tidy up the remains and tries to impart the atrocity of cannibalism to him. Crusoe is thrilled with Friday, his new sidekick, and introduces him to goat meat as an alternative to human flesh. Crusoe identifies the need to broaden his grain farming, which Friday assists with.

chapter 24

Crusoe warms up to Friday and, through basic dialogue, learns that cannibals often visit the island. He also gathers geographical knowledge to understand his proximity to Trinidad. He learns from Friday about the mainland Spaniards' violent acts. Crusoe tries teaching Friday religious concepts and finds that Friday readily grasps the idea of God, likening him to his own god, Benamuckee. Friday struggles to comprehend the devil and questions why God doesn't eliminate this evil entity. Crusoe struggles to answer and admits his limited religious understanding. Friday informs Crusoe that the cannibals have given refuge to the shipwreck survivors Crusoe had found before freeing Friday. Upon Friday's expression of longing to go back to his homeland, Crusoe becomes afraid of losing him. Moreover, when Crusoe thinks of joining the shipwreck survivors, Friday requests him not to abandon him. Consequently, they decide to build a boat together, intending to sail to Friday's land in late fall or early winter.

chapter 25

Crusoe and Friday find themselves hosting cannibals on their island before they could set off on their planned journey. The unwanted guests, twenty-one in number, arrive in three canoes to carry out a cannibalistic ritual on three hostages. Despite his initial reluctance to commit mass murder, Crusoe justifies the act as a necessity of war since Friday is from a rival tribe. Upon closer inspection, he realizes that one of the hostages is a fellow European. Crusoe and Friday attack the cannibals, defeating them with their advanced weaponry and allowing only a handful to escape. To Friday's delight, he discovers one of the hostages to be his father. They feed and shelter the stunned hostages, setting up a tent for them at Crusoe's home. Crusoe is satisfied with the expansion of his 'kingdom' with faithful subjects.

chapter 26

Following his interaction with Friday's father and the Spaniard, Crusoe reconsiders his old desire to go back to the mainland. He questions the Spaniard if the men left in the cannibals' domain would back him. The Spaniard affirms, but warns Crusoe that they'd need to amplify their food supply to feed the additional men. Assisted by his fresh workforce, Crusoe expands his farming operations. He equips each newcomer with a firearm.

chapter 27

Friday rushes to Crusoe, announcing an approaching boat. Crusoe discerns it's from England through his telescope. However, he remains wary. At the shore, they find eleven occupants in the boat, three tied as captives. Friday thinks the captors are cannibals. Spotting an opportunity as the eight free men wander, Crusoe talks to the prisoners, who misidentify him as an angel. One captive shares he's the ship's captain and they've suffered a mutiny. Crusoe suggests a deal: freedom for the captives in return for safe passage to England. The captain agrees, and Crusoe arms him with a gun. Crusoe foresees the sailors may notice something amiss and sends more crew. To pre-empt this, they make the boat unusable.

As expected, ten sailors from the ship find their boat ruined. With three left to guard the second boat, the other seven venture ashore. Crusoe uses Friday and another to yell at the men from different directions, tiring and disorienting them until they split up. The guards from the boat join their companions but are overcome by Crusoe's tactics. Crusoe's captain then negotiates with the remaining men, promising to spare all but the ringleader if they surrender. The mutineers acquiesce, and the captain concocts a tale about the island being a royal colony with the governor planning the ringleader's execution the next day.

chapter 28

Crusoe, after overpowering the mutineers, aims to retake the ship, a plan which the captain supports. With a fake warning about the island's governor planning to sentence them to death, Crusoe and the captain scare the captive mutineers into compliance. Crusoe takes five of them as hostages for assurance. The scheme is successful: the rebel leader aboard the ship is killed and the vessel is regained. Seeing the ship makes Crusoe almost faint from disbelief.

As a token of his gratitude, the captain offers him wine, food, and clothing. The mutineers are given the option to stay on the island to dodge the inevitable death penalty for their crimes in England. They gratefully choose to stay. Crusoe, with his wealth and some belongings, leaves the island on December 19, 1686, sailing for England after living there for twenty-eight years.

Upon his return, he learns that his money-keeper, a widow, is alive although not well-off. His family has passed away, save for two sisters and his brother's offspring. Crusoe then decides to travel to Lisbon to inquire about his Brazilian plantations.

chapter 29

Reaching Lisbon, Crusoe reconnects with his Portuguese captain friend who first brought him to Brazil. The captain informs Crusoe that his Brazilian properties, managed in trust, have yielded significant profits. The captain, owing Crusoe a substantial amount, initiates repayment. Touched by this honesty, Crusoe gives back some of the money. With a certified letter, Crusoe manages to regain control over his Brazilian assets, finding himself wealthy. He shares his wealth by sending monetary presents to his friend the widow and his sisters. Despite being tempted to relocate to Brazil, Crusoe chooses not to due to his aversion to converting to Catholicism. He opts to go back to England, yet is wary of sea travel, leading to him withdrawing his luggage from three ships at the last minute. He later discovers that two of these ships either succumbed to pirates or sank. Crusoe opts to travel by land instead, composing a travel party of Europeans and their staff.

chapter 30

Crusoe's crew departs from Lisbon, arriving in the Spanish city of Pamplona during late fall. Crusoe struggles with the freezing temperatures. The heavy snowfall causes them to remain in Pamplona for several weeks. They resume their journey toward France on the 15th of November, despite harsh weather conditions. In the forest, they encounter three wolves and a bear, which Friday manages to scare off after killing one wolf. Friday also provides some entertainment by taunting a bear before he kills it.

As the group continues their journey, they come across a terrified horse without a rider, and later, the remnants of two men who have been prey to wolves. A pack of three hundred wolves then engulfs Crusoe's group. They protect themselves by shooting at the wolves and creating an explosion with gunpowder, which eventually forces the wolves to retreat. Once they reach Toulouse in France, Crusoe discovers that their escape from the wolves was nothing short of a miracle.

chapter 31

Arriving in Dover, England, on January 14, Crusoe entrusts his belongings to a caring widow friend. He mulls over a return to Lisbon and Brazil, but faith-based worries hold him back. He opts to stick around in England and instructs the sale of his Brazilian assets, earning him a handsome fortune of 33,000 pieces of eight. With no family ties and accustomed to a nomadic lifestyle, Crusoe considers leaving England, regardless of his widow friend's efforts to stop him. He marries, but upon his wife's passing, he ventures to the East Indies as an independent trader in 1694. On this trip, he pays a visit to his former island. He learns the remaining Spaniards have dominated the mutineers with kindness. Crusoe showers them with presents like livestock, essential supplies, and even female companions. Despite a cannibal attack, the colony thrives.

Robinson Crusoe Short Questions & Answers

1.What made Robinson Crusoe think that the print on the ground was a footprint?

Ans: Robinson Crusoe thought that the print on the ground was a footprint because it exactly resembled a human foot. It had all the parts of a human foot: the toes, heels, etc.

2. Why was Robinson afraid when he looked at the bushes and trees?

Ans: Robinson was very fearful after discovering the footprint. While he was returning to his cave, out of fear, he mistook every bush and tree to be a human.

3. Why did Robinson pray when he saw the footprint?

Ans: Robinson prayed to God for protection. He was fearful that the footprint might be of a savage and the savage along with others would kill and eat him.

4.Where was Robinson Crusoe living?

Ans: Robinson Crusoe was living alone on a stranded island.

5 How did he end up there?

Ans: Robinson Crusoe's ship crashed in the sea near the island. He was the lone survivor and he ended up there on the deserted island.

6.What did Robinson Crusoe call 'My castle'?

Ans: The den in which Robinson Crusoe lived was called 'My castle' by him.

7. What were the two ways to enter Robinson's den?

Ans: The two ways to enter Robinson's den were:

a.   To use the ladder.
b.   To go in by the hole in the rock which he called 'door'.

8. How did Robinson's boat pose a threat to him?

Ans: Robinson feared that if the savages saw his boat on the shore, they would realise that someone lived on the island. Then they would come looking for him and if they found him, they would kill and eat him.

9.Why was Crusoe frightened whenever he looked at every bush and tree?

Ans: – After looking that footprint Crusoe returned homer very frightened and whenever he looked at every bush and tree he mistaken those to be a man.

10.Did Crusoe sleep that night well? Why?

Ans: – Crusoe did not sleep well that night. Because the more he thought about footprints that he had seen, the more afraid he becomes.

11.Why did Robinson Crusoe pray for protection?

Ans: – He thought the footprint could be of one of the savages of the mainland. He felt himself to be lucky that he was not a share at that time. He thought if the savage had seen his boat he would have realised that someone lived on this island and would soon return with others to kill and eat Crusoe. That is why Crusoe prayed for protection.

12.What did Crusoe decide when he went about two or three days and saw nothing on the shore?

Ans: – When Crusoe went about two or three days and saw nothing on the share he decided to go down to the shore again and examine the footprint once more .He decided to measure it with his own footprint.

13.What did Robinson crusoe realise when he came closer to the footprint? What did he do them?

Ans: – As he came closer to the footprint he realised that it could be not his footprint because he had not came to this part of the beach since a long time. Then he placed his foot alongside that footprint and the footprint seemed larger than his own footprint.

14.What made Robinson Crusoe think that the print on the ground was a footprint?

Ans:-Robinson Crusoe thought so because there was exactly the print of a foot – toes, heel, every part of a foot.

15.Why was Robinson afraid when he looked at the bushes and trees?

Ans:-Robinson was afraid when he looked at the bushes and trees because he mistook bushes and trees for a man following him.

16. Why did Robinson pray when he saw the footprint?

Ans:-Robinson thought that it could be the savages and knew someone lived on the island and would return with others to kill and eat him. Hence, he became afraid and prayed for his protection.

Long Questions & Answers

1.What does Crusoe's father mean by the "middle state"?

The term "middle state," when used by Crusoe's father in the beginning of the novel, can most closely be read to mean "middle class." Mr. Crusoe is telling his son the benefits of being neither rich nor poor. To Mr. Crusoe, the middle class has less to worry about than others of the superior or inferior classes. Middle-class individuals don't have to worry about making a living or finding an income, nor do they feel pressure about their growing greed or dissatisfaction with the life they life. To Mr. Crusoe, "middle state" is a term that conveys comfort and reliability.

2.Why does Crusoe take Xury with him on his escape but not the Moor?

The differences between Xury and the Moor are multiple, and these differences contribute to Xury's superior desirability as a fellow escapee. Xury, for starters, is a boy, whereas the Moor is an adult. Because the Moor has spent a longer period of his life as a slave, Crusoe feels he may show too much loyalty to his master and prohibit Crusoe from escaping. Xury, on the other hand, is too young to have developed such loyalty. Xury's youth also lends his character to a more subordinate nature. Furthermore, Xury is physically much weaker than the Moor, and possesses a smaller likelihood of physically preventing Crusoe's escape.

3.Why did Crusoe reject his father's advice to become a lawyer?

Crusoe exhibits a grander sense of adventure and rebelliousness than the rest of his family. Mr. Crusoe advises his son into law for the stability it offers, and also because Crusoe's brother was killed when he set off on an adventure to join the military. Crusoe's stubbornness and rebellious nature prompts him to reject this advice. This decision may also be influenced by the fact that Crusoe is the youngest child, and therefore has and will receive the least inheritance. This predicament causes Crusoe to feel resentment toward his family.

4.What does Crusoe's hallucination on the island mean?

After much time on the island, Crusoe eventually suffers a hallucination in which an angelic figure comes down from the sky and admonishes Crusoe for his actions and separation from God. This hallucination comes after Crusoe's sense of time has become so muddled he can no longer keep track of the Sabbath. To Crusoe, this hallucination is proof that his shipwreck was God's punishment for Crusoe's poor behavior. The hallucination influences Crusoe to read more scripture and repent for his sins. The hallucination's stand-in as a warning and promotion for the importance of repentance is supported by the fact that once Crusoe begins to repent and repair his relationship with God, his circumstances on the island and his overall outlook on life improve.

5.Does Crusoe see Friday as an equal on the island?

After rescuing Friday from the cannibals, Crusoe establishes a relationship with Friday that is anything but equal. By this point, Crusoe has already adopted the attitude of king of the island. Additionally, Crusoe's sense of heroism for saving Friday causes him to feel entitled to ownership of the man. This attitude is exhibited by the fact that, when teaching Friday English, Crusoe teaches him the word "master" before more useful words like "yes" and "no." Crusoe continues to expect Friday to do his bidding, including menial labor, during the rest of their time on the island. While it is true that Crusoe has an emotional connection to Friday and admits to loving him, it is clear that Crusoe does not see Friday as an equal. 6.What is the "middle state" Mr. Crusoe describes in Chapter 1 of Robinson Crusoe, and why does he recommend it to his son?

The middle state is what might today be called the middle class, and Mr. Crusoe considers it "the best state in the world." According to Mr. Crusoe, most of the evils and worries of life are visited upon people who live at the extremes of class, those who are very rich or very poor. The poor are exposed to "miseries and hardships" of labor and want. The very wealthy are afflicted with "pride, luxury, ambition, and envy" of maintaining a fortune and keeping up appearances. In the middle state, all needs are met without adding the social pressures of wealth, so Mr. Crusoe believes this is the best way to live, even though it lacks the excitement that his son so clearly craves.

7.How does Robinson Crusoe feel about his fate when the pirate takes him as a slave in Chapter 2?

Robinson Crusoe is surprised to find that the pirate treats him reasonably well, as the circumstances of his capture—a pirate raid on his ship—would create the expectation of rough treatment. Indeed, for a slave he is allowed remarkable latitude, generally left unattended in the house while his master is at sea, and left unattended on the ship while his master is in port. Because he is a European in an African country, Crusoe's opportunities to escape from his circumstances are limited, and he has no fellow Europeans with whom to plan an escape. Even though his circumstances are not brutal, Crusoe laments his labor and bondage and says he should have listened to his father. He has ignored his father's advice in pursuit of a life of adventure, and he now finds himself confined to one place, so it seems his disobedience was for naught.

8.Why does Robinson Crusoe save Xury but throw the other slave overboard when he escapes slavery in Chapter 2?

Early in his captivity, Robinson Crusoe laments that he has no other slaves, specifically of English, Irish, or Scottish descent, to plan an escape with, so he can only dream of escape rather than setting his plans into motion. This thinking indicates that he believes he will need assistance in carrying out an escape plan. When he is given access to the boat with only two slaves to hinder his escape, he chooses to push the Moor overboard and trust Xury. The Moor is also a slave, but he is an adult and of the same ethnicity as the pirate who has enslaved them, so Crusoe may fear that the Moor's loyalties will lie with their master. Crusoe may also fear that the Moor is strong enough to overpower him and so thwart his plans for escape. Xury, on the other hand, is a boy and so represents less of a physical threat to Crusoe. As a boy, Xury is also more malleable in his thinking, so Crusoe can influence him more easily, as evidenced by Xury's declaration of eternal loyalty to Crusoe.

9. What unlucky things happened to Robinson Crusoe in chapter 2 and what lucky things happened to him?

Ans: The unlucky things that happened to Robinson Crusoe were –i) He sailed to Guinea for the second time and lost all his money.ii) As he was sailing for Africa a pirate's ship attacked them and took all of them as prisoners.iii) Robinson Crusoe had to work for two years as the pirate captain's slave.

The lucky things that happen to Robinson Crusoe were-i) First time he went to Guinea he sold all his things and made a lot of money.ii) He managed to run away from the Pirate captain's house in a small boat and reached Brazil, where he sold his boat and got lots of money with which he bought some land and started farming.

10.Will a farmer's life make Robinson Crusoe happy?

Ans- Robinson Crusoe reached Brazil, sold his boat and bought some land, for sometime he was happy with his new life as a farmer but as he was not a person to stay back at one place but loved to go round the world so he was not happy with his life as a farmer.

Long Essay type Questions and Answers

1.Character Sketch of Robinson Crusoe

Daniel Defoe's "Robinson Crusoe" introduces readers to the indomitable and resourceful character of Robinson Crusoe. Stranded on a deserted island for years, Crusoe's tale is a narrative of survival, self-discovery, and resilience. In this character sketch, we explore the complexities of Robinson Crusoe's personality and the transformative journey that defines his character.

Adventurous Spirit: From a young age, Robinson Crusoe exhibits an adventurous spirit that compels him to defy his father's wishes and set out to sea. His insatiable desire for exploration becomes a driving force that shapes his destiny.

Quest for Independence: Crusoe's decision to embark on a sea voyage against his family's wishes is fueled by a deep-seated desire for independence. His quest for personal freedom propels him into a series of adventures that ultimately lead to his isolation on a deserted island.

Resourcefulness and Ingenuity: Stranded on the uninhabited island, Crusoe's resourcefulness and ingenuity come to the forefront. From constructing shelters to crafting tools, he utilizes his practical skills to adapt to the challenges of survival, showcasing an innate ability to make the best of adverse circumstances.

Struggle for Survival: Crusoe's years on the island are marked by a relentless struggle for survival. He battles the elements, scarcity of resources, and the psychological toll of isolation. His perseverance in the face of adversity becomes a defining aspect of his character.

Isolation and Self-Reflection: Isolation prompts Crusoe to engage in deep self-reflection. The solitude forces him to confront his own weaknesses, reassess his values, and question the choices that led him to this solitary existence. This introspection contributes to the evolution of his character.

Religious Transformation: Robinson Crusoe undergoes a profound religious transformation during his time on the island. His initial disregard for spiritual matters gives way to a fervent belief in divine providence. The Bible becomes a constant companion, and Crusoe sees his ordeal as a penance for his earlier disobedience.

Entrepreneurial Spirit: Even in the most challenging circumstances, Crusoe retains his entrepreneurial spirit. He establishes a semblance of civilization on the island, cultivating crops, domesticating animals, and creating a system of governance. This reflects his innate drive to shape his environment and maintain a sense of order.

Encounter with Friday: The arrival of Friday, a native he rescues from cannibals, introduces a new dynamic to Crusoe's life. His relationship with Friday evolves from one of master and servant to a more egalitarian and mutually beneficial partnership, highlighting Crusoe's capacity for compassion and camaraderie.

Yearning for Civilization: As years pass, Crusoe's initial desire for adventure transforms into a profound yearning for civilization. The isolation, though initially a consequence of his choices, becomes a crucible that reshapes his priorities, emphasizing the importance of human connection and community.

Narrative of Colonialism: Crusoe's interactions with Friday and the portrayal of the island's inhabitants contribute to a broader narrative of colonialism within the novel. The power dynamics and cultural clashes reflect the prevailing attitudes of the time, adding a layer of complexity to Crusoe's character.

Quick Overview:

1. Adventurous Spirit: Crusoe exhibits an adventurous spirit from a young age.
2. Quest for Independence: His journey is fueled by a desire for independence.

3. Resourcefulness and Ingenuity: Crusoe demonstrates resourcefulness and ingenuity for survival.

4. Struggle for Survival: His years on the island are marked by a relentless struggle for survival.

5. Isolation and Self-Reflection: Isolation prompts deep self-reflection and character evolution.

6. Religious Transformation: Crusoe undergoes a profound religious transformation.

7. Entrepreneurial Spirit: Even on the island, he maintains an entrepreneurial spirit.

8. Encounter with Friday: The relationship with Friday highlights compassion and partnership.

9. Yearning for Civilization: Over time, his desire for adventure transforms into a yearning for civilization.

10. Narrative of Colonialism: Crusoe's interactions contribute to a broader narrative of colonialism.

Conclusion: Robinson Crusoe emerges as a literary archetype of resilience and transformation. Defoe crafts a character who, through the crucible of isolation, undergoes a profound metamorphosis—from an adventurous but disobedient youth to a reflective, resourceful, and spiritually awakened man. Crusoe's journey resonates as a timeless exploration of human nature, the quest for independence, and the transformative power of adversity. In the vast realm of literature, Robinson Crusoe stands as a testament to the enduring appeal of characters whose narratives transcend the boundaries of time and continue to captivate readers across generations.

2.Character Analysis of Robinson Crusoe's Friday

A handsome, in about 26 years old, with straight and strong limbs, tall and well-shaped fellow who bare name Friday which he got for the memory of a day he was rescued.

The native was saved from certain death by Robinson Crusoe during one of the cannibal rituals of a local tribe. By the man who was actually on his way to Africa to buy Negroes!

His hair was long and black but not curled, he had a very high forehead and great sparkling sharp eyes. Friday's appearance was somewhere in between Negro and European, black but tawny skin, round face, and small but not flat nose as most of the Negroes have. Of course, as all Negroes have, had he fine teeth well set and white as ivory, but oddly enough – thin lips.

To lay his head flat upon the ground, close to person's foot, and set other foot upon his head – this was Friday's way of showing the servitude and submission. Robinson understood him in many things and let him know how very pleased he was with him. This was something Friday understood before he could speak Robinson's language. Still, he was a cannibal in his nature, full of lot abhorrence.

We can see how the other culture is suppressed from the very beginning. Robinson cures Friday of his cannibalistic habits and gives him a new Western name. But the first words he taught him in English were words that one servant has to know and use!

So Friday was domesticated and incorporated into Western society. The main fear and an idea throughout the book is Crusoe's goal to re-educate Friday to a civilized human being and if he wouldn't have, he would have no mercy but to kill him! Submissive Friday, full of gratitude was treated with the attitude close to colonial that is – possession.

In my opinion, Friday's total submission released Robinson from the sort of guilt and the need to use violence. He was Crusoe's slave because he was saved by him and lifelong servitude was accepted by Robinson. The servant-master relationship was symbolically sealed by an oath, a substitute for the written contract.

3.The relationship between Robinson Crusoe and Friday in Robinson Crusoe

Robinson Crusoe is the best novel of Daniel Defoe. This novel is considered a milestone in the history of English literature. It is one of the first few novels of English literature. The noble does not have too many characters. It tells the story of Robinson Crusoe who lives alone in an island for a long time. The other character that attracts readers' attention in the novel was Friday. The relationship between Friday and Robinson Crusoe is one of the key aspects of the novel hence making it very important.

Robinson Crusoe lived in England. He belonged to a lower race. Friday was brought by his enemies on that island. They would have killed him and ate his flesh. Robinson Crusoe saved Friday from those people. After that, Friday became Crusoe's loyal servant. Throughout the novel, the master-slave or master-servant relation was dominant.

Like his contemporaries, Daniel Defoe believed that the Europeans were the superior race. The non-white people do not have the capability to rule themselves. It is the duty of the European to turn these people into slave and civilize them.

In this novel, we see that Robinson Crusoe civilizes Friday. He tells him that he cannot eat human flesh. Because of Crusoe's education, Friday converts to Christianity. In the end, we see Friday desperately tries to become a European instead of following his own religion. In this manner, Crusoe turns Friday into a true European servant. However, European society never accepted him as one of their own.

Robinson Crusoe considered himself as superior. He ordered Friday to address him as master. From the day they met till the end of the novel Friday addressed him as "Master." Not by any other name.

In the beginning of the novel, we can see that Robinson Crusoe disobeyed his father and goes out for a voyage at the sea. That voyage destroyed his life. Friday was like a son to Crusoe. On the contrary, Robinson Crusoe was like a father to him. However, Crusoe's ideal about European supremacy never changed. He always considered himself better than Friday. He could never become a true father but remained Friday's master all his life. In the end, Crusoe becomes lonely. However, Crusoe was never cruel to Friday. He was very gentle with him and tried to win his heart and mind through his gentleness.

Robinson Crusoe was written at a time when the English did not see much success in establishing their colonies around the world. However, they competed with other European nations such as Portugal and Spain to establish colonies in Asia and America. Crusoe gives us a glimpse of how the colonies of the English would be in the coming years.

4.Relationship of Robinson Crusoe and Friday as master and slave

In the novel, "Robinson Crusoe," by Daniel Defoe, the main character, Robinson Crusoe, is a middle class, white man from England. Crusoe aspires to become a sailor, and against his father's wishes and advice, he embarks on a journey which ultimately takes him to the other side of the world. On his last expedition, he ends up shipwrecked on a desolate tropical island. For many years, he is alone of the island with no human contact, until one day he witnesses savages chasing a man. Crusoe rescues this man and kills off the savages, and the man, Friday, becomes a companion to him. The relationship that ensues between them is diverse and unbalanced; it brings out the great and lesser qualities of Robinson Crusoe and reveals his racist, colonial, white mindset typical of those times. Crusoe and Friday's relationship starts off by Crusoe taking him under his wing and protecting him from his fellow savages. Due to this rescue, Friday becomes very loyal towards him and submits. At times, the relationship between the two is almost like father and son, and Crusoe seems to have respect and trust for Friday. However, at other times, it is apparent that Crusoe is the master and Friday is merely his slave. This relationship is made clear in the text, from the moment where Crusoe gives him the name Friday, not caring what his real name may be. Crusoe also insists on being referred to as ˜Master', and Friday never discovers his actual name. This naming showed a certain hierarchy, placing Crusoe above Friday. This shows Crusoe's true nature, coming from an English, Christian background. Friday does not fight this master-slave relationship; in fact, he welcomes it and remains very devote as thanks to Crusoe for saving his life. This is shown when Crusoe states, "at last he lay his Head flat upon the ground, close to my Foot; and sets my other Foot upon his Head to let me know, how he would serve me as long as he liv'd " (Defoe 218).

5.Robinson Crusoe as the Prototype British Colonist

The novel, Robinson Crusoe, written by Daniel Defoe and first published in 1719, is an important literary piece of the Enlightenment period, as it expresses the Enlightenment themes of individualism, exploration and the rejection of authority. The poet James Joyce has described the character of Robinson Crusoe as the "true prototype of the British colonist"1, and Robinson Crusoe certainly shares many of the characteristics associated with British colonists of the period in which the novel was written. Robinson Crusoe exerts his manly independence by being the lone survivor from the shipwreck, his intelligence in ensuring his sustenance, and shows his well balanced approach to religion in order to comfort himself. These are all characteristics which explain why Joyce describes Crusoe as "the prototype of the British colonist"2. The relationship between Crusoe and Friday is also an important factor which explains what Joyce meant by his description of Crusoe, as Robinson attempts to convert Friday to Christianity, teach him the English language, and rid him of his savage tendencies. Crusoe leaves his comfortable life in England to travel the world, and in his travels he partakes in many of the activities of a British colonist, developing a plantation, and taking part in slavery and the international slave trade. All of these factors I will discuss explain why the character of Robinson Crusoe reflects the roles and characteristics of the British colonist.

Manly independence is often considered to be a common and necessary trait of the true British colonist at the time of the novel, and this is shown in the character of Robinson Crusoe at various points. An example of this manly independence can be found at the beginning of the novel, when Crusoe discusses the conversations which he had with his Father regarding his desire to travel the world in search of new pastures

6.Hypocrisy in Robinson Crusoe

We all have it, but rarely know what to do about it, and worse, rarely acknowledge it. As humans, we have the ability to come up with some rather creative ways to justify our hypocrisy. In Daniel Defoe's novel, Robinson Crusoe, religion plays a prominent role throughout the story; however, Crusoe, like the majority of individuals, practices selective religious conviction, clinging to actions and moral principals he finds appealing and ignoring those that do not conform to his beliefs. .

Robinson Crusoe is more than a story about a shipwreck, survival and rescue; it is a novel about one man's spiritual journey, a spiritual journey complete with spiritual apathy. Throughout the story, Crusoe's level of spiritual devotion is dependent upon his need. This hypocritical attitude is reflective in his actions. His theological dedication diminishes once he no longer requires assistance or deduces a non-supernatural cause for mysterious events. He lives a life of religious hypocrisy. On Crusoe's very first voyage, God gave him his first test to bring him to repentance. When the seas became rough and stormy, Crusoe said, "I made many vows and resolutions that, if it would please God to spare my life in this one voyage.I would go directly home to my father, and never set [my foot] into a ship again" (Defoe 52). He made a promise to God that if he were to survive the storm he would return home. Crusoe does survive; however, he does not follow through with his word. Instead he decides to get drunk with a friend. Crusoe does acknowledge his apathy by admitting: "In a word, as the Sea was returned to its Smoothness of Surface and settled Calmness by the Abatement of that Storm, so the Hurry of my Thoughts being over, my Fears and Apprehensions of being swallow'd up by the Sea being forgotten, and the Current of my former Desires return'd, I entirely forgot the Vows and Promises .

CHAPTER ELEVEN

GULLIVER'S TRAVELS - JONATHAN SWIFT

Gulliver's Travels

Summary of the novel:

Gulliver's Travels recounts the story of Lemuel Gulliver, a practical-minded Englishman trained as a surgeon who takes to the seas when his business fails. In a deadpan first-person narrative that rarely shows any signs of self-reflection or deep emotional response, Gulliver narrates the adventures that befall him on these travels.

Gulliver's adventure in Lilliput begins when he wakes after his shipwreck to find himself bound by innumerable tiny threads and addressed by tiny captors who are in awe of him but fiercely protective of their kingdom. They are not afraid to use violence against Gulliver, though their arrows are little more than pinpricks. But overall, they are hospitable, risking famine in their land by feeding Gulliver, who consumes more food than a thousand Lilliputians combined could. Gulliver is taken into the capital city by a vast wagon the Lilliputians have specially built. He is presented to the emperor, who is entertained by Gulliver, just as Gulliver is flattered by the attention of royalty. Eventually Gulliver becomes a national resource, used by the army in its war against the people of Blefuscu, whom the Lilliputians hate for doctrinal differences concerning the proper way to crack eggs. But things change when Gulliver is convicted of treason for putting out a fire in the royal palace with his urine and is condemned to be shot in the eyes and starved to death. Gulliver escapes to Blefuscu, where he is able to repair a boat he finds and set sail for England.

After staying in England with his wife and family for two months, Gulliver undertakes his next sea voyage, which takes him to a land of giants called Brobdingnag. Here, a field worker discovers him. The farmer initially treats him as little more than an animal, keeping him for amusement. The farmer eventually sells Gulliver to the queen, who makes him a courtly diversion and is entertained by his musical talents. Social life is easy for Gulliver after his discovery by the court, but not particularly enjoyable. Gulliver is often repulsed by the physicality of the Brobdingnagians, whose ordinary flaws are many times magnified by their huge size. Thus, when a couple of courtly ladies let him play on their naked bodies, he is not attracted to them but rather disgusted by their enormous skin pores and the sound of their torrential urination. He is generally startled by the ignorance of the people here—even the king knows nothing about politics. More unsettling findings in Brobdingnag come in the form of various animals of the realm that endanger his life. Even Brobdingnagian insects leave slimy trails on his food that make eating difficult. On a trip to the frontier, accompanying the royal couple, Gulliver leaves Brobdingnag when his cage is plucked up by an eagle and dropped into the sea.

Next, Gulliver sets sail again and, after an attack by pirates, ends up in Laputa, where a floating island inhabited by theoreticians and academics oppresses the land below, called Balnibarbi. The scientific research undertaken in Laputa and in Balnibarbi seems totally inane and impractical, and its residents too appear wholly out of touch with reality. Taking a short side trip to Glubbdubdrib, Gulliver is able to witness the conjuring up of figures from history, such as Julius Caesar and other military leaders, whom he finds much less impressive than in books. After visiting the Luggnaggians and the Struldbrugs, the latter of which are senile immortals who prove that age does not bring wisdom, he is able to sail to Japan and from there back to England.

Finally, on his fourth journey, Gulliver sets out as captain of a ship, but after the mutiny of his crew and a long confinement in his cabin, he arrives in an unknown land. This land is populated by Houyhnhnms, rational-thinking horses who rule, and by Yahoos, brutish humanlike creatures who serve the Houyhnhnms. Gulliver sets about learning their language, and when he can speak he narrates his voyages to them and explains the constitution of England. He is treated with great courtesy and kindness by the horses and is enlightened by his many conversations with them and by his exposure to their noble culture. He wants to stay with the Houyhnhnms, but his bared body reveals to the horses that he is very much like a Yahoo, and he is banished. Gulliver is grief-stricken but agrees to leave. He fashions a canoe and makes his way to a nearby island, where he is picked up by a Portuguese ship captain who treats him well, though Gulliver cannot help now seeing the captain—and all humans—as shamefully Yahoolike. Gulliver then concludes his narrative with a claim that the lands he has visited belong by rights to England, as her colonies, even though he questions the whole idea of colonialism.

Detailed summary of Part 1 and 2.

Chapter 1

The novel begins with Lemuel Gulliver recounting the story of his life, beginning with his family history. He is born to a family in Nottinghamshire, the third of five sons. Although he studies at Cambridge as a teenager, his family is too poor to keep him there, so he is sent to London to be a surgeon's apprentice. There, under a man named James Bates, he learns mathematics and navigation with the hope of traveling. When his apprenticeship ends, he studies physics at Leyden.

He then becomes a surgeon aboard a ship called the *Swallow* for three years. Afterward, he settles in London, working as a doctor, and marries a woman named Mary Burton. His business begins to fail when his patron dies, so he decides to go to sea again and travels for six years. Although he has planned to return home at the end of this time, he decides to accept one last job on a ship called the *Antelope*.

In the East Indies, the *Antelope* encounters a violent storm in which twelve crewmen die. Six of the crewmembers, including Gulliver, board a small rowboat to escape. Soon the rowboat capsizes, and Gulliver loses track of his companions. They are never seen again. Gulliver, however, swims safely to shore.

Gulliver lies down on the grass to rest, and soon he falls asleep. When he wakes up, he finds that his arms, legs, and long hair have been tied to the ground with pieces of thread. He can only look up, and the bright sun prevents him from seeing anything. He feels something move across his leg and over his chest. He looks down and sees, to his surprise, a six-inch-tall human carrying a bow and arrow. At least forty more little people climb onto his body. He is surprised and shouts loudly, frightening the little people away. They return, however, and one of the little men cries out,

"Hekinah Degul."

Gulliver struggles to get loose and finally succeeds in breaking the strings binding his left arm. He loosens the ropes tying his hair so he can turn to the left. In response, the little people fire a volley of arrows into his hand and violently attack his body and face. He decides that the safest thing to do is to lie still until nightfall. The noise increases as the little people build a stage next to Gulliver about a foot and a half off the ground. One of them climbs onto it and makes a speech in a language that Gulliver does not understand.

Gulliver indicates that he is hungry, and the little people bring him baskets of meat. He devours it all and then shows that he is thirsty, so they bring him two large barrels of wine. Gulliver is tempted to pick up forty or fifty of the little people and throw them against the ground, but he decides that he has made them a promise of goodwill and is grateful for their hospitality. He is also struck by their bravery, since they climb onto his body despite his great size.

An official climbs onto Gulliver's body and tells him that he is to be carried to the capital city. Gulliver wants to walk, but they tell him that that will not be permitted. Instead, they bring a frame of wood raised three inches off the ground and carried by twenty-two wheels. Nine hundred men pull this cart about half a mile to the city. Gulliver's left leg is then padlocked to a large temple, giving him only enough freedom to walk around the building in a semicircle and lie down inside the temple.

Chapter 2

Once the Lilliputians chain Gulliver to the building, he is finally allowed to stand up and view the entire countryside, which he discovers is beautiful and rustic. The tallest trees are seven feet tall, and the whole area looks to him like a theater set.

Gulliver meticulously describes his process of relieving himself, which initially involves walking inside the building to the edge of his chain. After the first time, he makes sure to relieve himself in open air, and servants carry away his excrement in wheelbarrows. He says that he describes this process in order to establish his cleanliness, which has been called into question by his critics.

The emperor visits on horseback from his tower. He orders his servants to give Gulliver food and drink. The emperor is dressed plainly and carries a sword to defend himself. He and Gulliver converse, though they cannot understand each other. Gulliver tries to speak every language he knows, but nothing works. After two hours, Gulliver is left with a group of soldiers guarding him. Some of them, disobeying orders, try to shoot arrows at him. As a punishment, the brigadier ties up six of these offenders and places them in Gulliver's hand. Gulliver puts five of them into his pocket and pretends that he is going to eat the sixth, but then cuts loose his ropes and sets him free. He does the same with the other five, which pleases the court.

After two weeks, a bed is made for Gulliver. It consists of 600 small beds sewn together. News of his arrival also spreads throughout the kingdom and curious people from the villages come to see him. Meanwhile, the government tries to decide what to do with him. Frequent councils bring up various concerns: that he will break loose, for instance, or that he will eat enough to cause a famine. Some suggest that they starve him or shoot him in the face to kill him, but others argue that doing so would leave them with a giant corpse and a large health risk.

Officers who witnessed Gulliver's lenient treatment of the six offending soldiers report to the council, and the emperor and his court decide to respond with kindness. They arrange to deliver large amounts of food to Gulliver every morning, supply him with servants to wait on him, hire tailors to make him clothing, and offer teachers to instruct him in their language.

Every morning Gulliver asks the emperor to set him free, but the emperor refuses, saying that Gulliver must be patient. The emperor also orders him to be searched to ensure that he does not have any weapons. Gulliver agrees to this search, and the Lilliputians take an inventory of his possessions. In the process, all of his weapons are taken away.

Chapter 3

Gulliver hopes to be set free, as he is getting along well with the Lilliputians and earning their trust. The emperor decides to entertain him with shows, including a performance by Rope-Dancers, who are Lilliputians seeking employment in the government. For the performance, which doubles as a sort of competitive entrance examination, the candidates dance on "ropes"—slender threads suspended two feet above the ground. When a vacancy occurs, candidates petition the emperor to entertain him with a dance, and whoever jumps the highest earns the office. The current ministers continue this practice as well, in order to show that they have not lost their skill.

As another diversion for Gulliver, the emperor lays three silken threads of different colors on a table. He then holds out a stick, and candidates are asked to leap over it or creep under it. Whoever shows the most dexterity wins one of the ribbons.

Gulliver builds a platform from sticks and his handkerchief and invites horsemen to exercise upon it. The emperor greatly enjoys watching this new entertainment, but it is cut short when a horse steps through the handkerchief, after which Gulliver decides that it is too dangerous for them to keep riding on the cloth.

Some Lilliputians discover Gulliver's hat, which washed ashore after him, and he asks them to bring it back. Soon after, the emperor asks Gulliver to pose like a colossus, or giant statue, so that his troops might march under Gulliver.

Gulliver's petitions for freedom are finally answered. Gulliver must swear to obey the articles put forth, which include stipulations that he must assist the Lilliputians in times of war, survey the land around them, help with construction, and deliver urgent messages. Gulliver agrees and his chains are removed.

Chapter 4

After regaining his freedom, Gulliver goes to Mildendo, the capital city of the Lilliputians. The residents are told to stay indoors, and they all sit on their roofs and in their garret windows to see him. The town is 500 feet square with a wall surrounding it, and can hold 500,000 people. The emperor wants Gulliver to see the magnificence of his palace, which is at the center of the city, so Gulliver cuts down trees to make himself a stool, which he carries around with him so that he can sit down and see things from a shorter distance than a standing position allows.

About two weeks after Gulliver obtains his liberty, a government official, Reldresal, comes to see him. He tells Gulliver that two forces, one rebel group and one foreign empire, threaten the kingdom. The rebel group exists because the kingdom is divided into two factions, called Tramecksan and Slamecksan. The people in the two factions are distinguished by the heights of their heels.

Reldresal tells Gulliver that the current emperor has chosen to employ primarily the low-heeled Slamecksan in his administration. He adds that the emperor himself has lower heels than all of his officials but that his heir has one heel higher than the other, which makes him walk unevenly. At the same time, the Lilliputians fear an invasion from the Island of Blefuscu, which Reldresal calls the "Other Great Empire of the Universe." He adds that the philosophers of Lilliput do not believe Gulliver's claim that there are other countries in the world inhabited by other people of his size, preferring to think that Gulliver dropped from the moon or a star.

Reldresal describes the history of the two nations. The conflict between them, he tells Gulliver, began years ago, when the emperor's grandfather, then in command of the country, commanded all Lilliputians to break their eggs on the small end first. He made this decision after breaking an egg in the old way, large end first, and cutting his finger. The people resented the law, and six rebellions were started in protest. The monarchs of Blefuscu fueled these rebellions, and when they were over the rebels fled to that country to seek refuge. Eleven thousand people chose death rather than submit to the law. Many books were written on the controversy, but books written by the Big-Endians were banned in Lilliput. The government of Blefuscu accused the Lilliputians of disobeying their religious doctrine, the *Brundrecral,* by breaking their eggs at the small end. The Lilliputians argued that the doctrine reads, "That all true believers shall break their eggs at the convenient end," which could be interpreted as the small end.

Reldresal continues that the exiles gained support in Blefuscu to launch a war against Lilliput and were aided by rebel forces inside Lilliput. A war has been raging between the two nations ever since, and Gulliver is asked to help defend Lilliput against its enemies. Gulliver does not feel that it is appropriate to intervene, but he nonetheless offers his services to the emperor.

Chapter 5

Gulliver spies on the empire of Blefuscu and devises a plan. He asks for cables and bars of iron, out of which he makes hooks with cables attached. He then wades and swims the channel to Blefuscu and catches their ships at port. The people are so frightened that they leap out of their ships and swim to shore. Gulliver attaches a hook to each ship and ties them together. The Blefuscu soldiers fire arrows at him, but he keeps working, protecting his eyes by putting on the spectacles he keeps in his coat pocket. He tries to pull the ships away, but they are anchored too tightly, so he cuts them away with his pocketknife and pulls the ships back to Lilliput.

In Lilliput, Gulliver is greeted as a hero. The emperor asks him to go back to retrieve the other ships, intending to destroy Blefuscu's military strength and make it a province in his empire. Gulliver dissuades him from this action, saying that he does not want to encourage slavery or injustice. This position causes great disagreement in the government, with some officials turning staunchly against Gulliver and calling for his destruction.

Three weeks later, a delegation arrives from Blefuscu, and the war ends with Blefuscu's surrender. The Blefuscu delegates are privately told of Gulliver's kindness toward the Lilliputians, and they ask him to visit their kingdom. He wishes to do so, and the emperor reluctantly allows it.

As a *Nardac*, or person of high rank, Gulliver no longer has to perform all the duties laid down in his contract. He does, however, have the opportunity to help the Lilliputians when the emperor's wife's room catches fire. He forgets his coat and cannot put the flames out with his clothing, so instead he thinks of a new plan: he urinates on the palace, putting out the fire entirely. He worries afterward that since the act of public urination is a crime in Lilliput he will be prosecuted, but the emperor tells him he will be pardoned. He is told, however, that the emperor's wife can no longer tolerate living in her rescued quarters.

Chapter 6

Gulliver describes the general customs and practices of Lilliput in more detail, beginning by explaining that everything in Lilliput— their animals, trees, and plants—is sized in proportion to the Lilliputians. Their eyesight is also adapted to their scale: Gulliver cannot see as clearly close-up as they can, while they cannot see as far as he can.

The Lilliputians are well educated, but their writing system is odd to Gulliver, who jokes that they write not left to right like the Europeans or top to bottom like the Chinese, but from one corner of the page to the other, "like the ladies in England."

The dead are buried with their heads pointing directly downward, because the Lilliputians believe that eventually the dead will rise again and that the Earth, which they think is flat, will turn upside down. Gulliver adds that the better-educated Lilliputians no longer believe in this custom.

Gulliver describes some of the other laws of Lilliput, such as a tradition by which anyone who falsely accuses someone else of a crime against the state is put to death. Deceit is considered worse than theft, because honest people are more vulnerable to liars than to thieves, since commerce requires people to trust one another. The law provides not only for punishment but also for rewards of special titles and privileges for good behavior.

Children are raised not by individual parents but by the kingdom as a whole. They are sent to live in schools at a very young age. The schools are chosen according to the station of their parents, whom they see only twice a year. Only the laborers' children stay home, since their job is to farm. There are no beggars at all, since the poor are well looked after.

Chapter 7

Gulliver goes on to describe the "intrigue" that precipitates his departure from Lilliput. While he prepares to make his trip to Blefuscu, a court official tells Gulliver that he has been charged with treason by enemies in the government. He shows Gulliver the document calling for his execution: Gulliver is charged with public urination, refusing to obey the emperor's orders to seize the remaining Blefuscu ships, aiding enemy ambassadors, and traveling to Blefuscu.

Gulliver is told that Reldresal has asked for his sentence to be reduced, calling not for execution but for putting his eyes out. This punishment has been agreed upon, along with a plan to starve him to death slowly. The official tells Gulliver that the operation to blind him will take place in three days. Fearing this resolution, Gulliver crosses the channel and arrives in Blefuscu.

Chapter 8

Three days later, he sees a boat of normal size—that is, big enough to carry him—overturned in the water. He asks the emperor of Blefuscu to help him fix it. At the same time, the emperor of Lilliput sends an envoy with the articles commanding Gulliver to give up his eyesight. The emperor of Blefuscu sends it back with the message that Gulliver will soon be leaving both their kingdoms. After about a month, the boat is ready and Gulliver sets sail. He arrives safely back in England, where he makes a good profit showing miniature farm animals that he carried away from Blefuscu in his pockets.

Part 2

Chapter 1

Two months after returning to England, Gulliver is restless again. He sets sail on a ship called the *Adventure,* traveling to the Cape of Good Hope and Madagascar before encountering a monsoon that draws the ship off course. The ship eventually arrives at an unknown land mass. There are no inhabitants about, and the landscape is barren and rocky. Gulliver is walking back to the boat when he sees that it has already left without him. He tries to chase after it, but then he sees that a giant is following the boat. Gulliver runs away, and when he stops, he is on a steep hill from which he can see the countryside. He is shocked to see that the grass is about twenty feet high.

He walks down what looks like a high road but turns out to be a footpath through a field of barley. He walks for a long time but cannot see anything beyond the stalks of corn, which are forty feet high. He tries to climb a set of steps into the next field, but he cannot mount them because they are too high. As he is trying to climb up the stairs, he sees another one of the island's giant inhabitants. He hides from the giant, but it calls for more people to come, and they begin to harvest the crop with scythes. Gulliver lies down and bemoans his state, thinking about how insignificant he must be to these giant creatures.

One of the servants comes close to Gulliver with both his foot and his scythe, so Gulliver screams as loudly as he can. The giant finally notices him, and picks him up between his fingers to get a closer look. Gulliver tries to speak to him in plaintive tones, bringing his hands together, and the giant seems pleased. Gulliver makes it clear that the giant's fingers are hurting him, and the giant places him in his pocket and begins to walk toward his master.

The giant's master, the farmer of these fields, takes Gulliver from his servant and observes him more closely. He asks the other servants if they have ever seen anything like Gulliver, then places him onto the ground. They sit around him in a circle. Gulliver kneels down and begins to speak as loudly as he can, taking off his hat and bowing to the farmer. He presents a purse full of gold to the farmer, which the farmer takes into his palm. He cannot figure out what it is, even after Gulliver empties the coins into his hand.

The farmer takes Gulliver back to his wife, who is frightened of him. The servant brings in dinner, and they all sit down to eat, Gulliver sitting on the table not far from the farmer's plate. They give him tiny bits of their food, and he pulls out his knife and fork to eat, which delights the giants. The farmer's son picks Gulliver up and scares him, but the farmer takes Gulliver from the boy's hands and strikes his son. Gulliver makes a sign that the boy should be forgiven, and kisses his hand. After dinner, the farmer's wife lets Gulliver nap in her own bed. When he wakes up he finds two rats attacking him, and he defends himself with his "hanger," or sword.

Chapter 2

The farmer's nine-year-old daughter, whom Gulliver calls Glumdalclitch, or "nursemaid," has a doll's cradle that becomes Gulliver's permanent bed. Glumdalclitch places the cradle inside a drawer to keep Gulliver safe from the rats. She becomes Gulliver's caretaker and guardian, sewing clothes for him and teaching him the giants' language.

The farmer begins to talk about Gulliver in town, and a friend of the farmer's comes to see him. He looks at Gulliver through his glasses, and Gulliver begins to laugh at the sight of the man's eyes through the glass. The man becomes angry and advises the farmer to take Gulliver into the market to display him. He agrees, and Gulliver is taken to town in a carriage, which he finds very uncomfortable. There, he is placed on a table while Glumdalclitch sits down on a stool beside him, with thirty people at a time walking through as he performs "tricks."

Gulliver is exhausted by the journey to the marketplace, but upon returning to the farmer's house, he finds that he is to be shown there as well. People come from miles around and are charged great sums to view him. Thinking that Gulliver can make him a great fortune, the farmer takes him and Glumdalclitch on a trip to the largest cities.

The three arrive in the largest city, Lorbrulgrud, and the farmer rents a room with a table for displaying Gulliver. By now, Gulliver can understand their language and speak it fairly well. He is shown ten times a day and pleases the visitors greatly.

Chapter 3

The strain of traveling and performing "tricks" takes its toll on Gulliver, and he begins to grow very thin. The farmer notices Gulliver's condition and resolves to make as much money as possible before Gulliver dies. Meanwhile, an order comes from the court, commanding the farmer to bring Gulliver to the queen for her entertainment.

The queen is delighted with Gulliver's behavior and buys him from the farmer for 1,000 gold pieces. Gulliver requests that Glumdalclitch be allowed to live in the palace as well. Gulliver explains his suffering to the queen, and she is impressed by his intelligence. She takes him to the king, who at first thinks he is a mechanical creation. He sends for great scholars to observe Gulliver, and they decide that he is unfit for survival, since there is no way he could feed himself. Gulliver tries to explain that he comes from a country in which everything is in proportion to himself, but they do not seem to believe him.

Glumdalclitch is given an apartment in the palace and a governess to teach her, and special quarters are built for Gulliver out of a box. They also have clothes made for him from fine silk, but Gulliver finds them very cumbersome. The queen grows quite accustomed to his company, finding him very entertaining at dinner, especially when he cuts and eats his meat.

He finds her way of eating repulsive, since her size allows her to swallow huge amounts of food in a single gulp.

The king converses with Gulliver on issues of politics, and laughs at his descriptions of the goings-on in Europe. He finds it amusing that people of such small stature should think themselves so important, and Gulliver is at first offended. He then comes to realize that he too has begun to think of his world as ridiculous.

The queen's dwarf is not happy with Gulliver, since he is used to being the smallest person in the palace and a source of diversion for the royal court. He drops Gulliver into a bowl of cream, but Gulliver is able to swim to safety and the dwarf is punished. At another point, the dwarf sticks Gulliver into a marrowbone, where he is forced to remain until someone pulls him out.

Chapter 4

Gulliver describes the geography of Brobdingnag, noting first that since the land stretches out about 6,000 miles there must be a severe error in European maps. The kingdom is bounded on one side by mountains and on the other three sides by the sea. The water is so rough that there is no trade with other nations. The rivers are well stocked with giant fish, but the fish in the sea are of the same size as those in the rest of the world—and therefore not worth catching.

Gulliver is carried around the city in a special traveling-box, and people always crowd around to see him. He asks to see the largest temple in the country and is not overwhelmed by its size, since at a height of 3,000 feet it is proportionally smaller than the largest steeple in England.

Chapter 5

Gulliver is happy in Brobdingnag except for the many mishaps that befall him because of his diminutive size. In one unpleasant incident, the dwarf, angry at Gulliver for teasing him, shakes an apple tree over his head. One of the apples strikes Gulliver in the back and knocks him over. Another time, he is left outside during a hailstorm and is so bruised and battered that he cannot leave the house for ten days.

Gulliver and his nursemaid are often invited to the apartments of the ladies of the court, and there he is treated as a plaything of little significance. They enjoy stripping his clothes and placing him in their bosoms, and he is appalled by their strong smell, noting that a Lilliputian told him that he smelled quite repulsive to them. The women also strip their own clothes in front of him, and he finds their skin extremely ugly and uneven.

The queen orders a special boat to be built for Gulliver. The boat is placed in a cistern, and Gulliver rows in it for his own enjoyment and for the amusement of the queen and her court.

Yet another danger arises in the form of a monkey, which takes Gulliver up a ladder, holding him like a baby and force-feeding him. He is rescued from the monkey, and Glumdalclitch pries the food from his mouth with a needle, after which Gulliver vomits. He is so weak and bruised that he stays in bed for two weeks. The monkey is killed and orders are sent out that no other monkeys be kept in the palace.

Chapter 6

He said, he knew no Reason, why those who entertain Opinions prejudicial to the Publick, should be obliged to change, or should not be obliged to conceal them.

Gulliver makes himself a comb from the stumps of hair left after the king has been shaved. He also collects hairs from the king and uses them to weave the backs of two small chairs, which he gives to the queen as curiosities. Gulliver is brought to a musical performance, but it is so loud that he can hardly make it out. Gulliver decides to play the spinet for the royal family, but must contrive a novel way to do it, since the instrument is so big. He uses large sticks and runs over the keyboard with them, but he can still strike only sixteen keys.

Thinking that the king has unjustly come to regard England as insignificant and laughable, Gulliver tries to tell him more about England, describing the government and culture there. The king asks many questions and is particularly struck by the violence of the history Gulliver describes. He then takes Gulliver into his hand and, explaining that he finds the world that Gulliver describes to be ridiculous, contemptuous, and strange, tells him that he concludes that most Englishmen sound like "odious Vermin."

I cannot but conclude the Bulk of your Natives, to be the most pernicious Race of little odious Vermin that Nature ever suffered to crawl upon the Surface of the Earth.

Chapter 7

Gulliver is disturbed by the king's evaluation of England. He tries to tell him about gunpowder, describing it as a great invention and offering it to the king as a gesture of friendship. The king is appalled by the proposal, and Gulliver is taken aback, thinking that the king has refused a great opportunity. He thinks that the king is unnecessarily scrupulous and narrow-minded for not being more open to the inventions of Gulliver's world.

Gulliver finds the people of Brobdingnag in general to be ignorant and poorly educated. Their laws are not allowed to exceed in words the number of letters in their alphabet, and no arguments may be written about them. They know the art of printing but do not have many books, and their writing is simple and straightforward. One text describes the insignificance and weakness of Brobdingnagians and even argues that at one point they must have been much larger.

Chapter 8

Gulliver wants to recover his freedom. The king orders any small ship to be brought to the city, hoping that they might find a woman with whom Gulliver can propagate. Gulliver fears that any offspring thus produced would be kept in cages or given to the nobility as pets. He has been in Brobdingnag for two years and wants to be among his own kind again.

Gulliver is taken to the south coast, and both Glumdalclitch and Gulliver fall ill. Gulliver says that he wants fresh air, and a page carries him out to the shore in his traveling-box. He asks to be left to sleep in his hammock, and the boy wanders off. An eagle grabs hold of Gulliver's box and flies off with him, and then suddenly Gulliver feels himself falling and lands in the water. He worries that he will drown or starve to death, but then feels the box being pulled. He hears a voice telling him that his box is tied to a ship and that a carpenter will come to drill a hole in the top. Gulliver says that they can simply use a finger to pry it open, and he hears laughter. He realizes that he is speaking to people of his own height and climbs a ladder out of his box and onto their ship.

Gulliver begins to recover on the ship, and he tries to tell the sailors the story of his recent journey. He shows them things he saved from Brobdingnag, like his comb and a tooth pulled from a footman. He has trouble adjusting to the sailors' small size, and he finds himself shouting all the time. When he reaches home, it takes him some time to grow accustomed to his old life, and his wife asks him to never go to sea again.

Analysis of Part 1

Gulliver's narrative begins much like other travel records of his time. The description of his youth and education provides background knowledge, establishes Gulliver's position in English society, and causes the novel to resemble true-life accounts of travels at sea published during Swift's lifetime. Swift imitates the style of a standard travelogue throughout the novel to heighten the satire. Here he creates a set of expectations in our minds, namely a short-lived belief in the truth of Gulliver's observations. Later in the novel, Swift uses the style of the travelogue to exaggerate the absurdity of the people and places with which Gulliver comes into contact. A fantastical style—one that made no attempt to seem truthful, accurate, or traditional—would have weakened the satire by making it irrelevant, but the factual, reportorial style of *Gulliver's Travels* does the opposite.

Gulliver is surprised to discover the Lilliputians but is not particularly shocked. This encounter is only the first of many in the novel in which we are asked to accept Gulliver's extraordinary experiences as merely unusual. Seeing the world through Gulliver's eyes, we also adopt, for a moment, Gulliver's view of the world. But at the same time, we can step back and recognize that the Lilliputians are nothing but a figment of Swift's imagination. The distance between these two stances—the gullible Gulliver and the skeptical reader—is where the narrative's multiple levels of meaning are created: on one level, we have a true-life story of adventure; on another, a purely fictional fairy tale; and on a third level, transcending the first two and closest to Swift's original intention, a satirical critique of European pretensions to rationality and goodwill.

Swift wrote *Gulliver's Travels* at a time when Europe was the world's dominant power, and when England, despite its small size, was rising in power on the basis of its formidable fleet. England's growing military and economic power brought it into contact with a wide variety of new animals, plants, places, and things, but the most significant change wrought by European expansion was the encounter with previously unknown people—like the inhabitants of the Americas—with radically different modes of existence. The miniature stature of the Lilliputians can be interpreted as a physical incarnation of exactly these kinds of cultural differences.

The choice of physical size as the way of manifesting cultural differences has a number of important consequences. The main consequence is the radical difference in power between Gulliver and the Lilliputian nation. His physical size and strength put Gulliver in a unique position within Lilliputian society and give him obligations and capabilities far beyond those of the people who keep him prisoner. Despite Gulliver's fear of the Lilliputians' arrows, there is an element of condescension in his willingness to be held prisoner by them. The power differential may represent

England's position with respect to the people it was in the process of colonizing. It may also be a way for Swift to reveal the importance of might in a society supposedly guided by right. Finally, it may be a way of destabilizing humanity's position at the center of the universe by demonstrating that size, power, and significance are all relative. Although the Lilliputians are almost pitifully small in Gulliver's eyes, they are unwilling to see themselves that way; rather, they think of themselves as normal and of Gulliver as a freakish giant. That Gulliver may himself be the Lilliputian to some other nation's Englishman—a notion elaborated fully in Part 2—is already implied in the first chapter.

Analysis: Part 1: Chapters 2 & 3

In these chapters, Gulliver learns more about Lilliputian culture, and the great difference in size between him and the Lilliputians is emphasized by a number of examples, many of which are explicit satires of British government. For instance, Lilliputian government officials are chosen by their skill at rope-dancing, which the Lilliputians see as relevant but which Gulliver recognizes as arbitrary and ridiculous. The would-be officials are almost literally forced to jump through hoops in order to qualify for their positions.

Clearly, Swift intends for us to understand this episode as a satire of England's system of political appointments and to infer that England's system is similarly arbitrary. Gulliver, however, never suggests that *he* finds the Lilliputians ridiculous. Throughout the entire novel, Gulliver tends to be very sympathetic in his descriptions of the cultures he visits, never criticizing them or finding anything funny, no matter how ludicrous certain customs seem to us. Nor does Gulliver point out the similarities between the ridiculous practices he observes in his travels and the ridiculous customs of Europe. Instead, Swift leaves us to infer all of the satire based on the difference between how things appear to us and how they appear to Gulliver.

The difference in size between Gulliver and the Lilliputians helps to emphasize the importance of physical power, a theme that recurs throughout the novel. Over time, Gulliver begins to earn the Lilliputians' trust, but it is clearly unnecessary: for all their threats, Gulliver could crush the Lilliputians by simply walking carelessly. The humor comes from the Lilliputians' view of the situation: despite the evidence before their eyes, they never realize their own insignificance. They keep Gulliver tied up, believing that they can control him, while in truth he could destroy them effortlessly. In this way, Swift satirizes humanity's pretensions to power and significance.

In these chapters, Swift plays with language in a way that again pokes fun at humanity's belief in its own importance. When the Lilliputians draw up an inventory of Gulliver's possessions, the whole endeavor is treated as if it were a serious matter of state. The contrast between the tone of the inventory, which is given in the Lilliputians' own words, and the utter triviality of the possessions that are being inventoried, serves as a mockery of people who take themselves too seriously. Similarly, the articles that Gulliver is forced to sign in order to gain his freedom are couched in formal, self-important language. But the document is nothing but a meaningless and self-contradictory piece of paper: each article emphasizes the fact that Gulliver is so powerful that, if he so desires, he could violate all of the articles without much concern for his own safety.

Despite the fact that the history of the conflict between Lilliput and Blefuscu is blatantly ridiculous, Gulliver reports it with complete seriousness. The more serious the tone, the more laughable this conflict appears. But Swift expects us to understand immediately that the entire history Gulliver relates parallels European history exactly, down to the smallest details. The High-Heels and the Low-Heels correspond to the Whigs and Tories of English politics. Lilliput and Blefuscu represent England and France. The violent conflict between Big-Endians and Little-Endians represents the Protestant Reformation and the centuries of warfare between Catholics and Protestants.

By recasting European history as a series of brutal wars over meaningless and arbitrary disagreements, Swift implies that the differences between Protestants and Catholics, between Whigs and Tories, and between France and England are as silly and meaningless as how a person chooses to crack an egg. Once we make this connection, though, we face the question of *why* Swift thinks that these conflicts are trivial and irrelevant. After all, religion, politics, and national identity would have been considered the most important issues in Swift's time, and we continue to think of these things as important today.

The answer to this question is less obvious, and the text does not give us a simple explanation. The debate between the Big-Endians and Little-Endians does provide some clues, however. The egg controversy is ridiculous because there cannot be any right or wrong way to crack an egg, so it is unreasonable to legislate how people must do it. Similarly, we may conclude that there is no right or wrong way to worship God—at least, there is no way to prove that one way is right and another way is wrong. Moreover, the Big-Endians and Little-Endians both share the same religious text, but they disagree on how to interpret a passage that can clearly be interpreted two ways. Similarly, Swift is suggesting that the Christian Bible can be interpreted in more than one way, and that it is ridiculous for people to fight over how to interpret it when no one can really be certain that one interpretation is right and others are wrong.

The text contains a number of allusions to events in Swift's life and to the politics of Europe. For instance, it has been suggested that the empress represents Queen Anne of England, Gulliver's urination on her quarters represents Swift's work *A Tale of a Tub,* and the empress's disgust at Gulliver's urination is analogous to Queen Anne's criticism of Swift's work and her attempts to limit his prospects in the Church of England. Within the story, Gulliver's urination on the palace is not merely an offense to the Lilliputians' sense of decency, it is also a suggestion of their insignificance, to which they respond indignantly. Although Gulliver's urination is intended to prevent a disaster, it is also an assertion of his ability to control the Lilliputians—even by the most profane of actions. The episode illustrates again the importance of physical power, which can turn a normally insignificant and vulgar action into a lifesaving act.

Gulliver's refusal to obey the emperor's orders to destroy the fleet of Blefuscu is a sign that he feels some responsibility toward all beings. However small, the inhabitants of Blefuscu still have rights, one of which is freedom from tyranny. Granted almost godlike power by his unusual size, Gulliver finds himself in a position to change the Lilliputians' society forever.

Throughout much of Part 1, Swift satirizes European practices by implicitly comparing them to outrageous Lilliputian customs. In Chapter 4, however, Gulliver describes a number of unusual Lilliputian customs that he presents as reasonable and sensible. This chapter, which describes improvements that could be made in European society, is less satirical and ironic than the previous chapters. We may infer that Swift approves of many of these institutions. Clearly, there is a good case to be made for treating fraud as a more serious crime than theft and for making false testimony a capital crime. The very fabric of society depends upon trust, so dishonesty may be even more damaging than theft and violence.

In general, the customs of Lilliput that Swift presents as good are those that contribute to the good of the community or the nation as opposed to those that promote individual rights or freedoms. Ingratitude is punishable by death, for instance, because anybody who would treat a benefactor badly must be an enemy to all mankind. Children are raised by the community rather than by their parents because parents are thinking only of their own appetites when they conceive children. Children are raised in public nurseries, but parents are financially penalized if they burden society by bringing children for whom they cannot pay into the world.

Gulliver's analysis of Lilliputian customs also serves to illuminate the arbitrary nature of such practices, as well as the fact that societies tend to assume, nonetheless, that certain customs are simply natural. The Lilliputians do not question their cultural norms because they have no reason to believe that there is any other way to conduct affairs. When alternatives are discussed, as in the case of the egg-breaking controversy, the discussion ends in violent conflict.

The articles of accusation against Gulliver, like the inventory of his possessions and the articles of his freedom in the previous chapters, are written in formal language that serves only to emphasize their absurdity. Swift makes a mockery of formal language by showing how it can be used to mask simple fears and desires, such as the Lilliputians' desire to eliminate the threat that Gulliver poses. The help that Gulliver gets from Reldresal is an illustration of a persistent motif in *Gulliver's Travels:* the good person surrounded by a corrupt society.

Part 2

In Gulliver's adventure in Brobdingnag, many of the same issues that are brought up in the Lilliputian adventure are now brought up again, but this time Gulliver is in the exact opposite situation. Many of the jokes from Gulliver's adventure in Lilliput are played in reverse: instead of worrying about trampling on the Lilliputians, Gulliver is now at risk of being trampled upon; instead of being feared and admired for his gargantuan size, he is treated as a miniscule and insignificant curiosity; instead of displaying miniature livestock in England to make money, he is put on display for money by the farmer. As a whole, the second voyage serves to emphasize the importance of size and the relativity of human culture.

Gulliver's initial experiences with the Brobdingnagians are not positive. First they almost trample him, then the farmer virtually enslaves him, forcing him to perform tricks for paying spectators. This enslavement emphasizes the fundamental humanity of the Brobdingnagians—just like Europeans, they are happy to make a quick buck when the opportunity arises—and also makes concrete Gulliver's lowly status. Whereas in Lilliput, his size gives him almost godlike powers, allowing him to become a hero and a *Nardac* to the Lilliputian people, in Brobdingnag his different size has exactly the opposite effect. Even his small acts of heroism, like his battle against the rats, are seen by the Brobdingnagians as, at best, "tricks."

Swift continues to play with language in a way that both emphasizes his main satirical points about politics, ethics, and culture and makes fun of language itself. In the first few pages of this section, while Gulliver is still at sea, he describes in complicated naval jargon the various attempts his ship makes to deal with an oncoming storm. The rush of words is nearly incomprehensible, and it is meant to be so—the point is to satirize the jargon used by writers of travel books and sailing accounts, which in Swift's view was often overblown and ridiculous. By taking the tendency to use jargon to an extreme and putting it in the mouth of the gullible and straightforward Gulliver, Swift makes a mockery of those who would try to demonstrate their expertise through convoluted language. Attacks like this one, which are repeated elsewhere in the novel, are part of Swift's larger mission: to criticize the validity of various kinds of expert knowledge that are more showy than helpful, whether legal, naval, or, as in the third voyage, scientific.

Analysis: Part 2: Chapters 3–5

Gulliver's continued adventures in Brobdingnag serve to illustrate the importance of physical size. Reduced to a twelfth of the size of the people who surround him, Gulliver finds all of his pride and importance withering away. Without physical power to back him up—whether the normal level that he experiences in England or the extraordinary level of his time in Lilliput—it is impossible for Gulliver to maintain the illusion of his own importance.

These chapters contain, in addition to the continuing satire of European culture, some of the most entertaining portions of the novel. Gulliver is treated like a doll, tormented by the court dwarf, and adopted, briefly, by a monkey. For the most part, these scenes serve to hammer home the image of Gulliver's miniscule size as compared to the Brobdingnagians, but they also achieve several more significant accomplishments. The conflict with the dwarf is a good example of such a point. The dwarf, unable to gain the power that generally accompanies great physical size, has tried to make a place for himself in society by capitalizing instead on the distinctive lack of power that accompanies his tiny size. When Gulliver enters the court, he challenges the dwarf's distinctiveness, and the dwarf responds aggressively. If there is a moral to the episode, it is that the politics of those who attempt to achieve power not through physical strength but through their distinctiveness can be just as immoral as the mainstream.

Another key episode takes place with Gulliver's visit to the ladies of the court. The fantasy of domination and submission—realized when Gulliver becomes the sexual plaything of the ladies—is overshadowed by his outright disgust at their smell and appearance. He knows, theoretically, that if he were their size they would be just as attractive as the well-pampered court ladies of England, but since he is not, their flaws are literally magnified, and they appear to him malodorous, blemished, and crude. Swift's point is that anything, even the smoothest skin or the most appealing political system, has imperfections, and these imperfections are bound to be exposed under close enough scrutiny. In a sense, what looks perfect to us is not actually perfect—it is simply not imperfect enough for our limited senses to notice.

At the time that Swift was writing *Gulliver's Travels,* however, technology that could accentuate these imperfect senses was burgeoning, and Gulliver's microscopic view of flies and flesh may be a reference to the relatively recent discovery of the microscope. The late seventeenth century saw the first publication of books containing magnified images illustrating that various items—fleas, hair, skin—contained details and flaws that had previously been hidden. Gulliver lives this microscopic experience directly. In a magnified world, everything takes on new levels of complexity and imperfection, demonstrating that the truth about objects is heavily influenced by the observer's perspective.

Analysis: Part 2: Chapters 6–8

In the previous section, Gulliver's personal insignificance is illustrated by his reduction to the status of a plaything in the court. In this section, the same lesson is repeated on a larger scale when he describes the culture and politics of Europe to the king of Brobdingnag. Suddenly, all of the life-and-death issues that seemed so important when Gulliver was in Europe are revealed to be the trivial conflicts of miniscule people. They are not only insignificant, but the king also derides them as "odious." In his eyes, the tiny size of the Europeans is matched by their moral weakness. Gulliver's long discussions with the king leave him feeling humiliated.

Nonetheless, Gulliver manages to maintain some sense of the importance of England in the face of the king's criticisms. But his protests seem so transparently groundless that each argument he gives for England's superiority, including his argument that the king is too dull-witted to see the beauty of English culture, serves only to emphasize the futility of his resistance. In the end, the king's assessment of the Europeans as "odious vermin" wins the day. Gulliver's personality plays an important role in pushing this satirical point home. His naïveté, his gullibility, and his ingenuous praise for England all accentuate his similarity to the Lilliputians: convinced of his own significance, he is unable to realize the pettiness and imperfection of the society he represents.

This imperfection is not just one of organization or law. If that were the only problem with English society as Swift saw it, then *Gulliver's Travels* would have been a much more boring and less significant work. The imperfection, rather, is fundamentally one of morals: the British, and by extension humanity in general, are not only bad at getting what they want, they also want bad things. This truth is illustrated in Gulliver's offer of the secret of gunpowder to the king. The king refuses without a second thought, not because the Brobdingnagians have superior technology, but because he is horrified by the potential moral and physical consequences of gunpowder. Most preindustrial societies would treat gunpowder as an achievement of high order. But the king indicates that he feels it would be better to live where violence and destruction are minimized instead of exaggerated. Gulliver's inability to understand the king's position—he sees the refusal as a weakness in the king's understanding—illustrates how the values of a violent society are deeply ingrained in Gulliver. Observing both the king and Gulliver, we are invited to choose between them.

Nevertheless, the Brobdingnagians are not perfect, however much more developed their moral sense may be than Gulliver's. They are, rather, humans who have achieved a gargantuan level of moral achievement. Unlike the petty and miniscule Lilliputians, in whom the human vices of pride and self-righteousness are exaggerated, the Brobdingnagians have constructed a society in which those vices are minimized as much as possible. They still exist—for instance, the farmer exploits Gulliver by showing him off for profit—but they are not, as they are in England, encoded in the structure of government itself. The Brobdingnagians—more moral than the Lilliputians, more practical than the Laputans of the third voyage, and more human than the Houyhnhnms of the fourth voyage—are in some ways the most admirable of the societies Gulliver encounters.

Some important questions and answers:

Question 1: Analyze the theme of satire in "Gulliver's Travels". How does Swift use satire to critique the politics, society, and culture of his time?

Answer: Swift uses satire in "Gulliver's Travels" to critique the politics, society, and culture of his time. He uses the fictional lands of Lilliput, Brobdingnag, Laputa, and Houyhnhnm to comment on the flaws and follies of human society. For example, the tiny people of Lilliput represent the petty squabbles and corruption of European politics, while the giant people of Brobdingnag represent the virtues of simplicity, honesty, and integrity. Through satire, Swift critiques the excesses and vices of his time, including the corruption of politicians, the superficiality of high society, and the absurdity of scientific and philosophical theories.

Question 2: Discuss the character of Lemuel Gulliver. What are his strengths and weaknesses, and how does he change or grow throughout the story?

Answer: Lemuel Gulliver is a complex and nuanced character in "Gulliver's Travels". His strengths include his curiosity, bravery, and adaptability, which enable him to navigate the strange and fantastical worlds he encounters. However, his weaknesses include his naivety, gullibility, and tendency to be swayed by the opinions of others. Throughout the story, Gulliver undergoes significant changes and growth, as he encounters different cultures and societies that challenge his assumptions and broaden his perspectives. He becomes increasingly disillusioned with the flaws and vices of human society, and ultimately returns home a wiser and more cynical man.

Question 3: Analyze the theme of imperialism in "Gulliver's Travels". How does Swift critique the colonial policies and practices of European powers during the 18th century?

Answer: Swift critiques the colonial policies and practices of European powers during the 18th century through the theme of imperialism in "Gulliver's Travels". He uses the fictional lands of Lilliput and Brobdingnag to comment on the exploitation and oppression of colonized peoples by

European powers. For example, the tiny people of Lilliput are exploited by the European colonizers, who use them for their own gain and amusement. Similarly, the giant people of Brobdingnag are portrayed as being more virtuous and civilized than the Europeans, highlighting the hypocrisy and double standards of colonialism. Through satire, Swift critiques the colonial policies and practices of European powers, highlighting their flaws and vices.

Question 4: Discuss the symbolism of the Houyhnhnms in "Gulliver's Travels". What do they represent, and how do they relate to the themes of the story?

Answer: The Houyhnhnms are a symbol of reason, virtue, and civilization in "Gulliver's Travels". They represent a utopian society that is governed by reason and justice, and that values simplicity, honesty, and integrity. The Houyhnhnms are also a critique of the flaws and vices of human society, highlighting the hypocrisy and double standards of human behavior. Through the Houyhnhnms, Swift satirizes the excesses and vices of human society, including the corruption of politicians, the superficiality of high society, and the absurdity of scientific and philosophical theories.

Question 5: Analyze the ending of "Gulliver's Travels". What significance does Gulliver's final return home hold, and how does it relate to the themes of the story?

Answer: The ending of "Gulliver's Travels" is significant because it highlights Gulliver's final disillusionment with human society. After his experiences in the various fantastical lands, Gulliver returns home a wiser and more cynical man. He is disillusioned with the flaws and vices of human society, and he struggles to reconcile his experiences with the reality of his own world. The ending of the story thus relates to the themes of satire, imperialism, and the critique of human society. Through Gulliver's final return home, Swift highlights the need for reform and change in human society, and he critiques the excesses and vices that have led to its corruption and decay.

Question 6: Discuss the theme of identity in "Gulliver's Travels". How does Gulliver's journey affect his sense of self and his understanding of his place in the world?

Answer: The theme of identity is a significant element in "Gulliver's Travels". Gulliver's journey affects his sense of self and his understanding of his place in the world in profound ways. As he travels to different lands and encounters various cultures, Gulliver is forced to confront his own assumptions and biases. He begins to question his own identity and his place in the world, and he ultimately emerges with a more nuanced and complex understanding of himself and his society.

Question 7: Analyze the use of irony in "Gulliver's Travels". How does Swift use irony to critique the politics, society, and culture of his time?

Answer: Swift uses irony extensively in "Gulliver's Travels" to critique the politics, society, and culture of his time. For example, the tiny people of Lilliput are portrayed as being ridiculously proud of their miniature accomplishments, highlighting the absurdity of human vanity. Similarly, the Houyhnhnms are depicted as being more virtuous and civilized than humans, irony that highlights the flaws and vices of human society. Through irony, Swift critiques the excesses and vices of his time, including the corruption of politicians, the superficiality of high society, and the absurdity of scientific and philosophical theories.

Question 8: Discuss the theme of morality in "Gulliver's Travels". How does Swift portray the moral implications of human actions, and what message does he convey about the importance of ethics and morality?

Answer: The theme of morality is a significant element in "Gulliver's Travels". Swift portrays the moral implications of human actions through Gulliver's experiences in the various lands he visits. For example, the Houyhnhnms are depicted as being morally superior to humans, highlighting the importance of ethics and morality. Swift also critiques the moral flaws and vices of human society, including the corruption of politicians, the superficiality of high society, and the absurdity of scientific and philosophical theories. Through the theme of morality, Swift conveys the importance of ethics and morality in human society, and he highlights the need for individuals to take responsibility for their actions.

Question 9: Analyze the character of the Emperor of Lilliput. What does he represent, and how does he relate to the themes of the story?

Answer: The Emperor of Lilliput represents the absurdity and vanity of human power and authority. He is depicted as being ridiculously proud of his miniature accomplishments, highlighting the absurdity of human ambition. The Emperor also represents the corruption and decadence of human society, as he is more concerned with his own power and prestige than with the welfare of his people. Through the character of the Emperor, Swift critiques the excesses and vices of human society, including the corruption of politicians and the superficiality of high society.

Question 10: Discuss the theme of cultural relativism in "Gulliver's Travels". How does Swift portray the diversity of cultures and societies, and what message does he convey about the importance of understanding and respecting different cultures?

Answer: The theme of cultural relativism is a significant element in "Gulliver's Travels". Swift portrays the diversity of cultures and societies through Gulliver's experiences in the various lands he visits. For example, the Houyhnhnms are depicted as being morally superior to humans, highlighting the importance of understanding and respecting different cultures. Swift also critiques the tendency of humans to judge other cultures by their own standards, highlighting the importance of cultural relativism. Through the theme of cultural relativism, Swift conveys the importance of understanding and respecting different cultures, and he highlights the need for individuals to approach other cultures with an open mind and a willingness to learn.

Some short questions and answers:

Q1: Who is the protagonist of "Gulliver's Travels"?
A1: Lemuel Gulliver.
   Q2: What is the name of the first land Gulliver visits?
A2: Lilliput.
   Q3: What is the significance of the Houyhnhnms in the story?
A3: They represent a utopian society that is governed by reason and justice.
   Q4: What is the theme of the story?
A4: Satire, imperialism, and the critique of human society.
   Q5: What is the symbolic significance of Gulliver's journey?
A5: It represents a journey of self-discovery and a critique of human society.
   Q6: Who is the Emperor of Lilliput?
A6: A tiny king who rules over the land of Lilliput.
   Q7: What is the name of the land of the giants?
A7: Brobdingnag.
   Q8: What is the significance of the ending of the story?
A8: It highlights Gulliver's final disillusionment with human society.
   Q9: What is the tone of the story?
A9: Satirical, ironic, and critical.

Q10: What is the message of the story?

A10: A critique of human society and its flaws, and a call for reform and change.

Q11: What is the name of Gulliver's ship?

A11: The Antelope.

Q12: Who rescues Gulliver from the Lilliputians?

A12: The Emperor of Blefuscu.

Q13: What is the name of the wise old Houyhnhnm who befriends Gulliver?

A13: The Master Houyhnhnm.

Q14: What is the significance of the Laputians?

A14: They represent the absurdity and uselessness of abstract knowledge.

Q15: What is the name of the land of the Yahoos?

A15: Houyhnhnmland.

Q16: What is the symbolic significance of Gulliver's size?

A16: It represents the relative nature of human importance and power.

Q17: Who is the target of Swift's satire in the story?

A17: The politicians, scientists, and philosophers of Swift's time.

Q18: What is the tone of the ending of the story?

A18: Melancholic and introspective.

Q19: What is the significance of Gulliver's return home?

A19: It represents his final disillusionment with human society and his desire to escape from it.

Q20: What is the overall message of "Gulliver's Travels"?

A20: A critique of human society and its flaws, and a call for reform and change.

Q21: What is the name of the kingdom that Gulliver visits after Lilliput?

A21: Brobdingnag.

Q22: Who is the king of Brobdingnag?

A22: The King of Brobdingnag.

Q23: What is the significance of the Brobdingnagians' size?

A23: It represents the idea that physical size is not necessarily an indicator of moral or intellectual greatness.

Q24: What is the name of the flying island that Gulliver visits?

A24: Laputa.

Q25: What is the significance of the Laputians' obsession with music and mathematics?

A25: It represents the idea that abstract knowledge and artistic pursuits can be pursued to the point of absurdity.

Q26: Who are the Yahoos?
A26: A group of savage, humanoid creatures that inhabit Houyhnhnmland.

Q27: What is the significance of the Houyhnhnms' treatment of the Yahoos?
A27: It represents the idea that even in a seemingly utopian society, there can be elements of oppression and inequality.

Q28: What is the name of the horse who befriends Gulliver in Houyhnhnmland?
A28: The Master Houyhnhnm.

Q29: What is the significance of Gulliver's decision to leave Houyhnhnmland?
A29: It represents the idea that even in a seemingly perfect society, there can be elements of imperfection and dissatisfaction.

Q30: What is the overall theme of "Gulliver's Travels"?
A30: A satire of human society and its flaws, with a focus on politics, morality, and the nature of humanity.

CHAPTER TWELVE

SHE STOOPS TO CONQUER

She Stoops to Conquer

Oliver Goldsmith

She Stoops to Conquer is a comedy play by Anglo-Irish writer Oliver Goldsmith. First performed in London in 1773, it is Goldsmith's best-known play and a cornerstone of both English literature and theatre classes in the English-speaking world. It is one of the few plays from the 18th century that has retained its popularity and is still regularly performed. Regarded as a classic of the period, the work has been adapted for films on numerous occasions, including in 1910, 1914, and 1923. The play is notable as the origin of the common phrase, "Ask me no questions and I'll tell you no lies."

She Stoops to Conquer is a stage play in the form of a comedy of manners, which ridicules the manners (way of life, social customs, etc.) of a certain segment of society, in this case the upper class. The play is also sometimes termed a drawing-room comedy. The play uses farce (including many mix-ups) and satire to poke fun at the class-consciousness of eighteenth-century Englishmen and to satirize what Goldsmith called the "weeping sentimental comedy so much in fashion at present."

Setting

Most of the action takes place in the Hardcastle mansion in the English countryside, about sixty miles from London. The mansion is an old but comfortable dwelling that resembles an inn. A brief episode takes place at a nearby tavern, The Three Pigeons Alehouse. The time is the eighteenth century.

Characters

Mr. Hardcastle: Middle-aged gentleman who lives in an old mansion in the countryside about sixty miles from London. He prefers the simple rural life and its old-fashioned manners and customs to the trendy and pretentious ways of upper-crust London.

Mrs. Dorothy Hardcastle: Wife of Mr. Hardcastle. Unlike her husband, she yearns to sample life in high society. She also values material possessions and hopes to match her son (by her first husband) with her niece, Constance Neville, in order to keep her niece's inheritance in the family.

Charles Marlow: Promising young man who comes to the country to woo the Hardcastles' pretty daughter, Kate. His only drawback is that he is extremely shy around refined young ladies, although he is completely at ease—and even forward—with women of humble birth and working-class status. He is a pivotal character in the play, used by author Goldsmith to satirize England's preoccupation with, and overemphasis on, class distinctions. However, Marlow's redeeming qualities make him a likeable character, and the audience tends to root for him when he becomes the victim of a practical joke resulting in mix-ups and mistaken identities.

Kate Hardcastle: Pretty daughter of the Hardcastles who is wooed by Charles Marlow. When he mistakes her for a woman of the lower class, she allows him to continue to mistake her identity, thus freeing his captive tongue so she can discover what he really thinks about her.

Tony Lumpkin: Son of Mrs. Hardcastle by her first husband. He is a fat, ale-drinking young man who has little ambition except to play practical jokes and visit the local tavern whenever he has a mind. When Tony comes of age, he will receive 1,500 pounds a year. His mother hopes to marry him to her niece, Constance Neville, who is in line to inherit a casket of jewels from her uncle. Tony and Miss Neville despise each other.

George Hastings: Friend of Marlow who loves Constance Neville.While Marlow is busy with Kate, Hastings is busy with Constance. Hastings hatches a plan to elope with Constance and receives the help of Tony, who wants to erase Constance from his life—and his mother's constant efforts to match him with Constance.

Constance Neville: Comely young lady who loves Hastings but is bedeviled by Mrs. Hardcastle's schemes to match her with Tony. Constance, an orphan, is the niece and ward of Mrs. Hardcastle (who holds Miss Neville's inheritance in her possession until she becomes legally qualified to take possession of it) and the cousin of Kate.

Sir Charles Marlow: Father of young Charles.

Servants in the Hardcastle Household

Maid in the Hardcastle Household

Landlord of the Three Pigeons Alehouse

First Fellow, Second Fellow, Third Fellow, Fourth Fellow: Drinking companions of Tony Lumpkin.

SUMMARY OF "She Stoops to Conquer"

She Stoops to Conquer opens with a prelude in which an on-screen character laments the dismissal of the conventional low Comedy at the consecrated place of nostalgic, "dull" show. He assumes that Dr. Goldsmith can cure this issue through the play going to be shown.

ACT ONE

Act I is stacked with set-up for whatever is left of the play. Mr. and Mrs. Hardcastle live in an old house that takes after a lodging, and they are sitting tight for the arrival of Marlow, offspring of Mr. Hardcastle 's old partner and a possible suitor to his daughter Kate. Kate is close to her father, to such a degree, to the point that she dresses clearly in the evening times (to suit his direct tastes) and capriciously in the mornings for her allies. Then, Mrs. Hardcastle's niece Constance is in the old woman's care, and has her little heritage (including some essential pearls) held until the point when the moment that she is hitched, preferably to Mrs. Hardcastle's spoilt kid hailed from a preceding marriage, Tony Lumpkin. The issue is that neither Tony nor Constance reveres the other, and in fact Constance has a dearest, will's character flying out to the house that night with Marlow. Tony's worry is also that he is a flushed and an admirer of low living, which he shows when the play develops to a bar contiguous. At whatever point Marlow and Hastings (Constance's venerated) get in contact at the bar, lost while in travel to Hardcastle's, Tony plays a feasible joke by telling the two men that there is no space at the bar and that they can find lodging at the old inn not far place (which is clearly Hardcastle's home).

ACT TWO

Act II sees the plot get jumbled. At whatever point Marlow and Hastings arrive, they are inconsiderate and impolite with Hardcastle, whom they accept is a proprietor and not a host (because of Tony's trap). Hardcastle foresees that Marlow will be an obliging youthful individual, and is paralyzed at the direct. Constance finds Hastings, and reveals to him that

Tony almost certainly played a trap. Regardless, they keep reality from Marlow, in light of the way that they figure revealing it will pester him and crush the trip. They will attempt to get her pearls and slip away together. Marlow has an odd tendency to converse with exaggerated aversion to "unpretentious" women, while talking in vivacious and liberal tones to women of low-class. When he has his first assembling with Kate, she is dressed well, and subsequently drives him into a crippling stupor by virtue of his feebleness to address humble women. She is regardless of being pulled in to him, and endeavors and draws out his real character. Tony and Hastings pick together that Tony will take the jewels for Hastings and Constance, with the objective that he can be liberated of his mother's strain to marry Constance, whom he doesn't love.

ACT THREE

Act III opens with Hardcastle and Kate each confused for the side of Marlow they saw. Where Hardcastle is staggered at his impoliteness, Kate is confused to have seen just inconspicuousness. Kate approaches her father for the chance to show to him that Marlow is more than both acknowledge. Tony has stolen the jewels, anyway Constance doesn't know and continues imploring her nearby relatives for them. Tony induces Mrs. Hardcastle to envision they were stolen to discourage Constance, a demand she vivaciously recognizes until the point that she comprehends they have truly been stolen. Meanwhile, Kate is presently wearing her plain dress and is stirred up by Marlow (who never looked her in the face in their earlier assembling) as a barmaid to whom he is pulled in. She fills the part, and they have an excited, fun discourse that terminates with him attempting to get a handle on her, a move Mr. Hardcastle watches. Kate asks for the night to exhibit that he can be both cognizant and eager.

ACT FOUR

Act IV finds the plots moderately going into decay. News has spread that Sir Charles Marlow (Hardcastle's sidekick, and father to energetic Marlow) is on the way, which will reveal Hastings' lifestyle as treasured of Constance and moreover force the subject of whether Kate and Marlow are to marry. Hastings has sent the pearls in a pine box to Marlow for supervision yet Marlow, dumbfounded, has offered them to Mrs. Hardcastle (whom in spite of all that he acknowledges is the proprietor of the lodging). Exactly when Hastings takes in this, he comprehends his expectation to slip away with wealth is done, and picks he ought to induce Constance to take away speedily. Meanwhile, Marlow's discourteousness towards Hardcastle (whom he acknowledges is the proprietor) accomplishes its pinnacle, and Hardcastle demonstrates him out of the house, in the midst of which fight Marlow begins to recognize what is truly happening. He finds Kate, who directly puts on a show to be a poor association with the Hardcastles, which would make her a suitable match also as class anyway, not an OK marriage to the degree of wealth. Marlow is starting to love her, but can't look after her since it is prohibited to his father in light of her nonappearance of wealth, so he surrenders her. In the meantime, a letter from Hastings arrives that Mrs. Hardcastle catches, and she examines that he sits tight for Constance in the garden, arranged to take away. Incensed, she requests that she will bring Constance far away, and makes game plans for that. Marlow, Hastings and Tony go up against each other, and the shock with respect to all the confusion prompts an extraordinary conflict, settled quickly when Tony assures them to deal with the issue for Hastings.

ACT FIVE - FINAL ACT

Act V discovers reality getting to be uncovered, and everyone merry. Sir Charles has arrived, and he and Hastings laugh together and complete the confusion young Marlow was in. Marlow gets in contact to apologize, and in the trade over Kate, claims he barely talked with Kate. Hardcastle points the finger at him for lying, since Hardcastle saw him get a handle on Kate (yet Marlow does not understand that was definitely Kate). Kate arrives after Marlow leaves the room and induces the more settled men; she will reveal the full truth if they watch a gathering between the two from a covered vantage behind a screen. Then, Hastings holds up in the garden, per Tony's rule, and Tony gets in contact to uncover to him that he drove his mother and Constance all completed in circles, so they think they are lost far from home when as a general rule they have been left close-by. Mrs. Hardcastle, upset, arrives and is convinced she ought to keep away from a scoundrel who is moving closer. The "criminal" winds up being Mr. Hardcastle, who panics her in her disorder for quite a while by the day's end finds out what is happening. Hastings and Constance, close-by, pick they won't keep running off yet rather demand to Mr. Hardcastle for generosity. Back at the house, the gathering between Kate (playing the poor association) and Marlow reveals his extremely extraordinary character, and after some exchange, everyone agrees to the match. Hastings and Constance ask for that approval to marry and, since Tony is truly of age and thus jug of his own volition pick not to marry Constance, the assent is permitted. All are playful (beside parsimonious Mrs. Hardcastle), and the "slips of a night" have been corrected.

Epilogues 1 and 2

In Epilogue 1, delivered by the performer playing Kate Hardcastle, <u>Goldsmith</u> summarizes the progress of the plot, emphasizing how Kate "stooped to conquer." In Epilogue 2, delivered by the character of Tony Lumpkin, the speaker boasts of his carefree spirit and independence.

Some important short questions and answers from She Stoops to Conquer by Oliver Goldsmith:

1. **Who is Mr. Hardcastle?**

   Mr. Hardcastle is a country gentleman who prefers old-fashioned values. He dislikes modern fashion and city manners.

2. **Why does Marlow feel shy around Kate?**

   Marlow feels shy because he thinks Kate is a high-born lady. He becomes nervous and awkward in the presence of respectable women.

3. **Why does Kate stoop to conquer?**

   Kate pretends to be a barmaid to win Marlow's love. She "stoops" to his level so he can speak confidently with her.

4. **How does Tony Lumpkin trick Marlow and Hastings?**

   Tony misleads them into thinking Mr. Hardcastle's house is an inn. This creates confusion and humor in the play.

5. **Who is Constance Neville in love with?**

   Constance Neville is in love with Hastings. She does not want to marry Tony Lumpkin.

6. **What is the main theme of the play?**

   The main theme is love and misunderstanding. It also shows the contrast between town and country life.

1. **Who is Mrs. Hardcastle?**

   Mrs. Hardcastle is Mr. Hardcastle's wife. She is fond of fashion and wants her son Tony to marry Constance Neville.

2. **Why does Marlow behave confidently with Kate when she is disguised?**

   Marlow believes Kate is a barmaid. He feels comfortable speaking boldly to women of lower social status.

3. **What problem does Constance face regarding her jewels?**

Constance's jewels are kept by Mrs. Hardcastle. She cannot marry Hastings without getting them back.

4. **Why does Tony refuse to marry Constance?**

Tony knows they are cousins and does not love her. He also wants to enjoy his freedom.

5. **How does Mr. Hardcastle react to Marlow's behavior?**

Mr. Hardcastle feels insulted because Marlow treats his house like an inn. He becomes angry at Marlow's rude manners.

6. **How does the play end?**

Marlow learns the truth about Kate and admits his love. Constance gets her jewels, and both couples are happily united.:

13. **Who is George Hastings?**

George Hastings is Marlow's friend. He is in love with Constance Neville and wants to marry her.

14. **Why does Mrs. Hardcastle take Constance to London?**

She plans to take her to London to keep her away from Hastings. She hopes to force her to marry Tony instead.

15. **What misunderstanding creates the main comedy in the play?**

Marlow and Hastings believe Mr. Hardcastle's house is an inn. This mistake leads to many funny situations.

16. **How does Kate test Marlow's true character?**

Kate observes how Marlow behaves in different situations. She wants to know if he is truly worthy of her love.

17. **Why is Tony Lumpkin important to the plot?**

Tony's trick starts the confusion in the story. His actions help bring about the happy ending.

18. **What lesson does the play teach?**

The play teaches that true love requires honesty and understanding. It also criticizes pride and social class differences.

19. **Why does Mr. Hardcastle prefer country life?**

He believes country life is simple and sincere. He dislikes the artificial manners of the city.

20. **How does Marlow insult Mr. Hardcastle?**

Marlow treats him as an innkeeper instead of a gentleman. He orders him about and complains about the house.

21. **What is Tony's relationship to Constance Neville?**
Tony and Constance are cousins. Mrs. Hardcastle wants them to marry, but they both refuse.

22. **How does Kate reveal her true identity to Marlow?**
She gradually lets him realize she is the same woman he loved as the "barmaid." This shocks and humbles him.

23. **Why is Marlow considered a complex character?**
He is shy and respectful with upper-class women. Yet he is bold and confident with women of lower status.

24. **What role does deception play in the play?**
Deception creates humor and moves the plot forward. It ultimately leads to self-discovery and happy marriages.

25. **What kind of son is Tony Lumpkin?**
Tony is playful and irresponsible. He enjoys practical jokes and dislikes his mother's control.

26. **Why does Mr. Hardcastle want to arrange Kate's marriage with Marlow?**
He believes Marlow is a suitable and respectable match. He wants his daughter to marry into a good family.

27. **How does Hastings try to help Constance?**
Hastings plans to elope with Constance. He also tries to get her jewels from Mrs. Hardcastle.

28. **What mistake does Mrs. Hardcastle make during the journey to London?**
She gets lost and unknowingly returns to her own house. This adds to the comic confusion.

29. **How does Tony prove he is of age?**
Tony reveals that he is already twenty-one years old. This frees Constance from the forced marriage.

30. **Why is the play called "She Stoops to Conquer"?**
The title refers to Kate's decision to lower her social position temporarily. By "stooping," she wins Marlow's love.

Important quotation and explanation

1."She stoops to conquer, and by that means wins the heart of the man she loves."

This quotation embodies the central theme and the title of the play *She Stoops to Conquer* by Oliver Goldsmith.Kate Hardcastle, the heroine, consciously decides to "stoop" — that is, to lower herself in social status — by pretending to be a barmaid in order to engage Marlow, a young man who is extremely shy and awkward around women of high social standing. Marlow's dual nature is crucial here: while he is tongue-tied and reserved in front of upper-class ladies, he is bold and confident with women of lower status. Goldsmith uses this situation to expose the absurdities of social pretensions and the rigidity of class-conscious behavior in 18th-century English society. By pretending to be socially inferior, Kate allows Marlow to express himself freely, revealing his true personality and virtues. This action not only demonstrates her intelligence and resourcefulness but also shows her emotional intelligence: she understands that genuine love cannot flourish under the constraints of formality, pride, or societal expectations. The phrase "stoops to conquer" also highlights a subtle inversion of power dynamics: though Kate pretends to lower herself, she ultimately gains control over the situation, shaping Marlow's perceptions and securing his affection. Goldsmith uses comedy and irony to deliver this message, making Kate both a clever strategist and a moral exemplar. Beyond the romantic plot, the quotation serves as a commentary on human behavior: often, humility, understanding, and empathy are more effective than pride or coercion in influencing others. In essence, the line encapsulates the interplay of social hierarchy, love, and personal ingenuity, which are central to the play's enduring appeal. Kate's actions remind the audience that intelligence and virtue can operate within, and sometimes transcend, societal structures, and that love is most sincere when it emerges from understanding rather than superficial etiquette.

2. "The greatest pleasure in life is doing what people say you cannot do."

This line has been extracted from Oliver Goldsmith's famous play *She Stoops to Conquer.*

This line reflects Tony Lumpkin's mischievous personality and the play's emphasis on playful rebellion against social expectations. Tony is the archetypal comic character, enjoying pranks, freedom, and the subversion of authority, particularly his mother's attempts to control him. The quotation underscores a theme that runs throughout *She Stoops to Conquer*: the tension between societal norms and individual desire. Tony's enjoyment of defying expectations provides comic relief, but it also subtly critiques rigid social hierarchies and the pressure to conform. By delighting in challenges and restrictions, Tony embodies the human desire for autonomy and personal agency. Goldsmith uses Tony's behavior as a mirror to other characters' pretensions. While Tony is openly rebellious, other characters, like Marlow or Mrs. Hardcastle, are constrained by social anxiety or obsession with appearances. This contrast emphasizes the value of authenticity and natural behavior, a key moral of the play. Furthermore, Tony's philosophy extends to broader life lessons: courage, wit, and resilience often emerge when one dares to act independently, even in the face of societal disapproval. This idea resonates beyond the comedic surface, suggesting that breaking conventions can lead to self-discovery and genuine relationships. By highlighting Tony's perspective, Goldsmith champions individuality, cleverness, and the humor inherent in life's challenges, making this quotation both entertaining and insightful.

3.*"I never saw a man who had less of the gentleman in him than Mr. Marlow."*

This line has been extracted from Oliver Goldsmith's famous play She Stoops to Conquer.

This quotation captures Kate Hardcastle's early assessment of Marlow, highlighting the play's use of first impressions and social perception. At first glance, Marlow appears shy, awkward, and ill-suited for polite society, especially in the formal presence of women of high status. Kate's observation reflects both her sharp wit and the theme of appearances versus reality. Marlow's seemingly timid demeanor is actually context-dependent: while he falters in refined company, he is confident and flirtatious with women he believes to be of lower social standing. Goldsmith uses this contrast to critique the artificial constraints of social etiquette, illustrating how social anxiety can mask true character. The line also underscores the comedic tension in the play, as the audience is aware of the impending confusion—Marlow will later behave boldly toward Kate when she "stoops" to appear as a barmaid, directly contradicting her judgment. Beyond comedy, the quotation reflects Goldsmith's deeper commentary on human behavior: rigid class expectations and societal pressure often distort interactions and lead to misunderstandings. Kate's perception, though initially critical, evolves as she interacts with Marlow in disguise, revealing her insight, patience, and emotional intelligence. This line also introduces a recurring motif: the necessity of probing beneath superficial impressions to understand people's true qualities. It serves as a caution against judging solely by manners or appearance, advocating instead for observation, empathy, and subtlety. By framing Marlow as an apparent "failure" in social grace, Goldsmith cleverly sets up the comic situations that drive the plot, while simultaneously exploring themes of identity, social performance, and the tension between natural behavior and societal expectation.

4.*"I am determined that nobody shall ever call me a fool again."*

:This line has been extracted from Oliver Goldsmith's famous play *She Stoops to Conquer.*This line is spoken by Tony Lumpkin and epitomizes his defiance and comic cunning. Tony is portrayed as a trickster figure throughout the play: he enjoys creating confusion and resisting authority, particularly that of his mother. Here, the quotation reflects his personal pride and desire for autonomy. Tony's declaration also serves as a humorous acknowledgment of human vanity—the need to protect one's reputation while engaging in mischievous behavior. More importantly, it introduces the motif of self-assertion, which runs throughout *She Stoops to Conquer.* Tony's practical jokes, such as misleading Marlow and Hastings into thinking Mr. Hardcastle's house is an inn, illustrate that rebellion against social expectation can be a tool for empowerment and self-expression. Goldsmith uses Tony's line to comment on societal pretensions: while upper-class characters worry about etiquette, wealth, and appearances, Tony, though of the same class, disregards these constraints and acts according to his own logic. The humor derived from his antics is underpinned by insight: independence and cleverness often triumph over rigid adherence to rules. This quotation also highlights Tony's pivotal role in the plot. His mischief creates situations that reveal the true nature of other characters—Marlow's dual personality, Kate's intelligence, and Constance's resilience. In essence, the line is both comic and thematic, illustrating Goldsmith's broader point that life is enriched by wit, courage, and the ability to challenge social norms without malice. It encourages readers to value ingenuity and self-determination, demonstrating how humor can be combined with social critique in drama.

5.*"I never had any real opinion of myself till I knew I was loved."*

This line has been extracted from Oliver Goldsmith's famous play *She Stoops to Conquer.*

This quotation speaks to the emotional core of *She Stoops to Conquer.* Kate Hardcastle's realization highlights the transformative power of love and the importance of mutual understanding in relationships. Throughout the play, Kate demonstrates intelligence, strategy, and patience as she navigates social expectations and Marlow's shyness. Her "stooping" to appear as a barmaid is not a humiliation but a calculated act of empathy: by meeting Marlow on his level, she allows him to reveal his true character. This line underscores the theme that self-awareness and confidence often emerge in the context of genuine human connection. Love, in this sense, acts as a mirror, reflecting hidden strengths and virtues. Goldsmith also uses the quotation to comment on gender and societal norms. Women of Kate's class were expected to conform to rigid standards of decorum and submission. By taking control of the situation, Kate asserts both her agency and her emotional intelligence. The line suggests that authentic recognition—being seen and accepted for who one truly is—can unlock personal growth and self-respect. Additionally, it reinforces the play's moral lesson: superficial impressions, social pretenses, and rigid etiquette are secondary to honesty, understanding, and emotional connection. Kate's self-awareness, catalyzed by love, contrasts with characters like Marlow and Mrs. Hardcastle, who are initially trapped by fear, shyness, or obsession with appearances. This quotation elegantly combines romantic sentiment with Goldsmith's social commentary, showing that humor, wit, and strategic thinking can coexist with emotional depth. It highlights the human need for affirmation, connection, and the courage to embrace vulnerability—a theme that continues to resonate with modern audiences.

6.*"I am never so happy as when I am in the company of a woman I can talk freely with."*

This line has been extracted from Oliver Goldsmith's famous play *She Stoops to Conquer.*

This quotation reveals Marlow's central conflict: his extreme shyness and social anxiety when dealing with upper-class women. Marlow is polite, respectful, and seemingly timid around women of his own class, especially Kate Hardcastle, whom he admires. However, in situations where he believes the woman to be of lower status, he becomes confident, assertive, and even flirtatious. Goldsmith uses this duality to explore themes of perception, social hierarchy, and the constraints of etiquette. Marlow's remark reflects his desire for genuine human connection unburdened by the formalities and expectations of polite society. It also provides a comic setup for the play's central plot device: Kate's decision to "stoop" to a lower social identity in order to interact with him on a level where he feels comfortable. Beyond comedy, this line is psychologically revealing, showing that Marlow's awkwardness is situational rather than inherent. It critiques social conventions that prioritize appearances over substance, suggesting that true behavior emerges only when people feel safe and understood. Furthermore, Marlow's statement underscores Goldsmith's interest in authenticity and naturalness, qualities that are rewarded in the play's resolution. By creating situations where characters are tested under mistaken identities or altered circumstances, Goldsmith exposes the absurdity of rigid social structures. Ultimately, the quotation illuminates the play's deeper moral lesson: love, respect, and understanding thrive when people engage sincerely and without pretense. Marlow's preference for honest interaction over performative politeness positions him as both a figure of comedy and of social critique. The line also prepares the audience for the play's climactic revelation: that Marlow's true character can only be appreciated when barriers of fear, expectation, and class are temporarily removed. Through humor, irony, and insight, this quotation demonstrates Goldsmith's skill in blending entertainment with commentary on human behavior and societal norms.

7. "I have been long a prisoner in the house of an old fool."

This line has been extracted from Oliver Goldsmith's famous play *She Stoops to Conquer.*

This line is spoken by Constance Neville and highlights her sense of entrapment, both literally and metaphorically. Constance has been confined in Mrs. Hardcastle's house due to the threat of being forced into a marriage with Tony Lumpkin. The quotation reflects the constraints placed on women in 18th-century society, where their personal desires were often subordinated to family control and social expectations. By calling Mr. Hardcastle "an old fool" (though she refers in part to the family authority structure), Constance emphasizes her frustration with patriarchal authority and the absurdity of rigid social rules. Goldsmith uses Constance's predicament to contrast with Kate's more active agency. While Kate "stoops to conquer" by taking strategic action, Constance must navigate her oppression with patience, wit, and occasional reliance on allies like Hastings. The line also foreshadows her cleverness and determination: she will ultimately secure her freedom and marry Hastings, illustrating that intellect, courage, and persistence can overcome social obstacles. Additionally, the quotation resonates with the play's broader themes of misunderstanding and misjudgment. Constance is perceived by some characters, particularly Mrs. Hardcastle, as weak or incapable, yet her intelligence and resolve are revealed through her strategies to recover her jewels and protect her love. Goldsmith combines humor and social critique here, using Constance's words to expose the absurdity of rigid social hierarchies and the oppression of women, while also creating dramatic tension. The line balances comic exaggeration with genuine empathy, encouraging audiences to recognize the unfair limitations imposed on women while appreciating Constance's resilience. In essence, it demonstrates how wit and courage allow characters to navigate societal constraints and achieve justice and happiness.

8.*"I love a little management; it is the spice of life."*

This line has been extracted from Oliver Goldsmith's famous play *She Stoops to Conquer*.

This line is spoken by Mrs. Hardcastle and reveals her obsession with control, social status, and appearances. She enjoys manipulating situations, particularly regarding the marriages of her son Tony and her niece Constance. Goldsmith portrays Mrs. Hardcastle as a comic figure whose "management" often backfires, creating confusion and humor. Her delight in control underscores a major theme of the play: the tension between social ambition and human folly. Mrs. Hardcastle represents the older generation's rigid adherence to societal norms, believing wealth, propriety, and marriage alliances can be dictated by authority and strategy. However, the play repeatedly shows that her schemes are undermined by natural behavior, wit, and mischief, particularly through Tony's pranks and Kate's intelligence. The quotation also emphasizes the contrast between appearance and reality: Mrs. Hardcastle believes she can orchestrate events perfectly, but she underestimates the initiative and cunning of others. Goldsmith uses her character to critique the artificiality of social manipulation, showing that life is unpredictable and that true understanding of people cannot be forced. Humor arises from her self-importance and the irony of her plans being foiled, making her a source of both comic relief and social commentary. Beyond comedy, the line suggests a universal human tendency: the desire to control circumstances and others is natural, yet it must be tempered with humility and insight. Mrs. Hardcastle's "management" contrasts sharply with Kate's strategic action, which is guided by intelligence, empathy, and moral purpose rather than ego or social pride. Ultimately, this quotation captures Goldsmith's skill in blending satire with characterization: Mrs. Hardcastle embodies social ambition and human vanity, while the plot rewards cleverness, honesty, and kindness over rigid control. Her line serves as both a humorous observation and a subtle warning about the limitations of manipulation and the value of understanding human nature.

9.*"I have found that I am always happiest when I can be myself."*

This line has been extracted from Oliver Goldsmith's famous play *She Stoops to Conquer.*

This quotation reflects Marlow's transformation and is central to the play's moral and comedic resolution. Throughout *She Stoops to Conquer*, Marlow struggles with a dual personality: he is shy and awkward around upper-class women, yet confident and assertive with women of lower social status. This behavior highlights the tension between natural self-expression and societal expectations of etiquette and class. When Kate Hardcastle pretends to be a barmaid, she creates a safe environment in which Marlow can act naturally. In doing so, she allows him to reveal his genuine character—bold, witty, and capable of affection—without the constraints of social anxiety. This quotation signifies Marlow's self-realization: true happiness and fulfillment come from authenticity, honesty, and being unafraid to act according to one's nature. Goldsmith emphasizes this point with humor and irony, showing that societal pressures often obscure true behavior and lead to misunderstanding. The line also illustrates the broader theme of the play: love, understanding, and human connection are most successful when built on truth rather than pretense. By learning to "be himself," Marlow achieves personal growth and emotional maturity, which enables him to engage sincerely with Kate and accept her as an equal partner in intellect and character. Furthermore, this realization critiques the rigid social hierarchy of 18th-century England, showing that confidence and virtue are not inherently tied to class or external formality. The audience is encouraged to recognize the comedic and moral value of authenticity, as Marlow's journey demonstrates that self-awareness and courage in social interaction are essential to meaningful relationships. Ultimately, the quotation encapsulates the play's blend of comedy, romance, and social commentary: it celebrates human intelligence, emotional honesty, and the ability to navigate society with wit and sincerity, offering a timeless message about personal freedom, love, and self-expression.

10.*"Let the past mistakes be forgotten; love and reason shall guide us henceforth."*

This line has been extracted from Oliver Goldsmith's famous play *She Stoops to Conquer.*

This quotation comes near the play's conclusion and signifies reconciliation, closure, and the triumph of reason and love over confusion and folly. Much of *She Stoops to Conquer* revolves around misunderstandings, mistaken identities, and social misperceptions. Characters such as Marlow, Kate, Constance, Tony, and Mrs. Hardcastle all experience moments of error or misjudgment, often caused by pride, social anxiety, or clever deception. This line signals a moral resolution: past errors are forgiven, and rational thought combined with genuine affection will shape future actions. Goldsmith uses this moment to underscore the play's themes of harmony, emotional intelligence, and social balance. Humor and comic chaos are replaced by clarity, as the characters now understand one another's true intentions and feelings. Marlow and Kate's union reflects the rewards of strategic empathy, honesty, and personal courage, while Constance and Hastings' successful pairing emphasizes persistence and moral integrity. Additionally, this quotation conveys Goldsmith's social commentary: societal constraints, rigid expectations, and misjudgments can be corrected when love, understanding, and reason prevail. It suggests that while human folly is inevitable, it can be overcome through communication, patience, and ethical insight. The line also reinforces the comic structure of the play: the chaos caused by mistaken identity and deception is ultimately resolved, creating a satisfying emotional and narrative closure for the audience. It combines moral instruction with comedic relief, leaving readers with the impression that life, though often messy and unpredictable, rewards honesty, cleverness, and virtuous intentions. Goldsmith's final sentiment encourages forgiveness, reflection, and the prioritization of love and reason over social pride or misunderstandings, making it a fitting conclusion to this celebrated comedy.

11.*"The world is a stage, and one must play one's part with wisdom and discretion."*

This line has been extracted from Oliver Goldsmith's famous play *She Stoops to Conquer*.

This quotation captures a central theme of *She Stoops to Conquer*: the interplay between appearance and reality. Goldsmith repeatedly contrasts characters' public behavior with their private selves. Marlow, Kate, and Tony all navigate social expectations differently: Marlow conceals his boldness under shyness, Kate adopts a disguise to reveal Marlow's true nature, and Tony uses mischief to manipulate perception. The line reflects the idea that life requires careful observation and strategic action; one must understand social rules without being enslaved by them. Goldsmith uses humor and irony to critique rigid adherence to status, etiquette, and superficial judgment. Characters who are overly concerned with appearances, such as Mrs. Hardcastle, are often outwitted, while those who act with intelligence, empathy, and emotional insight, like Kate, achieve success. The quotation also highlights the performative nature of social interaction in the 18th century: individuals must balance sincerity with tact, navigating societal structures without losing authenticity. Beyond comedy, it conveys a moral lesson: wisdom comes from understanding both human nature and the structures that shape behavior, and discretion allows one to act effectively in complex social situations. Kate's strategic disguise and Marlow's eventual self-awareness exemplify this philosophy. Goldsmith's use of theatrical metaphor—"the world is a stage"—emphasizes both the comic and instructive aspects of the play, reminding audiences that while social life involves performance, honesty, intelligence, and emotional insight are essential to meaningful action and lasting relationships. This quotation, therefore, synthesizes the play's thematic concerns: the tension between appearance and reality, the value of wit and prudence, and the rewards of authentic human connection.

Important long questions and answers

1. Discuss the role of mistaken identity in *She Stoops to Conquer*. How does it contribute to both comedy and the play's themes?

Mistaken identity is the central device around which the entire plot of *She Stoops to Conquer* revolves. Goldsmith ingeniously uses it to generate comic situations, develop characters, and explore social themes such as class, manners, and the contrast between appearance and reality. The primary instance of mistaken identity occurs when Tony Lumpkin deceives Marlow and Hastings into thinking that Mr. Hardcastle's house is an inn. Believing themselves to be in an inn, the two city gentlemen behave with rudeness and familiarity, expecting servile treatment. This error creates immediate comic tension, as the audience is fully aware of the truth, and watches characters navigate situations that are both awkward and amusing. Marlow, who is naturally shy and timid around women of social standing, treats Kate with boldness and flirtation, believing her to be a barmaid. This inversion of behavior—timidness before ladies of high status and confidence with those of lower status—forms the basis of much of the play's humor.

Beyond comedy, mistaken identity serves to reveal deeper truths about the characters. Kate's decision to disguise herself as a barmaid allows her to observe Marlow's true nature. While he struggles to express himself in the company of an upper-class woman, he speaks freely, confidently, and sincerely when he believes Kate is a social inferior. Goldsmith thus uses the mistaken identity plot device to explore the theme that social conventions and superficial judgments often conceal true character. By lowering herself in status, Kate "stoops to conquer," demonstrating intelligence, emotional insight, and strategic action. The mistaken identity scenario also highlights Marlow's dual personality, illustrating that courage, wit, and sincerity may be situationally dependent but are nonetheless present.

Additionally, the device allows other characters, like Constance and Hastings, to navigate obstacles created by societal expectations. Constance's struggle with Mrs. Hardcastle over her inheritance and her desire to marry Hastings is complicated by misperceptions and assumed identities. Tony's trickery, while playful, drives these misunderstandings and ultimately forces the characters to confront their assumptions.

Thematically, mistaken identity reinforces Goldsmith's critique of rigid social hierarchies and the artificiality of manners. By showing how a single misunderstanding can reverse behavior, Goldsmith questions the moral and social significance placed on class and decorum. It also emphasizes that true virtue, affection, and intelligence are revealed only when people are unshackled from pretense.

In conclusion, mistaken identity in *She Stoops to Conquer* functions as a comedic engine, a moral lens, and a means of character revelation. It drives the plot, provides humor through situational irony, and allows Goldsmith to critique social rigidity. The audience gains insight into human behavior, learning that appearances can be deceptive and that intelligence, empathy, and authenticity matter more than superficial status. It is this interplay of comedy, social commentary, and character development that makes the play enduringly entertaining and insightful.

2.Examine the character of Kate Hardcastle in *She Stoops to Conquer*. How does she embody intelligence, wit, and agency?

Kate Hardcastle, the heroine of *She Stoops to Conquer*, is one of the most memorable characters in 18th-century comedy, combining charm, intelligence, and strategic agency. Unlike many female characters of the period, Kate is neither passive nor purely decorative; she actively shapes the events of the play and guides the male protagonist, Marlow, toward self-realization and love. From the beginning, Kate demonstrates a sharp intellect and keen observation. She quickly assesses Marlow's dual personality: his extreme shyness in the company of upper-class women and his confidence with women of lower social rank. Recognizing this, she devises the plan to disguise herself as a barmaid, allowing Marlow to interact freely and reveal his true self. This act demonstrates foresight, emotional intelligence, and agency, as Kate strategically manipulates circumstances without deceiving for selfish or malicious ends.

Kate's wit is another defining feature. She engages in verbal sparring, subtle irony, and playful teasing, particularly in her interactions with Marlow. Her humor is intelligent rather than frivolous; it serves both to entertain and to instruct. For instance, her ability to maintain her disguise while observing Marlow's behavior shows self-control, cleverness, and a deep understanding of human nature. Kate's wit is complemented by her moral sensibility. While she uses deception to achieve her goal, her intentions are guided by fairness and genuine affection, illustrating that intelligence and morality can coexist.

Moreover, Kate subverts traditional gender expectations. In an era when women were often confined to passive roles, she assumes control of the narrative, guiding both plot and male characters. Marlow, though initially socially dominant in other contexts, is rendered vulnerable and self-revealing by her strategy. By orchestrating events, Kate demonstrates that women's agency is not limited to marriage decisions but extends to shaping social interactions and revealing truth.

Her character also embodies the theme of appearance versus reality. Kate's disguise allows her to manipulate social perception while revealing character authenticity. In doing so, she critiques societal norms that overvalue etiquette and social rank, suggesting that true understanding and love require insight, patience, and intelligence.

In conclusion, Kate Hardcastle represents a perfect blend of intellect, wit, and agency. She is central to the comedic structure, the romantic plot, and the thematic message of *She Stoops to Conquer*. Through her, Goldsmith conveys that women can be both perceptive strategists and morally upright individuals, capable of guiding others and challenging societal conventions. Kate's resourcefulness, cleverness, and moral vision make her an enduringly admired character in English literature, symbolizing the triumph of intelligence, wit, and virtue over superficial appearances and social rigidity.

3.Analyze the contrast between town and country life in *She Stoops to Conquer*. How does Goldsmith use this contrast to create comedy and social commentary?

The contrast between town and country life is a central theme in *She Stoops to Conquer*, and Goldsmith uses it to generate humor while offering social critique. The play juxtaposes the simplicity, sincerity, and hospitality of rural living with the sophistication, affectation, and pretentiousness associated with city life, particularly London. Mr. Hardcastle, the play's patriarch, epitomizes the virtues of the countryside. He values honesty, warmth, and moral integrity over social display or fashion. He is comfortable, confident, and straightforward, and he represents a life guided by reason and common sense rather than superficial manners. In contrast, characters from the city, such as Marlow and Hastings, embody the anxieties, affectations, and rigidities of urban life. Marlow, for instance, is paralyzed by formality and shyness in the presence of upper-class women, illustrating how social training and urban expectations can hinder natural behavior.

Goldsmith creates comedy through this contrast by highlighting the misunderstandings and social blunders that arise when city manners collide with country straightforwardness. Tony Lumpkin, a country youth, deliberately misleads Marlow and Hastings, exploiting their urban naïveté and resulting in humorous confusion. The city gentlemen treat the Hardcastle household as an inn, ignoring its social status and disrespecting the hosts. These interactions reveal their awkwardness and pretension while simultaneously allowing the audience to appreciate the natural grace, wit, and intelligence of the rural characters. Kate Hardcastle, though of high social standing, bridges this divide by combining city refinement with country pragmatism, ultimately guiding Marlow toward authentic expression and social ease.

Beyond comedy, Goldsmith uses the town-country contrast for social commentary. He critiques the rigid etiquette, superficiality, and excessive concern with appearances prevalent in city life. The urban characters' social nervousness and obsession with rank highlight the artificial constraints imposed by societal expectations, whereas rural characters' sincerity and common sense reflect more genuine values. By dramatizing these differences, Goldsmith suggests that authenticity, moral integrity, and natural behavior are preferable to pretension, affectation, and excessive concern with social hierarchies.

The contrast also reinforces themes of perception and misunderstanding. Urban characters misjudge the country's simplicity as naivety, while rural characters perceive city manners as ridiculous or excessive. Comedy arises from these misalignments, but Goldsmith's underlying message is clear: social refinement alone does not guarantee virtue or wisdom. Genuine character emerges when people act naturally, guided by reason and empathy rather than rigid convention.

In conclusion, the town-country contrast in *She Stoops to Conquer* serves both comedic and moral purposes. It generates humor through situational irony and character misunderstandings while allowing Goldsmith to critique social pretensions and celebrate authenticity, simplicity, and practical intelligence. By balancing comedy with insight, Goldsmith demonstrates that true social wisdom comes from understanding human nature, not blindly following rules or etiquette.

4.Discuss the character of Tony Lumpkin and his role in the comedy of *She Stoops to Conquer*.

Tony Lumpkin is one of the most memorable comic characters in *She Stoops to Conquer*, and he serves multiple purposes: he provides humor, drives the plot through mischief, and offers a critique of social pretensions. Tony is depicted as a playful, rebellious, and carefree young man, whose love of freedom and practical jokes often disrupts the orderly world of his family and guests. Unlike other characters, who are constrained by social expectation, etiquette, or romantic anxiety, Tony operates with spontaneity and natural wit. His humor is rooted in mischief, exaggeration, and verbal play, which makes him a source of constant amusement. For example, he deliberately misleads Marlow and Hastings into believing that Mr. Hardcastle's home is an inn. This single prank creates the central confusion of the play, driving much of the comedic action and allowing Goldsmith to explore themes such as mistaken identity, class perception, and the contrast between appearance and reality.

Tony's role is also crucial in revealing the characteristics of other figures. Marlow's dual personality—his shyness with upper-class women and confidence with lower-class women—is exposed because of Tony's deception. Similarly, the reactions of Mrs. Hardcastle, Hastings, and Constance to Tony's antics highlight their priorities, personalities, and values. In this sense, Tony functions not only as a comic figure but also as a catalyst for character development. He demonstrates how a seemingly frivolous figure can influence the plot and illuminate deeper truths about human nature.

Furthermore, Tony represents a certain critique of societal rigidity. While other characters are often preoccupied with social status, wealth, and propriety, Tony is unconcerned with convention. He enjoys life on his own terms, demonstrating a natural intelligence that contrasts with the pretentiousness of city gentlemen and the manipulative tendencies of his mother. Tony's humor, rooted in practical jokes and verbal wit, encourages audiences to question the seriousness with which society often treats appearances and decorum.

Tony also adds layers to the play's thematic structure. His youthful exuberance and love of freedom highlight the tension between societal expectation and individual desire, a recurring motif in Goldsmith's comedy. By challenging authority, questioning social norms, and creating situations of confusion, Tony contributes to the play's exploration of class, human behavior, and social manners. At the same time, his character remains morally harmless; his mischief is playful rather than destructive, allowing him to serve as both a comic relief and a moral mirror.

In conclusion, Tony Lumpkin is indispensable to *She Stoops to Conquer*. He provides humor, drives the plot through deception and mischief, exposes the true nature of other characters, and critiques social pretension. Through Tony, Goldsmith blends comedy with insight, showing that intelligence, wit, and playfulness can coexist with moral clarity. Tony's vibrant personality not only entertains but also reinforces the play's central themes: the contrast between appearance and reality, the folly of rigid social conventions, and the value of authenticity and natural behavior in human interaction.

5. Examine the theme of love and marriage in *She Stoops to Conquer*. How does Goldsmith portray different attitudes toward courtship?

Love and marriage form the central thematic core of *She Stoops to Conquer*, yet Goldsmith presents them with complexity, combining romantic idealism with social commentary and comic critique. The play explores not only the process of courtship but also the social conventions, misunderstandings, and personal qualities that influence relationships. Goldsmith portrays love as a union of intelligence, virtue, and mutual understanding rather than a mere transaction based on wealth, rank, or appearance. This perspective is particularly evident in the relationship between Kate Hardcastle and Marlow. Their courtship is initially obstructed by social anxiety, misperceptions, and the rigid expectations associated with their class. Marlow's shyness with upper-class women and Kate's clever disguise as a barmaid reflect the challenges of navigating societal norms while seeking authentic emotional connection. Goldsmith's treatment of their romance emphasizes intelligence, empathy, and strategic action as essential for successful courtship, suggesting that love flourishes when individuals engage sincerely and observe the true character of their partners.

The play also contrasts different attitudes toward marriage. Mrs. Hardcastle embodies social ambition and parental control, attempting to dictate marital choices for Tony and Constance based on wealth, inheritance, and convenience rather than affection. Her schemes, however, are consistently thwarted, underscoring Goldsmith's message that marriages imposed by societal expectation or material interest are likely to fail. In contrast, Constance and Hastings exemplify patience, loyalty, and moral clarity in love. Despite obstacles such as Constance's lack of access to her inheritance and Mrs. Hardcastle's manipulations, they navigate their challenges with honesty and perseverance, ultimately securing a happy union. Tony's playful rebellion, though primarily comic, also demonstrates that marriage and relationships must respect individual choice and personal desire rather than rigid adherence to social hierarchy.

Mistaken identity, a recurring plot device, serves as a tool to explore romantic dynamics. Marlow's dual personality, revealed through his interactions with Kate in disguise, emphasizes the importance of context and understanding in courtship. By "stooping" socially, Kate enables Marlow to express his true self, highlighting Goldsmith's assertion that authentic love requires insight, patience, and empathy. The play further critiques superficiality, showing that social manners, appearances, or inherited status are secondary to honesty, intelligence, and genuine emotional connection.

Goldsmith balances these serious insights with comedy, making the play entertaining while delivering moral lessons. Romantic misunderstandings, disguises, and witty dialogue provide humor, yet they simultaneously reveal the psychological and social complexities of love. The resolution reinforces the idea that successful marriages combine personal affection, mutual respect, and practical intelligence, rather than merely conforming to social expectation.

In conclusion, *She Stoops to Conquer* presents love and marriage as domains where intelligence, virtue, and authenticity triumph over superficiality, social rigidity, and coercion. Through the relationships of Kate and Marlow, Constance and Hastings, and the thwarted ambitions of Mrs. Hardcastle, Goldsmith explores multiple attitudes toward courtship, demonstrating that patience, wit, and empathy are essential for romantic success. Love, in the play, is not only a source of personal happiness but also a medium through which social norms, character, and human behavior are examined and celebrated.

6.How does Oliver Goldsmith use humor and comedy to comment on social class and human behavior in *She Stoops to Conquer*?

Humor and comedy are central to *She Stoops to Conquer*, yet Goldsmith employs them not merely to entertain but to offer incisive social commentary. The play's humor arises from character flaws, misunderstandings, mistaken identities, verbal wit, and situational irony, and it serves to critique human pretension, social rigidity, and the artificiality of manners. One of the most prominent comedic devices is mistaken identity, which drives much of the plot. Marlow and Hastings, city gentlemen, are misled by Tony Lumpkin into believing that Mr. Hardcastle's house is an inn. Their resulting behavior—rudeness toward the Hardcastles, inappropriate familiarity, and nervousness around women of supposed higher status—creates situational comedy while simultaneously exposing the fragility of social hierarchies. Goldsmith highlights how urban refinement and etiquette, when divorced from sincerity, can appear ridiculous and even absurd.

The contrast between town and country life is another source of humor. Country characters, such as Mr. Hardcastle and Tony Lumpkin, are portrayed as straightforward, practical, and honest, while urban characters are overly concerned with appearances, rank, and decorum. This contrast allows Goldsmith to satirize societal pretensions, showing that the confidence and wisdom associated with social status often mask naivety or foolishness. The audience is invited to laugh at the mistakes and exaggerations of city characters while appreciating the natural wit and common sense of rural figures.

Verbal humor, particularly through witty dialogue and irony, also serves social critique. Kate Hardcastle's clever manipulation of Marlow and her use of verbal play reveal both her intelligence and the limitations of social expectation. Similarly, Tony's mischievous commentary and practical jokes amuse the audience while pointing to the arbitrary and sometimes ludicrous nature of social control. Mrs. Hardcastle's obsession with fashion, wealth, and authority is lampooned, providing comic relief while illustrating the follies of social ambition.

Goldsmith's comedy also conveys moral lessons. Through humor, he encourages audiences to value authenticity, intelligence, and empathy over superficial manners, rank, or wealth. Characters rewarded in the play—Kate, Marlow, Constance, Hastings—combine wit with moral integrity, whereas those whose pretensions dominate their behavior, like Mrs. Hardcastle or socially anxious Marlow, must confront the consequences of their rigidity or misunderstandings. Humor thus functions as both entertainment and moral guidance, making the play enjoyable while prompting reflection on human behavior and social values.

In conclusion, Goldsmith masterfully uses comedy in *She Stoops to Conquer* to critique social class, human pretension, and artificial manners. Mistaken identities, verbal wit, situational irony, and the contrast between town and country life generate laughter while illuminating truths about human behavior, social hierarchy, and personal authenticity. Humor becomes a vehicle for moral insight, demonstrating that intelligence, sincerity, and cleverness are superior to rigid adherence to social norms or superficial refinement. Through this blend of comedy and social commentary, Goldsmith creates a timeless and engaging play that entertains while provoking thought about human nature and societal values.

7. How does Kate Hardcastle demonstrate intelligence and agency in *She Stoops to Conquer*, and how does this influence the play's outcome?

Kate Hardcastle is the embodiment of intelligence, wit, and agency in *She Stoops to Conquer*, and her actions are central to the development and resolution of the plot. Unlike many female characters in 18th-century literature, Kate is not passive or merely reactive. She actively shapes events, influences male characters, and ensures the resolution of conflicts, all while demonstrating moral integrity. Her intelligence is immediately evident in her observation of Marlow. She recognizes his dual nature: his extreme shyness and awkwardness in the company of upper-class women, contrasted with his boldness and confidence around those of lower status. Understanding this, Kate devises the clever plan to disguise herself as a barmaid. This "stooping" allows her to interact with Marlow in a context where he feels comfortable and expressive. In doing so, she not only reveals his true personality but also facilitates the emotional and romantic development necessary for their union.

Kate's agency is further evident in her careful management of the unfolding comedy. She controls her disguise, timing, and dialogue to maintain the illusion, all while observing and guiding Marlow's behavior. This demonstrates both strategic thinking and emotional intelligence: Kate can read people, anticipate reactions, and adjust her behavior to achieve desired outcomes. Unlike characters such as Mrs. Hardcastle, whose manipulations are ego-driven and superficial, Kate's actions are morally sound and aimed at fostering understanding, love, and genuine connection. Her wit complements her strategy; she employs verbal irony, playful teasing, and subtle manipulation to both entertain the audience and instruct the characters around her. This combination of intelligence, humor, and morality distinguishes Kate as the moral and emotional center of the play.

Kate's actions have a direct impact on the play's outcome. By orchestrating Marlow's revelation of his true self, she ensures that the romantic and social conflicts are resolved. Marlow gains self-confidence, Kate secures his affection, and the other misunderstandings—such as the issues around Constance and Hastings—can be addressed more easily. Kate's agency thus transforms potential chaos into a harmonious resolution. Goldsmith uses her character to challenge contemporary notions of female passivity, showing that women's intelligence and strategic insight are not only admirable but crucial to social and personal harmony.

Thematically, Kate's intelligence and agency reflect Goldsmith's interest in the interplay between appearance and reality. By manipulating appearances, Kate allows truth and virtue to emerge, illustrating that cleverness, observation, and moral integrity can navigate social complexities more effectively than rigid adherence to etiquette. Her ability to "stoop to conquer" encapsulates the play's central moral: humility, strategic insight, and intelligence are powerful tools for achieving personal and social fulfillment.

In conclusion, Kate Hardcastle demonstrates intelligence and agency through her clever manipulation of circumstances, emotional insight, and moral judgment. Her actions drive the plot, reveal true character, and ensure a harmonious resolution. She is both the intellectual and emotional linchpin of the play, embodying Goldsmith's belief that wit, intelligence, and ethical purpose are essential to personal and social success. Kate's influence is a key reason *She Stoops to Conquer* remains a celebrated example of 18th-century comedy and character-driven drama.

8.Explain how Goldsmith uses social class and manners to create humor and convey his social critique in *She Stoops to Conquer*.

Social class and manners are central to both the comedic structure and the social commentary of *She Stoops to Conquer*. Goldsmith masterfully contrasts rural and urban lifestyles, as well as natural and artificial behavior, to generate humor while critiquing societal pretensions. The city characters—Marlow and Hastings—embody the anxieties, awkwardness, and rigidity often associated with urban refinement. Marlow's extreme shyness and inability to converse comfortably with upper-class women showcase the artificial constraints of social etiquette. In contrast, he is bold, confident, and flirtatious when he believes a woman is of lower social status. Goldsmith uses this situational irony to create comedy while highlighting the absurdity of rigid social conventions. The contrast between appearance and reality underscores a broader critique: social rank and manners do not always reflect intelligence, virtue, or emotional maturity.

The rural characters—Mr. Hardcastle, Tony Lumpkin, and Kate Hardcastle in her practical wisdom—embody honesty, straightforwardness, and common sense. Their natural ease in social situations contrasts sharply with the nervousness and pretension of city visitors. Tony's practical jokes, such as misleading Marlow and Hastings into believing that Hardcastle's house is an inn, expose the artificiality and superficiality of social manners. The comedic confusion that follows relies on social hierarchy and expectation: the humor is both situational and character-driven, arising from the clash between urban anxiety and rural practicality.

Goldsmith's satire extends to the obsession with wealth, inheritance, and social advancement. Mrs. Hardcastle's exaggerated concern with fashion, her manipulative attempts to control her son's marriage, and her overestimation of social status provide comic relief while emphasizing the absurdity of placing appearances above human character. Her pretentiousness highlights the folly of valuing manners and wealth over intelligence, virtue, and emotional authenticity. Similarly, the play mocks the rigid deference to social rank, showing that genuine human qualities are often independent of social class.

The use of mistaken identity amplifies these contrasts. By manipulating perceptions of class and status, Goldsmith demonstrates how easily manners and behavior are influenced by social assumptions. Marlow's behavior when he believes Kate is a barmaid reveals that social performance often masks natural ability, wit, and sincerity. Through these comedic situations, the audience laughs at the absurdity of social rigidity while also recognizing the deeper truth: human behavior and character are revealed under circumstances that bypass superficial social constraints.

Ultimately, Goldsmith's comedy balances entertainment with social insight. He uses humor to critique the artificiality of manners, the limitations imposed by social hierarchy, and the folly of valuing appearance over substance. Characters who are sincere, intelligent, and morally upright—Kate, Marlow, Constance, Hastings—are rewarded, while pretension and excessive social ambition—embodied by Mrs. Hardcastle or socially anxious city visitors—are humorously exposed. Goldsmith thus uses class and manners not only as comedic devices but also as vehicles for moral and social critique.

In conclusion, Goldsmith's humor arises from the interplay between social class, manners, and human behavior. Comedy exposes pretension, celebrates authenticity, and emphasizes the importance of wit, intelligence, and moral integrity. The contrasts between town and country, artificiality and sincerity, and mistaken perception versus reality provide both entertainment and a subtle, enduring commentary on social values.

9.How does *She Stoops to Conquer* balance comedy with moral and social lessons? Provide examples.

She Stoops to Conquer masterfully balances comedy with moral and social lessons, using humor as a vehicle to critique human behavior, social pretension, and societal expectations. Goldsmith's comedy operates on multiple levels: situational, verbal, and character-driven. The central comedic device is mistaken identity, which creates confusion, irony, and laughter. When Tony Lumpkin tricks Marlow and Hastings into believing Mr. Hardcastle's house is an inn, the audience immediately anticipates the ensuing chaos. Marlow, shy and awkward with upper-class women, behaves boldly and flirtatiously toward Kate, whom he believes to be a barmaid. This inversion is both humorous and illuminating, as it exposes the absurdity of social hierarchies and the superficiality of manners.

Beyond humor, the play delivers moral lessons. Kate Hardcastle's intelligence and strategic action demonstrate that patience, insight, and ethical cleverness are more effective than deception or force driven by selfish motives. By "stooping" to a lower social identity, Kate allows Marlow to reveal his true character, emphasizing the importance of authenticity in love and human interaction. Similarly, Constance Neville and Hastings demonstrate the value of perseverance, honesty, and moral courage in pursuit of personal happiness, even when confronted with social obstacles and manipulative figures like Mrs. Hardcastle.

Goldsmith also critiques societal pretensions through comedy. Characters such as Mrs. Hardcastle, obsessed with fashion, wealth, and control, provide comic relief but simultaneously illustrate the folly of prioritizing appearances over virtue. Marlow's dual behavior underscores the play's central commentary on social anxiety and class-based etiquette. His transformation—becoming confident and sincere when social pretension is removed—suggests that personal worth cannot be measured by status or manners. The audience laughs at the absurdity of these situations while absorbing the underlying message: virtue, wit, and moral insight outweigh social rank or superficial behavior.

Comedy is also used to explore the theme of human folly. Tony Lumpkin's playful mischief and verbal wit disrupt authority and rigid social expectations, yet his actions are morally harmless. His pranks expose pretension, reveal character, and ultimately facilitate the resolution of romantic and social conflicts. Humor, therefore, becomes a tool for both entertainment and moral instruction, showing that laughter and ethical reflection can coexist.

In conclusion, *She Stoops to Conquer* balances comedy and moral lessons by integrating situational humor, verbal wit, and character-driven irony with social critique. Mistaken identities, clever deceptions, and playful pranks generate laughter while exposing human folly, social pretension, and the limitations of etiquette. Through characters such as Kate, Marlow, Constance, and Tony, Goldsmith emphasizes intelligence, moral insight, authenticity, and emotional understanding. The play demonstrates that comedy is not merely entertainment; it is a lens through which audiences can reflect on human behavior, social norms, and the virtues that truly matter in relationships and society.

CHAPTER THIRTEEN

HISTORY OF THE RELEVANT PERIOD

Elizabethan Age (1558-1603)

The Elizabethan Age is among the most important periods in English Literature known for its vigour and inclination for emulating the Classics like the Virgil and its sense of innovative form. Thus, it is important to understand the background and features of the Elizabethan Age. Let's jump in.

What is the Elizabethan Age?

Introduction

The greatest age in the history of English Literature. Yes, you heard it right- I am talking about the great Elizabethan age; also known as:

· The Golden Age of England

· The Renaissance

· The Shakespearean Age

· The 1st great age of Drama & the 2nd great age of Poetry

Elizabethan age was remarkable for its religious tolerance, strong national spirit, patriotism, social content, intellectual progress & unbounded enthusiasm. Incredible thoughts, feelings & vigorous actions were the pillar of this age. It flowers extraordinary development of drama. Equally, it is an age of poetry. The Elizabethan period was the period of glory and triumph in the life and literature of the English people.

The Elizabethan Age in English literature refers to the period that coincides with the reign of England's Queen Elizabeth I (1558-1603). Often, the periods or distinct ages in English literature are named after some towering identifiable figure from the literary world or after someone with socio-political status. The Elizabethan period is considered from 1550 to 1630. All the works written during this period are considered Elizabethan literature.

Historical Background of the Elizabethan Age

The Elizabethan Age (1550-1630) in English Literature provided a conducive environment for art and writers to flourish. The name of the age is after the reign of Queen Elizabeth. Two major themes can be observed as far as the historical background of the Elizabethan Age in connection with English Literature.

- **Sense of Settlement** – Though there were still a few dynastic problems during this period, the nation's political environment was stable. Compared to the wars and chaos of the previous period, it didn't culminate in open warfare. The union of the Crowns settled the ancient quarrels between Scotland and England. This helped literature big time, numerous patrons of literature and a period where people could focus on other things.
- **Expansion in the true sense** – An expansion in terms of mental and geographical horizons marked this era. Knowledge pouring from the East and voyages made discoveries of new lands and routes. Often these voyages were chronicled. Finally, the Elizabethan Period had just the right combination of socioeconomic conditions to support drama. This genre of English Literature flourished to new heights under the penmanship of Marlowe and other University wits, and of course, Shakespeare.

The religious background of the Elizabethan Age

Queen Elizabeth's father, Henry VIII broke away from the Catholic Church and separated the Church of England from Papal authority in 1534 to divorce his wife, Catherine of Aragon. This led to religious unrest in England. After King Henry VIII's reign, i.e., during Edward VI's and Mary I's succession, the religious unrest only increased. Queen Elizabeth I's religious tolerance led to a time of peace between religious factions. This is the reason people celebrate her reign.

The social background of the Elizabethan Age

The social aspects of life during the Elizabethan Age had their merits and demerits. While there were no famines, and harvest was bountiful during this period, people also lived in extreme poverty due to a wide wealth gap among the different social groups.

Families that could afford to, sent their sons to school, while daughters were either sent to work and earn money for the household or be trained to manage a household, do domestic chores and take care of children in the hopes of them marrying well.

The population of England increased. This increase led to inflation, as labour was available for cheap. Those who were able-bodied were expected to work and earn a living. Due to an increase in population, major cities, especially <u>London</u>, were overcrowded. This led to rat infestation, filthy environments and the rapid spread of diseases. There were multiple outbreaks of plague during the Elizabethan Age, during which outdoor gatherings were banned, including theatre performances.

The political background of the Elizabethan Age

During the reign of Queen Elizabeth I, the Parliament was not yet strong enough to pit itself against Royal authority. This changed after the succession of James I of the crown. An elaborate spy network and a strong military foiled numerous assassination attempts on the Queen. Furthermore, Queen Elizabeth I's army and naval fleet also prevented the invasion of England by the Spanish Armada in 1588, thus establishing England's and consequently Queen Elizabeth I's supremacy in Europe. The period was also marked by political expansion and exploration. The trade of goods thrived, leading to a period of commercial progress.

Literary Features of the Elizabethan Age

The Elizabethan Age is considered to be the height of the English Renaissance. An inclination marked it for the classics. Poets and dramatics took inspiration from Italian forms and genres such as the love sonnet, pastoral poems, and allegorical epics. Musicality, rhythm, verbal sophistication, and romantic exuberance are priorities by many writers over form, leading to new structures like the introduction of English English mode or Shakespearian mode. Let's briefly examine the major literary features of the various genres.

1.Popularity of Poetry

Though the poetical production was not quite equal to the dramatic, Poetry enjoyed its hey-day during the Elizabethan age. It was nevertheless of great and original beauty. Poetic fervor had bagged the entire age.

Lyrics, songs, & sonnets were produced in huge amount. England became the nest of the singing birds. There were notable improvements in versification.

Spenser introduced pictorialism and melody into poetry. Elizabethan poetries were extraordinary because of its freshness, distinct variety, youth as well as romantic feeling. This age saw the flowering of poetry.

Era of Sonnet

Sonnet was popularized in this period. It was introduced by Thomas Wyatt early in the 16th century. He introduced Petrarchan sonnet. Shakespeare made changes to the Italian model and introduced his own style, now known as the English Sonnet or Shakespearean Sonnet.

2.Prose

For the first time in the history of English literature, prose was of first-rate importance.

The heavy burden of the Latin was disappearing while English prose gained a tradition & universal application. Rapid development during this period was almost inevitable.

3. Emergence of Renaissance

In the Elizabethan age, there were two potent forces- the Renaissance and the Reformation. Both the forces blended and co-operated each other. These two movements produced a great uplifting of the spirit.

The word "renaissance" is originated from the Latin word "nasci" which means "Be Born" Renaissance was the time of great improvement of art, literature, and learning in Europe. The Renaissance Age began in the 14th century and extended till the 17th century.

The Renaissance-inspired the aesthetic and intellect potential whereas the reformation aroused the spiritual nature.

4. New Classicism

The new passion for classical learning was a rich and worthy enthusiasm. It became a danger to the language. In all branches of literature, Greek and Latin usages began to force themselves upon English, which was not totally beneficial. English language gave away its native sturdiness and allowed itself to be tempered and polished by the new influences.

5. Development of Drama

Drama, during the Elizabethan age, made a rapid & glorious leap into maturity. The drama was perfectly molded in the hands of Shakespeare & Ben Jonson perfectly developed drama

Although, it had many early difficulties to overcome. Because of the disturbances caused by the actors, the theatres were closed between 1590 – 1593. In 1594, the problems were solved by the licensing of two troupes of players:

- The Lord of Chamberlain's (among whom was Shakespeare)
- The Lord Admirals

Another early difficulty the drama had to face was its fondness for taking part in the quarrels of the time. For example "Marprelate Controversy" Owning to this meddling, the theatres were closed in 1589. Already, also a considerable amount of Puritan opposition was declaring itself.

The most important antidramatic book of that time was Gosson's "School of Abuse" to which Sidney replied with his "Apology for Poetry".

6. Abundance of Output

During the Elizabethan Age, the historical situation encouraged a rich & healthy production of the literature of all kinds. A lot of interest was shown in literary subjects. Treaties and pamphlets were written freely uplifting the quality of the literary output. Much abuse; of a personal and scurrilous character that were indulged in literary questions became almost of national importance.

7. New Romanticism

Elizabethan romantic quest is, for the magnificent & the beautiful. Elizabethan age is the first & the greatest period of romanticism. All these kind of desires were amply fulfilled by this age.

According to Albert, ***"there was a daring & resolute spirit of adventure in literary as well as the other regions, & most important of these was an unmistakable buoyancy & freshness in the strong wind of the spirit. It was the ardent youth of English Literature & the achievement was worthy of it."***

8. Translations in Elizabethan Age

The Elizabethan age observed several important foreign books translation in the English language. By 1579, many of the great books of ancient & modern times had been translated into English, almost all of them by 1603; the end of Queen Elizabeth's reign.

Just like the original works, the translations also gained popularity:

- Plutarch's Lives translation by Sir Thomas North
- Montaigne's Essais translation by John Florio

Poetical translations were also much popular

- E.g. Arthur Golding translated Metamorphoses
- Sir John Harrington translated Aristotle's Orlando Furioso
- Richard Carew translated Tasso's Jerusalem Libertad

9. Spirit of Independence

Even though the writers borrowed literature from abroad, this age depicted an unbound spirit of independence & creativeness. Shakespeare openly borrowed literature, but with his splendid creative imaginations, he transformed everything into gold. 'Spenserian Stanza' was introduced by Spenser. We gained the impression of creativity & boldness from his works. Inventiveness and intrepidity was his masterstroke. In short, during this age, the writers' outlook was broad & independent.

10.Scottish Literature

A curious minor feature of the age was the disappearance of the Scottish Literature after its brief but remarkable appearance in the previous age. At this point, it took to the ground and did not appear till late in the 18th century.

CONCLUSION

"Such were some of the conditions which combined to create the spirit of Shakespeare's age – An age in which men lived intensely, thought intensely and wrote intensely."

-W.H Hudson-

Famous Writers of the Elizabethan Age

The Elizabethan Age took English LIteratyure to new heights and gave what was missing up to that point; a national culture & tradition. Countless writers made contributions. Though the Elizabethan age is known for its impressive drama output, other genres, such as poetry and prose, also flourished through select writers. Let's take a quick look at the list of Famous writers of the Elizabethan Age.

Famous Writers of Elizabethan Age

Writer

Major Work
Edmund Spenser

- The Shepheards Calendar (1579)
- The Faerie Queen (1596)

John Donne

- Of the Progres of the Soule (1601)
- Ignatius his Conclave (1611)

John Lyly

- Euphues: The Anatomy of Wit (1578)
- Endymion (1592)

Christopher Marlowe

- Tamburlaine the Great (1587)
- The Jew of Malta (1589)

William Shakespeare

- King Lear (1605)
- Othello (1604)

Ben Jonson

- The Poetaster (1601)
- Volpone, or the Fox (1605)

Writers and Poets of the Elizabethan Age

The most important playwrights and poets of the Elizabethan Age include
William Shakespeare, Ben Jonson, Christopher Marlowe and Edmund
Spenser.

1.William Shakespeare

William Shakespeare (1564-1616) was known as the 'Bard of Stratford' as he hailed from a place called Stratford-Upon-Avon in England. He is credited with having written 39 plays, 154 sonnets and other literary works. A prolific writer, much of the vocabulary we use today in our everyday lives was coined by William Shakespeare.

William Shakespeare often performed a supporting character in the theatrical iterations of the plays he wrote. He was a part-owner of a theatre company that came to be known as the King's Men as it received great favour and patronage from King James I. Even during the reign of Queen Elizabeth I, Shakespeare received patronage from the monarch and often performed for her.

Because of the universal themes that characterise his works, such as jealousy, ambition, power struggle, love etc., William Shakespeare's plays continue to be widely read and analysed today. Some of his most famous plays include Hamlet (c. 1599-1601), Othello (1603), Macbeth (1606), As You Like It (1599) and Romeo and Juliet (c. 1595).

2.Ben Jonson

Ben Jonson had a significant influence on English theatre and poetry. His work popularised the genre of comedy of humours, such as Every Man in His Humour (1598).

Comedy of humours typically focuses on one or more characters, particularly highlighting their 'humours' or shifts in temperaments.

Jonson is identified by some as the first poet Laureate as he received patronage from aristocrats as well as a yearly pension. Ben Jonson's work was influenced by his social, cultural and political engagements. Jonson was well acquainted with Shakespeare and the latter's theatre company often produced Jonson's plays. While during his lifetime, Jonson was often critical of Shakespeare's works, he also credited Shakespeare as a genius in the preface to the First Folio.The First Folio is the first consolidated publication of Shakespeare's plays. It was published by John Heminges and Henry Condell.Some works authored by Ben Jonson include The Alchemist (1610), Volpone, or The Fox (c. 1606) and Mortimer His Fall (1641).

3.Christopher Marlowe

Christopher Marlowe was a contemporary of Jonson and Shakespeare and a prolific poet and playwright. He is best known for his translation of Goethe's tale of Dr. Faust, which Marlowe titled The Tragical History of the Life and Death of Doctor Faustus (c. 1592).

Marlowe employed the blank verse to compose his works, popularising the form in the Elizabethan Age. His works include Tamburlaine the Great (c. 1587), The Jew of Malta (c. 1589) and Dido, Queen of Carthage (c. 1585). Marlowe's untimely death at the age of 29 is a matter of debate among scholars, some of whom think that Marlowe was killed by a spy in the Privy Council.

4.Edmund Spenser

Edmund Spenser is most famous for his epic poem The Fearie Queene (c. 1590), which includes pastoral themes and whose titular character is inspired by Queen Elizabeth I. The poem celebrates the Tudor dynasty and was widely read at the time of publication, and continues to be an important part of the English literary canon emerging from the period.

Edmund Spenser is also the pioneer of the Spenserian stanza and the Spenserian sonnet, both of which are named after him.

The Spenserian stanza is composed of lines written in the iambic pentameter with the final line of the stanza written in the iambic hexameter (the iambic foot occurring 6 times). The rhyme scheme of the Spensarian stanza is ababbcbcc. The poem The Faerie Queene is written in Spensarian stanzas.

The Spenserian sonnet is 14 lines long, wherein the final line of each quatrain is linked to the first line of the quatrain. A quatrain is a stanza composed of 4 lines. The rhyme scheme of a Spensarian sonnet is ababbcbccdcdee.

5.Philip Sidney

Sir Philip Sidney, a Renaissance polymath, shaped English literature through his diverse works and innovative style. His life as a courtier, diplomat, and soldier infused his writing with unique perspectives and themes that resonated with readers of his time.

Sidney's major works, including "Astrophil and Stella" and "The Defence of Poesy," showcased his mastery of various genres. His poetic style blended classical influences with new techniques, establishing him as a pivotal figure in Elizabethan literature.

The Elizabethan Age today

The effects of the Elizabethan Age can be felt in contemporary works of literature. This is because of the many literary forms, devices and genres that were developed during the time and remained popular through the centuries. Literary works emerging from the Elizabethan Age are widely read and studied till the present day, particularly those of William Shakespeare.

Elizabethan Age - Key takeaways

- The Elizabethan Age is named after the reigning monarch of England, Queen Elizabeth I.
- The Elizabethan Age lasted from 1558 to 1603.
- The Elizabethan Age is also known as the Golden Age as works of art flourished during this period.
- The popular writers and poets of the Elizabethan Age include William Shakespeare, Ben Jonson, Christopher Marlowe and Edmund Spenser.
- Works emerging from the Elizabethan Age are read and studied to this day.

Frequently Asked Questions about Elizabethan Age

1.Why was the Elizabethan age considered a golden age?

Queen Elizabeth was a great patron of the arts, extending her patronage to remarkable artists and performers, thus leading to a surge in works of art produced. This is why the period is also referred to as the Golden Age.

2.What is the Elizabethan age

The Elizabethan Age is named after the reigning monarch of England at the time, Queen Elizabeth I. The epoch began in 1558 when Queen Elizabeth I ascended the throne and ended with her death in 1603.

During the Elizabethan Age, England was experiencing the effects of the Renaissance, which began as a movement in Italy and then swept the rest of Europe in the 16th century.

The Renaissance spurred artists to create great works of art and had a significant influence on the ideologies and products of painting, sculpture, music, theatre and literature. Figures representing the English Renaissance include Thomas Kyd, Francis Bacon, William Shakespeare and Edmund Spenser among others.

3.What are the characteristics of the Elizabethan age?

The Elizabethan Age is marked by numerous religious, social, political and economic shifts. Queen Elizabeth I's religious tolerance led to a time of peace between religious factions. Families sent sons to schools while daughters were educated in domestic responsibilities. During bouts of plague, outdoor gatherings were not permitted. Queen Elizabeth I's military and navy managed to consolidate her power and prevent the Spanish invasion by defeating the Spanish Armada.

4.Why was the Elizabethan age so important?

The effects of the Elizabethan Age can be felt in contemporary works of literature. This is because of the many literary forms, devices and genres that were developed during the time and remained popular through the centuries. Literary works emerging from the Elizabethan Age are widely read and studied to the present day.

The Elizabethan age was the golden age of English Literature:-

The Elizabethan Age is often called the golden age of English literature. This period took place during the reign of Queen Elizabeth I, from 1558 to 1603. There was a renaissance of Greek and Roman literature, mythology, and culture. Writers and poets produced works that are still famous today. This served as a source of inspiration to the countless writers of the period. Let us discuss why this era is seen as a golden age.

Golden Time for Drama: Drama was one of the most important parts of the Elizabethan Age. During this time, playwrights like William Shakespeare (1564-1616), Christopher Marlowe (1564-1593), and Ben Jonson (1573-1637) wrote plays that became classics. Shakespeare's plays, such as "Romeo and Juliet" (1594), "As You Like It" (1600), and "Hamlet" (1601) are known for their deep characters and powerful stories. In Hamlet, he remarked on frailty as our nature:

Frailty, thy name is woman.

Marlowe's "Doctor Faustus" (1592 c.) and Jonson's "Volpone" also stand out. Norton (1532-84) and Sackville (1536-1608) made "Gorboduc" (1562) the first English tragedy. These plays explored big ideas like ambition, love, and power. The theatres were full, and people loved watching these performances.

Golden Time for Poetry: Poetry also flourished during the Elizabethan Age. Poets like Edmund Spenser (1552 c.-1599) and Sir Philip Sidney (1554-1586) wrote beautiful and innovative poems. Spenser's "The Faerie Queene" (1590) is an epic poem that mixes mythology and history. It was written to honour Queen Elizabeth. Sidney's "Astrophel and Stella" (1591) is a famous sonnet sequence. Shakespeare's sonnets represented his love for natural beauty, vastness, and plenty. In Sonnet XVIII, he talks about his friend,

So long as men can breathe or eyes can see,
So long lives this, and this gives life to thee.

These poems discuss love, beauty, and emotions. The poets of this time experimented with new forms and ideas, which made their work exciting and fresh.

Golden Time for Prose: Prose writing also became important during this era. Writers like Francis Bacon (1561-1626) made significant contributions. Bacon wrote essays that discussed various topics, including science, politics, and human behaviour. For example, in

"Of Revenge," he said,
Revenge is a kind of wild justice.

Sir Philip Sidney's (1554-86) "An Apology for Poetry" (1595) was a critical writing for defending poetry. Thomas Nashe (1567-1601 c.) made fictional prose like "The Unfortunate Traveller" (1594). These works helped shape modern thinking. The prose of this time was clear and direct, which made it easier for people to understand complex ideas.

Humanism and Classical Influences: The humanist movement greatly influenced Elizabethan literature. It emphasized the study of classical texts. Writers drew inspiration from Greek and Roman literature. For example, Christopher Marlowe revealed his interest in classical characters in "Doctor Faustus." He mentioned,

Sweet Helen, make me immortal with a kiss.

Here, Faustus is astonished by Helen's beauty and wishes to kiss her sweet lips. The Renaissance focused on rediscovering ancient Greek and Roman ideas.

Lasting Legacy: The literary works of the Elizabethan Age have a lasting legacy. This period's plays, poems, and prose are still read, performed, and studied worldwide. Shakespeare's plays are regularly performed in theatres, and his sonnets are quoted in everyday life. The works of Spenser, Marlowe, and others continue to influence writers today. Charles Lamb addressed Spenser as "The poet of poets."The Elizabethan Age set a high standard for English literature, and its impact is still felt today.

In conclusion, the Elizabethan Age was a time when drama, poetry, and prose reached new heights. Writers were inspired by the Renaissance and supported by a stable society. This period laid the foundation for many literary traditions that continue to shape our world today. So, it was truly a golden age of English literature.

The Jacobean Age (1603-1625)

In English literature, the Jacobean Age is a distinctive period that came after the Elizabethan age and was characterized by notable historical and cultural developments. This period, which was named after King James I of England, reigned from 1603 to 1625 and was marked by a dramatic change in the political, religious, and societal environment. The Jacobean Age is sometimes considered as a continuation of the Renaissance ideal while also hinting at the complexity that would develop in later decades.

Understanding the Jacobean Age's importance requires knowledge of its historical background. Queen Elizabeth I's demise in 1603 marked the end of the Tudor dynasty. The crowns of England and Scotland were united when her cousin James Stuart, the King of Scotland, succeeded to the English throne as James I. The political and cultural dynamics of England saw tremendous changes as a result of this marriage, ushering in a new era. Thus, King James I's impact, as well as his reign's policies, ideologies, and difficulties, have a close connection to the Jacobean Age.

The literature of the Jacobean Age mirrored these changes as England adapted to the shifting political and social environment. Playwrights like Shakespeare continued to contribute, creating plays that delved into the complexity of human psychology and morals and tackled darker subjects. In reaction to the uncertainty of the period, the genre of tragicomedy, which combined aspects of tragedy and humour, became quite popular. The occult, corruption, and themes of power were prevalent in both theatre and poetry.

Cultural and Historical Background

1.Political climate and events

King James I's unification of the English and Scottish thrones was one of the major political developments of the Jacobean Age. When Queen Elizabeth I passed away in 1603, James VI of Scotland became James I of England, marking this historic milestone. As a result of this union, Scotland and England were unified under a single king, which signified a huge change in the geopolitical landscape. This union brought together two different countries with their own histories, traditions, and religious practices, which had deep cultural as well as political ramifications.

The Jacobean Age was also characterized by religious disputes and controversies. By making the Anglican Church the dominant church, the Reformation had already had a significant influence on England. However, religious divisions continued, with the supremacy of the Anglican establishment being challenged by Puritans and Catholics. Conflicts between these theological movements occurred during the Jacobean era, and as a result, political alliances and the King's relationships with various factions were affected. The literature of the time mirrored these conflicts, with themes of religious identity, moral quandaries, and concerns of authority frequently taking front stage.

2.Social and economic change

The social and economic structure of the Jacobean Age was significantly shaped by explorations and colonial expansion. During this time, England was heavily engaged in foreign exploration, which resulted in the founding of colonies in many regions of the world, including North America and the Caribbean. A rise in wealth, resources, and opportunity resulted with the conquest of new lands. The economic success of England and its people was directly impacted by this newly discovered wealth from colonial and international commerce

A direct result of England's increasing commercial networks and colonial endeavors was the birth of a new merchant class. Those who participated in international trade profited significantly from the success of their international endeavors. The merchant class was able to become more prominent thanks to their increased money, upending society's established hierarchical framework. The merchant class rose to prominence as a powerful economic force, influencing not just economic but also political and cultural issues.

The literature of the Jacobean Age mirrored these social and economic shifts. The expansion of the merchant class and the money generated by international commerce gave people the chance to question conventional wisdom and investigate new ideas. Literary works of the era frequently dealt with the intricacy of social hierarchies, desires for upward mobility, and the intersections of money and power. Poets and playwrights frequently utilized their works to investigate the conflicts between the old nobility and the burgeoning merchant class and to remark on how society was changing.

3.Intellectual and scientific advancements

Early advancements in natural philosophy and science that established the foundation for later scientific research were observed during the Jacobean Age. An increasing interest for observing and interpreting the natural world via empirical research emerged during this period. Francis Bacon, who is sometimes credited as one of the founders of the scientific method, favored methodical and experimental methods of nature research. Bacon broke with merely theoretical and speculative approaches by emphasizing actual observation and the acquisition of knowledge via experimentation.

The Jacobean Age saw a continuation of the Renaissance humanism that had gained popularity in previous decades. Humanism placed a strong emphasis on the need for free thinking, education, and the study of ancient literature. The core principles of Renaissance humanism were the investigation of human potential, rational thought, and the quest of knowledge. These values influenced many facets of society, such as literature and the arts, and they fostered an atmosphere that encouraged intellectual inquiry and artistic expression.

In the Jacobean Age, literature and culture were greatly influenced by the fusion of these intellectual and scientific developments with Renaissance humanism. The urge to delve further into the complexity of the human experience and the spirit of inquiry that underlies it served as an inspiration for playwrights, poets, and novelists. The investigation of the complexities of human nature, morality, and society institutions in the works of playwrights like William Shakespeare are evidence of this.

The emphasis on logic and the empirical method of understanding the universe have also led to the development of literary subjects and narrative techniques. Characters grappled with ethical issues, went on a journey of self-discovery, and challenged social conventions, reflecting the period's intellectual interests. A rich tapestry of literary works reflecting the larger intellectual currents of the time resulted from the merging of scientific inquiry and humanistic values.

Key Themes and Characteristics

1.Moral Ambiguity and Complexity

Jacobean literature's investigation of the moral and ethical decisions that characters are compelled to make is at its core. A lot of times, these decisions defy simple classification into categories of right or wrong. It reflects the complex nature of human morality that characters are faced with choices that put their ideas, morals, and ideals to the test. For instance, in Shakespeare's play "Hamlet," the title character struggles with the moral ramifications of taking revenge for his father's death, which causes him to feel conflicted and self-conscious. In a similar way, the protagonists in John Webster's drama "The Duchess of Malfi" must make morally challenging choices that are motivated by their goals for control, love, and survival.

This investigation of moral complexity is closely related to the tumultuous Jacobean political and theological atmosphere. Characters frequently found themselves caught between conflicting loyalties at this time because of the shifting allegiances, religious differences, and power conflicts that characterised the age. Shakespeare's historical plays, such "Richard II" and "Henry IV," which are filled with political intrigue and ambiguous power dynamics, provide as excellent examples of the difficulties that the main characters in those plays had to face.

Conflicts that questioned the fundamental foundation of the individuals' identities were fanned by the conflict between various religious factions and ideological rivalries. John Donne's metaphysical poetry, especially his religious sonnets, deals with issues of faith, doubt, and salvation in a time when one's religious affiliation had a big impact on society and politics in addition to being a matter of personal preference.

2.Macabre and Supernatural Elements

The literature of the era revealed a significant interest in investigating witchcraft, the occult, and supernatural occurrences. This interest in the enigmatic and unknown was in part fueled by a larger cultural curiosity. People's imaginations were captured by playwrights and poets who frequently integrated supernatural themes into their works. For instance, in <u>Shakespeare</u>'s play "Macbeth," the three witches behave as foreboding prophets, making supernatural prophecies that influence the protagonists' behaviour. The story's surreal and scary depth is enhanced by the witches' presence, which makes the distinction between the supernatural and real-world events blurry.

This fascination with the supernatural was not just an act of creativity; it was also a response to societal concerns. Political ambiguity, religious conflict, and apprehension about the future defined the Jacobean age. Literary works provided a forum for exploring and expressing these societal angsts in a society where the distinction between fact and superstition was frequently blurred. For instance, the Thomas Middleton and William Rowley drama "The Changeling" explores themes of treachery, insanity, and the supernatural while addressing the issues of the day on the brittleness of social order and the unpredictability of the forces that can destabilize it.

The inclusion of supernatural components allowed writers to explore the darkest facets of human nature in their works of fiction. The supernatural was frequently used as a symbol for internal conflict, mental anguish, and the negative effects of unbridled ambition. A ghostly appearance makes an appearance in John Webster's "<u>The Duchess of Malfi,</u>" adding to the ominous mood and reflecting the protagonists' psychological suffering.

3.Political and Religious Discourse

The idea of royalty and divine right was one of the major themes of Jacobean literature. King James I's merger of the Scottish and English thrones raised issues related to monarchy, power, and the existence of a divine right to govern. <u>Shakespeare</u>'s historical plays, including "Henry IV" and "Henry V," explore the difficulties and obligations of monarchy, capturing the struggles and victories of leaders as they wrestle with the weight of their divine duty.

Furthermore, the exploration of kingship was strongly related to the concept of divine right, which held that kings were appointed by God and so had an unchallengeable right to govern. The difficulties of this idea were frequently discussed in Jacobean literature, which also raised issues regarding the boundaries of regal authority and the duties that went along with it. <u>Shakespeare</u> explores the tragic nature of royalty in his play "King Lear," which shows the demise of a monarch who exaggerates the scope of his authority and the legitimacy of his throne.

Another major issue of Jacobean Age literature was religious discourse, which reflected the continuous theological conflicts and disagreements of the time. Religious identity was a contentious issue because of the long-lasting tensions caused by England's conversion from Catholicism to Protestantism. Literary works have been utilized by authors to explore the ramifications of various religious identities and how they affect society. In a time of theological turmoil, John Donne's poetry, notably his Holy Sonnets, reflected the intricacies of religious devotion by addressing issues of faith, doubt, and redemption.

Literature of the Jacobean Age

The literary environment of the Jacobean Age was rich and varied, highlighted by the flourishing of drama, poetry, and prose that captured the intricacies of the time. William Shakespeare's later plays, such "Macbeth" and "Antony and Cleopatra," are among the best examples. Shakespeare's remarkable investigation of human psychology and ethical difficulties is on display in these plays, which explore themes of power, ambition, and tragedy. Ben Jonson, another well-known dramatist, also contributed to comedies and tragedies at the same time. By examining topics like avarice and societal hypocrisy, works like "Volpone" and "The Alchemist" demonstrated Jonson's wit and sarcastic insight into society.

Tragicomedy, a separate theatrical subgenre that combines sad and humorous aspects, also became popular during the Jacobean era. Playwrights were able to skillfully intertwine profound human emotions and moral concerns in this genre. The contrast of bright and dark components echoed the altering socio-political scene and reflected the period's uncertainty. Metaphysical poetry had a noticeable impact on poetry at the same time. The poetry expression of the time was influenced by this intellectual and philosophical style, which is known for its elaborate wordplay and investigation of abstract ideas. The metaphysical tradition was represented by John Donne's poetry, which explored both religious devotion and love while diving into the spiritual and material worlds in astonishing depth.

The period produced prose and non-fiction in addition to drama and poetry. The enormous "King James Bible" of 1611 made a lasting impact on the English language and society by establishing norms for literary and religious expression. Along with religious writings, Jacobean authors also created intellectual essays and treatises that addressed modern issues. The variety of literary genres displayed a society in transition, one that was debating theological, philosophical, and political concepts. This diversity of literary genres also represented the general intellectual atmosphere.

Conclusion:

In conclusion, the Jacobean Age, which lasted from 1603 to 1625, was characterised by a time of exceptional literary depth and richness. The literature of this time period mirrored the complexity of the socio-political environment via its investigation of topics including moral ambiguity, the supernatural, political discourse, and religious conflicts. Dramatic narratives underwent a change as a result of playwrights like Shakespeare and Ben Jonson, as well as the rise of tragicomedy. As typified by John Donne, metaphysical poetry explored complex philosophical and spiritual spheres, while the publication of the "King James Bible" and several prose works broadened the field of literature. The Jacobean Age's importance is highlighted by its role in laying the groundwork for English literature and culture, providing insights into the complexity of human behaviour, politics, and faith that have had an impact on writing for centuries.

Here is a list of some of the most notable Jacobean writers:

- William Shakespeare (1564-1616): Shakespeare is widely regarded as the greatest playwright and poet in the English language. He wrote over 30 plays, including Hamlet, Macbeth, and King Lear.
- Ben Jonson (1572-1637): Jonson was a poet and playwright who was known for his satirical comedies. He wrote over 50 plays, including Volpone and The Alchemist.
- John Donne (1572-1631): Donne was a poet and preacher who is known for his metaphysical poetry. His poems are often complex and intellectual, and they explore themes of love, religion, and death.
- Francis Bacon (1561-1626): Bacon was a philosopher, statesman, and essayist who is considered to be one of the founders of the scientific method. He wrote a number of essays on a variety of topics, including science, politics, and morality.
- George Chapman (c. 1559-1634): Chapman was a poet and playwright who is best known for his translation of Homer's Odyssey. He also wrote

a number of original plays, including Bussy D'Ambois and The Revenge of Bussy D'Ambois.

- John Marston (c. 1576-1634): Marston was a poet and playwright who is known for his dark and satirical comedies. He wrote over a dozen plays, including The Malcontent and The Dutch Courtesan.
- Thomas Middleton (1580-1627): Middleton was a poet and playwright who wrote a variety of genres, including comedies, tragedies, and romances. He wrote over 50 plays, including The Changeling and Women Beware Women.
- John Webster (1580-1634): Webster was a playwright who is best known for his tragedies, which often deal with themes of revenge and violence. He wrote over a dozen plays, including The Duchess of Malfi and The White Devil.
- Cyril Tourneur (c. 1575-1626): Tourneur was a playwright who wrote a number of tragedies, including The Revenger's Tragedy and The Atheist's Tragedy.
- Philip Massinger (1583-1640): Massinger was a playwright who wrote a variety of genres, including comedies, tragedies, and romances. He wrote over 30 plays, including A New Way to Pay Old Debts and The City Madam.
- James Shirley (1596-1666): Shirley was a playwright who wrote over 40 plays, including comedies, tragedies, and romances. He was one of the last playwrights to write for the public stage before the English Civil War closed the theaters in 1642.

Other notable Jacobean plays include:

- King Lear by William Shakespeare
- Macbeth by William Shakespeare
- The Duchess of Malfi by John Webster
- The Changeling by Thomas Middleton and William Rowley
- Volpone by Ben Jonson
- The Alchemist by Ben Jonson

In addition to drama, the Jacobean Age also saw the flourishing of other literary genres, such as poetry and prose. John Donne is one of the most famous Jacobean poets, and his work is known for its wit, passion, and religious devotion. Francis Bacon is one of the most famous Jacobean prose writers, and his work is known for its insights into philosophy and science.

Important years to be looked at :-

November 5, 1605:-The Gunpowder Plot fails to kill James I:-A group of English Catholics led by Guy Fawkes attempts and fails to blow up the Houses of Parliament on November 5, 1605. This is one of many unsuccessful assassination attempts against James I, who, as a Protestant, refuses to grant equal rights to Catholics.

1607:-English colonists establish the Jamestown colony in North America.(Spring 1607):-in 1606, the Virginia Company of London receives a charter from James I to settle lands between present-day North Carolina and the Potomac River in North America. In spring 1607, 105 English colonists establish the Jamestown colony, the first permanent English settlement in North America.

1610:-John Donne publishes Pseudo-Martyr:-The poet John Donne publishes Pseudo-Martyr, in which he argues that Roman Catholics can support James I without compromising their faith. Donne displays his extensive knowledge of the laws of Church and state throughout his works.

1611:-The King James version of the Bible appears:-James I comes into conflict with the Puritans, who call for simpler services and a more democratic church without bishops. James rejects their demands and calls for a new translation of the Bible. The King James version appears in 1611 and has a lasting influence on English language and literature.

1611:-Marcus Gheeraerts is commissioned to paint portraits of the royal family:-Marcus Gheeraerts, a Dutch painter who came to prominence in Queen Elizabeth's court, becomes a favorite of James I's queen Anne of Denmark. In 1611 he is commissioned to paint portraits of the king, queen, and princess. He remains a royal favorite until around 1617.

1615:-James I pressures John Donne to enter the Church:-James I pressures the metaphysical poet John Donne to enter the Anglican Ministry, claiming that Donne cannot be employed outside the Church. Donne is appointed Royal Chaplain later that year.

1616:-Ben Jonson becomes England's first Poet Laureate:-The poet and playwright Ben Jonson, a favorite of King James I, begins receiving a yearly pension in 1616. Many historians have thus identified Jonson as England's first Poet Laureate.

1617:-Paul van Somer settles in England.(c. 1617):-By 1617, the Flemish painter Paul van Somer settles in England and quickly becomes one of James and Anne's favorite court painters. He is a forerunner of later, more famous Flemish and Dutch artists.

1619:-Cornelius Johnson begins his English portraits:-The Dutch painter Cornelius Johnson settles in England, where he is active until 1643. He begins to paint portraits of the gentry in 1619, capturing their reticent attitudes in head, full-length, and group portraits.

1620:-Francis Bacon publishes Novum Organum:-Philosopher and essayist Francis Bacon publishes Novum Organum, which describes his belief that facts must be gathered and observed before coming to a conclusion. This idea revolutionizes scientific experimentation, since previous scientists relied on the methodology of only searching for examples that confirmed their conclusions.

November 1620:-The Mayflower lands in North America:-After receiving a royal charter to settle in North America, a group of Separatists on the Mayflower land in present-day Massachusetts. They establish the religious colony of Plymouth, which, along with Jamestown, creates an English foothold in North America.

1622:-Inigo Jones completes the Banqueting House:-After the Banqueting House at Whitehall is destroyed by fire in 1619, architect Inigo Jones replaces it with what comes to be seen as his greatest achievement. The new Banqueting House, completed in 1622, is the first fully realized Renaissance classical example of architecture in England.

November 1623:-The First Folio of Shakespeare's work is published:-In 1623, seven years after Shakespeare's death, the First Folio of Shakespeare's works is published. Shakespeare is active throughout James I's reign, publishing some of his best plays, including Macbeth and The Tempest.

March 27, 1625:-James I dies:-James I dies on March 27, 1625, and his son Charles I inherits the throne. The Jacobean Era comes to an end.

A Short note on Gunpowder Plot :-

The Gunpowder Plot was a plan to blow up the Houses of Parliament in London and kill the king. It is one of the most famous attempts to kill a king in <u>British history</u>. King James I was due to hold a ceremony on 5th November 1605 in the Houses of Parliament, and the plan was to hide barrels of gunpowder in the basement, which would then be set alight.

The plot was not only to kill the king, but also the queen, their son Prince Charles and every member of the government who would be at the ceremony. Beneath the Houses of Parliament, there were cellars that were used as storage spaces. These were rented out for the plot and gradually filled with a total of 36 barrels of gunpowder, with the intent of blowing up the buildings as well as everyone in them.

Who was involved in the plot?

The most famous man who was involved in the plot was <u>Guy Fawkes</u>. He and a group of other Roman Catholics were led by a man named Robert Catesby. Some of the other people involved were:

- Thomas Percy
- Francis Tresham
- John and Christopher Wright
- Thomas and Robert Winter
- Thomas Bates
- Ambrose Rookwood
- Sir Everard Digby
- Robert Keyes
- John Grant

They all had different roles in the plot; for example, Guy Fawkes' role was to set the barrels of gunpowder on fire, although he was caught red-handed before he could do so. Others were responsible for buying the gunpowder and other weapons for the conspiracy

Why did the Gunpowder Plot happen?

Guy Fawkes, Robert Catesby and the rest of the men were angry at the English government and the Protestant king for their mistreatment of Roman Catholics. They believed that Catholics were being treated unfairly under the Protestant rule.

When James I came to the English throne in 1603, there were already many conflicts between the Protestants and Roman Catholics. He had succeeded Elizabeth I, another Protestant royal, who didn't allow Catholics to practise their religion as they wanted to. James I's mother had been Catholic, so the Roman Catholics of England had hoped that he would present a fairer rule, but he instead ordered for all Catholic priests to leave England.

As a result of this, Guy Fawkes, Robert Catesby and the rest of the conspirators were all furious at the king and his decision. They believed that if they removed him from the throne, the King of Spain would claim it and he would treat Catholics more fairly.

Why did the Gunpowder Plot fail?

Despite their hopes, the Gunpowder Plot failed and Guy Fawkes was caught before he could blow up Parliament and remove the king from the throne. Lord Meagle, the brother-in-law of one of the conspirators, received an anonymous letter which warned him not to attend the Houses of Parliament on the night of November 5th. Monteagle immediately alerted the government of the warning.

Soldiers found Fawkes in the cellar and the plot was a failure; they arrested him and took him to the Tower of London, where he underwent three days of torture. After this torture, Fawkes eventually gave up the names of the rest of the conspirators. The rest of the men were arrested for treason (plotting against the king and his country). They were imprisoned at the Tower of London alongside Fawkes.

Months later, January 30th and 31st, the entire group of conspirators were executed in front of hundreds of people in London. Their heads were displayed on poles around the city as a warning of what would happen to others if they too committed treason.

After this, James I ordered that the people of England should have a bonfire night on November 5th every year to celebrate and remember his survival. Now, this day is known as Guy Fawkes Nigh or Bonfire Night. People celebrate with large bonfires, fireworks, and it's also commemorated by the famous poem 'Remember, remember, the 5th of November'.

Caroline Age in English Literature(1625-1649)

The Caroline Age in English literature, spanning around 1625–1649, is distinguished by its unique historical setting and literary traits. The Caroline Age in English literature, which ran roughly from 1625 to 1649, is distinguished by its unique historical setting and literary traits. Following the Jacobean period and bearing the name of King Charles I of England, this era is distinguished by a transitional stage that reflects the changing socio-political climate of the time. The Caroline Age was a reaction to King

Charles I's rule, which began in 1625 with his accession to the throne.

The emergence of theological issues and differences, as well as obstacles and tensions between the monarchy and Parliament, arose with the reign of this new ruler. During this time, political and social discontent reached a high point with the outbreak of the English Civil War and its immediate aftermath. Thus, the literature of the Caroline Age depicts this atmosphere of ambiguity and transition, providing insights into the changing literary genres, subjects, and issues that evolved as England reached one of its most important historical turning points.

Cultural and Historical Background

1.Political challenges and conflicts

The Caroline Age's cultural and historical context was shaped by complex political issues and conflicts that served as the catalyst for important changes in England. The increasing hostility between the monarchy and Parliament was one of its notable aspects. King Charles I tried to enforce his royal privileges, while Parliament wanted more power and influence. The monarchy wanted to preserve its previous dominance while Parliament attempted to establish its influence in the decision-making process. This struggle for dominance ended in a lengthy confrontation. These conflicts sparked a constitutional crisis and a subsequent power struggle that eventually led to the English Civil War. Thus, the Caroline Age is seen as a turning point in English history when these smothering political disputes started to emerge and change the country's direction.

2.Impact of religious divisions

The continuing religious struggle that had been a defining feature of prior times had a profound influence on the Caroline Age as well. As England struggled with the coexistence of several religious faiths, religious disagreements and debates persisted during this time. Religious identity and political allegiances were closely linked, and the schisms between Catholics, Protestants, and other Protestant sects remained unsolved. The competing influences of Puritanism and Anglicanism were particularly significant. The established Anglican Church faced a threat from the emergence of Puritanism, which was distinguished by its emphasis on reform and more stringent religious practices. The conflict between these two religious opinions widened already-existing societal fault lines and made things even more polarized and unpredictable. Religious conflicts had a significant influence on the Caroline Age's literature because authors grappled with issues of religion, morality, and power in the midst of this turbulent religious atmosphere.

Literature of the Caroline Age

1.Metaphysical Poetry Continuation

The literature of the Caroline Age carried on to expand on the works of the earlier Jacobean period, notably in the field of metaphysical poetry. This peculiar literary form, characterized by its intricate metaphors, depth of thought, and study of abstract ideas, found continuance in the Caroline Age. The works of poets like George Herbert and Richard Crashaw were influenced by the tradition and impact of Jacobean metaphysical poetry, which was epitomized by authors like John Donne. These poets continued the metaphysical philosophical tradition by exploring spirituality, the human condition, and the intersection of the heavenly and the earthly. Their poetry demonstrated deft wordplay and deep philosophical reflection, representing the intellectual and spiritual fervor of the time while introducing fresh perspectives to the continuing conversation started by their predecessors.

2.Cavalier Poetry

A unique literary trend known as cavalier poetry evolved during the Caroline Age, expressing a different aesthetic from the time's metaphysical poetry. Cavalier poetry mirrored the ideas and beliefs of the Royalists who supported King Charles I and was distinguished by its lightness, humor, and joyful tone. The poetry frequently reflected themes of carpe diem, or "seize the day," highlighting the fleeting nature of life and its joys. Poets like Robert Herrick and Thomas Carew were influential members of this movement; Herrick's poems like "To the Virgins, to Make Much of Time" serve as the perfect example of the carpe diem theme, which urges readers to seize the transitory chances presented by life. The mood of cavalier optimism and courtly elegance was also present in Carew's poetry. Cavalier poetry captured the spirit of the Caroline Age's social and cultural context and offered a lively counterbalance to the period's more reflective philosophical writing.

3.Drama and Playwrights

From the previous Jacobean era, the Caroline Age saw a change in dramatic approaches, as well as a major shift in the kinds of plays and performers that graced the stage. The Caroline era saw a change towards a more balanced approach, since the Jacobean age had been distinguished for its investigation of difficult moral quandaries and psychological depths. Tragicomedies, a unique genre that combined tragic and humorous aspects, became more popular. These plays used both emotional and hilarious moments in an effort to represent the synthesis of human emotions. John Ford's "The Lover's Melancholy," which mixed themes of love, lunacy, and wit, is a perfect example. Additionally, Caroline theatre had a reputation for courtly entertainment, which reflected the sophisticated tastes of the royal court. A layer of extravagance and grandeur was added to the theatrical environment of the time by productions like James Shirley's masques and entertainments, which appealed to the courtly audience's thirst for spectacle and refinement. This shift in dramatic idioms reflected the Caroline Age's shifting tastes and provided spectators with a wide variety of theatrical experiences.

4 Prose and Essays

In the Caroline Age, prose and essays provided a potent platform for commenting on the pressing political and ecclesiastical issues of the day. In order to address the issues at hand as tensions between the king and Parliament grew, authors turned to writing. They conveyed their opinions on issues of government, human rights, and societal order through writings. One such instance is John Milton's "The Tenure of Kings and Magistrates," in which he argued for the legitimacy of removing oppressive rulers and set forth ideas that would later resonate during the English Civil War. A significant impact on prose writing was also caused by the Civil War itself. As the conflict unfolded, prose works started to capture the intricacies of the conflict's aftermath, the difficulties of reestablishing society, and the moral quandaries that people on both sides of the struggle confronted. As a result, prose works turned into a reflection of the troubled times, portraying the Caroline Age's intellectual and emotional landscapes in a way that was both instructive and thought-provoking.

Key Themes and Characteristics

1. Political and Social Unrest

Being on the cusp of the English Civil War, the Caroline Age was profoundly influenced by themes of political and social upheaval. The literature of the period was pervaded by growing hostilities between the crown and Parliament. Writings like John Milton's "Areopagitica" show how authors wrestled with the ambiguity and fragility of the political situation. This piece, which defends press freedom, is a reflection of the political unrest of the time and the fight for individual rights in the face of escalating repression. The literature of the Caroline Age also explored power dynamics and societal issues, reflecting the nuanced interactions between rulers and subjects as well as the moral conundrums that people had to deal with while navigating a society that was in turmoil. The works from this historical period provides a glimpse into the complicated emotions and thoughts of people coping with a period of profound upheaval and uncertainty.

1. Reflection of Religious Debates

The literary discourse of the Caroline Age included discussions of religion often, reflecting the ongoing social divisions. Both poets and prose authors discussed religious ideas, shedding light on the period's many theological stances. George Herbert's poetry, particularly the poems in his book "The Temple," is an excellent example of this interest in spiritual issues. The poetry of Herbert examine the intricacies of spirituality, the human experience, and the battle to balance worldly reality with heavenly truths. Similarly, prose works like John Bunyan's allegorical novel "The Pilgrim's Progress" provide a vivid illustration of religious questions. Bunyan discusses salvation, temptation, and the challenges of faith in the metaphorical journey of Christian; this topic resonates with readers from varied religious backgrounds and reflects the religious diversity of the time. Thus, the literary works of the Caroline Age present a tapestry of theological viewpoints, illuminating the intricate interaction between religion and society dynamics during this transformative period.

3. Carpe Diem Motif

The timeless "carpe diem" theme, which urges people to grasp the day and cherish life's transitory moments, was adopted by the literature of the Caroline Age. As the Civil War approached and society struggled with political and religious unrest, this motif struck a profound chord with the angst of the day. This philosophy was captured in the writings of poets like Robert Herrick, especially in poems like "To the Virgins, to Make Much of Time," which urged readers to enjoy the moment. Herrick's verses serve as a gentle reminder that life is transient and emphasise the value of savouring the moments of happiness and pleasure. The Caroline Age poets captured the spirit of life at a period when nothing was definite and emphasised the value of the present moment through the use of the carpe diem motif, which resonated with both the personal and the collective.

4. Notable Figures of the Caroline Age

The Caroline Age included a number of notable figures who had a lasting impact on English literature and culture. King Charles I, after whom the era is called, was an important figure of the period. His reign, which was characterized by political upheaval and religious strife, had a significant impact on the topics and issues of literature of the time. Famous poet and clergyman George Herbert is renowned for his profound philosophical poetry that examined the relationship between spirituality and the human experience. His "The Temple" series is an evidence of his capacity for blending devotion with creative expression. Significant Cavalier poets like Robert Herrick and Thomas Carew made their mark on the thriving poetry scene of the time. Carew's poetry emanated courtly elegance and reflected the refined attitude of the royal court, whereas Herrick's rhymes represented the carpe diem motif and urged readers to appreciate life's transitory joys. Collectively, these significant individuals represent the intricate and dynamic literary, political, and cultural influences that molded the Caroline Age, leaving behind a legacy that continues to deepen our understanding of this transformative period.

Conclusion:

To sum up, the Caroline Age, which roughly lasted from 1625 to 1649, was a time marked by the complex interaction of political issues, religious conflicts, and creative literary manifestations. The period's literature mirrored the anxieties, aspirations, and intellectual ferment of the time, which was characterised by the conflicts between the king and Parliament as well as the impact of continuous religious disputes. Metaphysical poetry remained popular, while Cavalier poets praised life's joys in a contrasting manner. This literary tapestry was woven by key figures including King Charles I, George Herbert, Robert Herrick, and Thomas Carew. The Caroline Age was important in moulding the development of English literature because it provided a nuanced portrayal of the intricacies of the time, which would later reverberate in the upheavals of the English Civil War and beyond.

Commonwealth Period in English Literature(1649-1660)

The Commonwealth Period in English literature, a distinctive and tumultuous period in the country's history, is defined by its political backdrop and repercussions. The Republican governance that was established after King Charles I's execution during this 1649–1660 time frame marked a shift from monarchical control. The English Civil War, a protracted, catastrophic battle that had torn the country apart, had ended when the Commonwealth Period began.

This conflict was fought between Parliamentarians, who wanted more political influence and religious change, and Royalists, who backed the monarchy and its established power. King Charles I's execution in 1649 marked the end of this conflict and marked a radical break from centuries of monarchical governance in England. This execution was a turning point in history that led to the establishment of the Commonwealth under Oliver Cromwell's direction and altered the cultural and political circumstances of the country. The literature of the Commonwealth Period reflects this turbulent context by examining themes of political upheaval, religious passion, and the pursuit of stability at a period of significant change.

Cultural and Historical Background

The growing impact of Puritanism was one of this era's most significant characteristics. Puritans, who upheld strict religious beliefs and worked to reform the Church of England, were crucial in establishing the social, moral, and cultural norms of the Commonwealth era. Their emphasis on morality, simplicity, and religious piety had a significant impact. Beyond theological issues, this Puritan influence had a big impact on a lot of different areas of life, including politics, education, and cultural expression.

Puritan principles led to the suppression of many creative and recreational pursuits because they were seen as morally destructive. Puritans held that entertainment and the arts frequently promoted moral slackness and diverted people from their spiritual obligations. In order to promote a more solemn and subdued social atmosphere, theaters were shut down and traditional social events were cut back. That is why, the Commonwealth Period saw a sharp decline in the vibrant cultural environment of earlier times due to the prohibition of artistic and theatrical activity.

Literature of the Commonwealth Period

1 Poetry of Dissent and Controversy

The Commonwealth Period is known for its distinctive style of poetry, which captures dissent and controversy while providing deep insights into the political and religious issues of the age. Poets of this period were intensely conscious of the turbulent terrain and utilized their verses to address the significant changes taking place in England. They participated in the discussion of the pressing political and religious issues, expressing their divergent opinions and questioning accepted conventions. Poetry evolved into a tool that poets could use to tackle the complicated issues of this period of acute intellectual and ideological change.

John Milton was one of the most significant writers in this literary period. His writings, particularly the epic masterwork "Paradise Lost," serve as an excellent example of the complexity and depth of the political and religious discussions that characterized the Commonwealth Period. Themes of human agency, the nature of evil, and the consequences of disobedience are all explored by Milton in "Paradise Lost," all of which resonated with the unstable circumstances of the Commonwealth era. Furthermore, Milton's "Areopagitica," a defense of freedom of expression, became the foundation of arguments for free speech and open conversation at this time.

2.Religious and Philosophical Prose

The Commonwealth Period was characterized by strong theological disputes and the publication of treatises that addressed difficult issues of faith, government, and personal conscience. A flurry of religious inquiry was stimulated by the period's turbulent ecclesiastical atmosphere, which was characterized by the emergence of Puritanism and the destruction of the Church of England's established structure. Scholars like Richard Baxter and John Owen participated in theological debates on a variety of subjects, including salvation, church structure, and the role of the individual in issues of religion. These treatises represented the theological plurality and fervor of the time, when several religious factions sought to express their beliefs and proclaim their ideals for the church and society.

John Bunyan's "The Pilgrim's Progress" is among the most enduring and illustrative pieces of Christian literature from the Commonwealth Period. The theological and intellectual ideals of the day were captured in this allegorical story, which served as both a religious and philosophical masterpiece. Christian's journey served as a metaphor for Bunyan's exploration of spiritual truths, obstacles to faith, and the quest for salvation. Readers looking for spiritual direction and comfort amidst the significant upheavals and difficulties of the Commonwealth era found "The Pilgrim's Progress" to be of great resonance. In addition to making a significant contribution to the theological and philosophical debate of the day, Bunyan's writing also received long-lasting literary praise, becoming a pillar of English literature and a representation of the spiritual search that characterized the time.

Key Themes and Characteristics

1. Exploration of Political and Religious Ideals

Reflecting the volatile and transformational nature of the time, the Commonwealth Period in English literature was characterized by an in-depth study of political and theological principles. Discussions regarding government and individual freedom were one major issue. After the monarchy was overthrown and a republic was founded, new issues regarding the function of the government and the rights of its people emerged in English society. The nature of political power, the boundaries of governance, and the duties of rulers and citizens were major subjects of debate among writers and intellectuals. These discussions created the intellectual foundation for democratic and republican principles to emerge, which would go on to influence political thought for centuries to come. John Milton's writings, especially his book "The Tenure of Kings and Magistrates," were representative of this issue since he upheld the legality of overthrowing oppressive rulers and argued for the legitimacy of a people's right to self-government. The literature of the Commonwealth Period became known for its examination of government and individual freedom, which was a reflection of the significant political upheavals occurring at the time.

The relationship between political order and religion was another major issue. Questions of religious belief and practice became more prominent in political debate with the emergence of Puritanism and the founding of the Commonwealth. The question of how religious ideas should influence governmental structure and ruler behavior has been debated by authors. This issue permeated philosophical discussions regarding the moral foundations of political power. The interaction between religion and the political system was explored in the writings of this time period, including Milton's "Areopagitica" and works by other religious and political intellectuals. They questioned the necessity of a religious foundation for governance, the propriety of enforcing religious conformity, and the viability of accommodating religious plurality within a republic. The investigation of these intricate and interconnected subjects highlighted the Commonwealth Period's intellectual depth and ideological diversity, making it a crucial period in the development of political and religious thinking in England.

2. Suppression of Artistic Expression

The Puritan principles that predominated during the Commonwealth Period directly contributed to the suppression of artistic expression. A stringent version of Protestantism known as Puritanism tried to purify the Church of England by eradicating perceived corruption and placing a focus on moral and theological purity. This religious movement had a significant impact on English society, culture, and the arts. Many creative and recreational pursuits, especially those connected to theater, were seen by Puritans as morally corrupting and diverting from spiritual matters. Thereby they deliberately tried to stifle these forms of expression. Theaters were shut down, and various types of amusement and celebration were curtailed to promote a more solemn and subdued cultural environment.

The literary and cultural climate of the time was significantly impacted by this suppression. Puritan principles imposed restrictions on writers and artists, and they frequently found alternate means to communicate their ideas. The change from secular to religious themes in literature and the arts was one important result. Many writers turned to religious themes and allegory as a source of expression once traditional entertainment and secular narrative were suppressed. This change is best illustrated by John Bunyan's "The Pilgrim's Progress," which employed allegorical narrative to teach significant religious and moral teachings. Other authors, who reflected the prevailing ethos of the time, wrote on moral and religious issues in their writings.

Notable Figures of the Commonwealth Period

A number of noteworthy figures contributed to religious and literary expression throughout the Commonwealth Period in English literature, profoundly influencing the intellectual and cultural milieu of their day.

John Milton was a genius poet, essayist, and pamphleteer whose works captured the turbulent spirit of the Commonwealth. He is perhaps one of the most renowned individuals from this time period. The complex theological and political topics he explored in his epic poem "Paradise Lost" were the essence of evil, human agency, and the effects of rebellion. Milton promoted free speech and the unrestricted flow of ideas in his prose, especially in "Areopagitica," and he argued that these aspects are crucial in a republican society.

Another notable author from the Commonwealth Era, John Bunyan, wrote the epic allegorical work "The Pilgrim's Progress." This classic work truly reflected the moral and religious ambitions of the day and gave readers a spiritual journey through the struggles and victories of the protagonist, Christian. An example of the enduring power of spiritual narrative, Bunyan's allegory is now considered a masterpiece of Christian literature.

Known for his lyrical poetry and political works, Andrew Marvell demonstrated a deep involvement with the political and theological issues of the day. His poems frequently combined introspective meditation with larger societal issues, capturing the ambiguities and complexities of the Commonwealth period.

A well-known Puritan theologian named Richard Baxter wrote a number of theological treatises that addressed questions of salvation, religion, and church organization. His writings, such as "The Reformed Pastor," are still studied today for their insights into pastoral care and Puritan theology.

Conclusion

In conclusion, the Commonwealth Period in English literature, which covers from 1649 to 1660, is characterized by political upheaval, intense religious fervor, and in-depth intellectual inquiry. The literature of this time period is characterized by major themes of political opposition, discussions of governance and individual liberty, the interaction between faith and political order, and the repression of artistic expression.

The English Civil War:-A short Note

The English Civil War was a pivotal conflict that fundamentally reshaped the relationship between the monarchy and Parliament. By 1642, Charles I and Parliament were in open conflict, and the King's decision to leave London and raise his battle standard in Nottingham marked the official beginning of the war. Despite early hopes, the fighting soon reached a stalemate, with neither side able to decisively overpower the other. However, the arrival of the New Model Army, led by Oliver Cromwell, shifted the balance of power, and the Royalist forces were ultimately defeated. In the end, Charles I was captured, and England's monarchy was brought to its knees.

The Cavaliers

Those who supported King Charles I were known as Royalists, or more commonly, Cavaliers.

- The term Cavalier comes from the Spanish word caballero, meaning armed trooper or horseman. It reflected the Royalist tendency to fight mounted on horseback, particularly among the aristocracy.

- The Cavaliers were typically gentry and wealthy landowners, who wanted to preserve the traditional social hierarchy and maintain the power of the monarchy over Parliament.
- Geographically, most of the King's support came from the north and west of England, regions where royalist sentiment was stronger and where many large estates were located.

The Roundheads

On the opposing side, those who fought for Parliament were known as Parliamentarians or Roundheads.

- The term Roundhead was coined due to the distinctive short, cropped haircuts of the Parliamentary supporters, particularly the London apprentices who had become prominent in Parliament's struggle against the King.
- The Roundheads were a broad mix of people, including merchants, traders, and small landowners, many of whom were frustrated with Charles I's heavy taxation and his attempts to bypass Parliamentary control over spending.
- Support for Parliament was strongest in the south of England, especially London, where the economy was dominated by trade and commerce, and where the Parliamentary cause had significant backing.

The conflict often divided families and communities, with some choosing sides based on personal, political, or religious beliefs. In many areas, there was significant internal strife, as people struggled to reconcile their loyalties to the King or to Parliament.

Oliver Cromwell and the New Model Army

A key figure in the Parliamentary cause was Oliver Cromwell, a Puritan and a strong advocate for the abolition of the monarchy.

- Cromwell was the Member of Parliament for Cambridge and was deeply committed to seeing the monarchy dismantled in favour of a republic. His dedication and organisational skills made him one of the leading figures in Parliament's military campaigns.

Creation of the New Model Army:

- In February 1645, Cromwell played a crucial role in establishing the New Model Army, Britain's first professional army. Unlike previous armies, which were often poorly organised and undisciplined, the New Model Army was highly structured, disciplined, and ideologically motivated.

Key Features of the New Model Army:

- Skilled Soldiers: The army consisted of battle-hardened soldiers, many of whom were devout Protestants with strong religious convictions.
- Merit-based Promotion: Unlike traditional armies, where promotion often depended on social status, Cromwell's army promoted soldiers based on ability and achievement. This led to a more effective and capable force.
- Religious Influence: Every regiment had its own religious minister who helped ensure that soldiers stayed true to their beliefs and the cause they were fighting for.
- High Pay: Soldiers in the New Model Army were paid better than in previous armies, which helped ensure their loyalty and morale.

The creation of the New Model Army not only revolutionised military tactics and discipline but also played a decisive role in determining the outcome of the war.

The Battle of Naseby

On 16 June 1645, the New Model Army, led by Cromwell, engaged in the Battle of Naseby, which marked a turning point in the war.

- The Battle of Naseby, fought near the village of Naseby in Northamptonshire, was the first major engagement for the New Model Army. It resulted in a decisive victory for the Parliamentarians.
- The Royalist forces were routed, and Charles I's army was effectively destroyed. This victory shattered the Royalist hopes of winning the war and significantly boosted the morale of the Parliamentarians.
- After Naseby, the Royalist strongholds, such as Bristol and Oxford, fell into Parliamentarian hands, and by 1647, Charles I himself was captured, bringing the war to a turning point.

The Second Civil War

Even after Charles I's capture, conflict was not over, and the Second Civil War erupted due to political and religious developments.

Charles's Negotiations:

- While a prisoner, Charles I attempted to negotiate with Parliament and sought to end the war. However, he also secretly pursued a strategy to gain Scottish support for his cause, promising to establish a Presbyterian Church in England similar to the Church of Scotland if the Scots would support him against Parliament.

Scottish Invasion:

- In 1648, the Scottish army, backed by Charles I, invaded England in an attempt to reinforce the Royalist cause and re-ignite the civil war. This led to the Second Civil War.

- However, the Scottish army was defeated at the Battle of Preston in 1648, marking the final defeat of Royalist military efforts.

Division within Parliament:

- The Scottish invasion and Charles's continued attempts to incite rebellion convinced many Roundheads that Charles could not be trusted. They felt that negotiating with him would be dangerous and that he should be punished rather than pardoned.

By the time the Second Civil War ended, Charles I was firmly in the hands of Parliament, but the political divisions between the king and Parliament had escalated to the point where negotiations were no longer seen as possible. His continued pursuit of his royalist cause, even after being captured, solidified the belief among many Parliamentarians that he was a tyrant unfit for rule.

The end of the war and the execution of Charles I in 1649 marked the dramatic conclusion of the English Civil War and the start of a brief period without a monarchy. This period, known as the Commonwealth, would radically change the course of British history.

Restoration Age in English Literature(1660-1700)

In English literature, the Restoration Age was a significant period of revival and change that was characterized by its historical backdrop and the rise of the monarchy. Following the chaotic <u>Commonwealth Period</u>, it began in 1660 with King Charles II's restoration of the monarchy. The restoration of the monarchy brought significant political and cultural shifts to England after years of unrest. The restoration of the monarchy had a significant effect since it represented a return to order and a reaffirmation of traditional ideals. It ushered in a thriving period of creative and literary rebirth, as theaters reopened their doors, the arts thrived once again, and a spirit of optimism swept the country.

During this time, new literary forms and subjects emerged, interacting dynamically with the courtly culture of Charles II's court. The writing of the Restoration Age, which was characterized by humor, satire, and a rethinking of social conventions, represented the intricacies of this period and was essential in influencing the development of English literature and culture in the years that followed.

The Cultural and Historical Background

The Restoration Age's cultural and historical context was a dynamic and evolving one that significantly influenced the literature and artistic creations of the time.

Social developments and the court's influence

After the monarchy was restored under King Charles II, English society underwent a significant transition. Charles II's court, known for its refinement, hedonism, and pursuit of pleasure, had a big influence on social norms and preferences of the time. Fashion, etiquette, the arts, and literature were all impacted by court culture in addition to fashion and manners. The courtly culture of wit and elegance became a salient aspect of Restoration society, and this influence extended to the period's literary works, giving rise to the "Comedy of Manners" in which social behavior and norms were parodied and criticized.

Reopening of theaters and rebirth of the arts

Reopening of theaters was one of the most important developments of the Restoration Age. Theaters had been shut down during the Commonwealth Period, but once the monarchy was restored, they were once more allowed to run. The performing arts and English play had a revival as a result. Theatrical groups, playwrights, and actors all enjoyed great success, creating a wide variety of works that reflected the tastes and spirit of the time. The theater developed into a thriving setting for satire, social commentary, and investigation of modern values.

Change in literary preferences and sensibilities:

There was a noticeable change in literary preferences and sensibilities throughout the Restoration Era. The political and religious themes that had dominated prior eras, such the Commonwealth Period, were abandoned. Instead, writing of this time period emphasized the complexity of human behavior, etiquette, and social norms. Authors started to examine the nuances of individual psychology and relationships in their writings as wit, satire, and humor were appreciated. The emergence of the "Comedy of Manners" and the examination of the vices and follies of the higher classes are two examples where this shift in sensibility was most noticeable.

Literature of the Restoration Age

1. <u>Comedy of Manners</u>

During the Restoration Period, the <u>Comedy of Manners</u> developed into a distinctive literary form that captured the wit, intelligence, and social norms of the time. Sharp sarcastic comments on the manners and conduct of the English upper classes was a defining feature of this genre. The complexity of social interaction, love, and relationships within the aristocracy was expertly portrayed in plays by playwrights like William Wycherley, William Congreve, and George Etherege.

<u>Comedies of Manners</u> frequently featured morally dubious protagonists who engaged in clever and occasionally scathing dialogue while navigating the complexities of courting, marriage, and social rank. Themes including the pursuit of pleasure, marriage as a business transaction, and the fragility of societal standards were frequently investigated. These works challenged conventional norms and parodied the vices of the upper classes, offering not only amusement but also a critical mirror to the society of their day.

For instance, <u>"The Way of the World"</u> by William Congreve explores the complexities of courting and marriage while exposing the at times mercenary nature of love relationships among the affluent. These plays not only kept spectators amused, but they also provided insightful reflection on the moral standards and manners of Restoration society. <u>The Comedy of Manners</u>, with its clever banter and cutting sarcasm, perfectly reflecting the social complexity and cultural vitality of the time.

2. **Heroic Drama**

During the Restoration Era, heroic drama was a notable literary subgenre distinguished by its distinctive fusion of dramatic elements, epic subjects, and the influence of French neoclassical drama. The neoclassical values of restraint, unity of time and place, and devotion to traditional dramatic structure had a significant impact on this genre.

Heroic theater's structure and themes can be traced to French neoclassical theater, particularly the works of Pierre Corneille and Jean Racine. In addition to adhering to the traditional unities of time, place, and action, these plays frequently featured noble and heroic individuals caught up in serious conflicts. One of the leading playwrights of the time, John Dryden, is known for writing several famous Heroic Dramas, such as "The Conquest of Granada" and "Aureng-Zebe." Drawing on classical models, Dryden mixed elements of tragedy and epic in these works while addressing themes of dignity, love, and political intrigue. With reference to classical models and an exploration of topics such as honor, love, and political intrigue, Dryden blended aspects of tragedy and epic in his works.

In contrast to the farcical and sarcastic comedies of the day, heroic drama offered viewers a more somber and refined kind of entertainment. Heroic drama contributed to the variety of dramatic forms in the Restoration era, demonstrating the age's obsession with themes of courage, honor, and virtue even though it didn't have the same enduring appeal as the <u>Comedy of Manners.</u>

3. Restoration Poetry

With a focus on humor, satire, and sharp social commentary, restoration poetry in the late 17th and early 18th centuries mirrored the shifting sensibilities and tastes of the time. The literary landscape of this time period was significantly shaped by poets like John Dryden and Alexander Pope, who dealt with the complicated issues of the time.

Restoration poetry was greatly enriched by wit and satire. Wit, which is characterized by deft wordplay and sharp humor, was highly valued and frequently used to mock the follies and pretensions of the upper classes and society at large. In poems like "Absalom and Achitophel," poets like John Dryden employed satire to make statements about political and social issues. They frequently drew caricatures of famous people to illustrate their arguments. The sarcastic and humorous poetry of Dryden in particular were well-known for criticizing the social, political, and moral milieu of the day.

Alexander Pope, a notable figure in Restoration poetry, contributed to the growth of the satirical genre with his cutting-edge wit and astute assessment of society. By comically exaggerating an apparently inconsequential event, his "The Rape of the Lock" mocked the frivolities and vanity of high society. Pope's "The Dunciad" was a caustic parody of the deterioration of literary and intellectual standards and a condemnation of the society at the time.

Key Themes and Characteristics

1. Exploration of Morality and Social Mores

In English literature, the Restoration Period is known for its thorough study of morality and social mores, as well as its sarcastic depiction of societal conventions and reflection of shifting moral beliefs. Literature evolved into a medium through which these developments were both examined and critiqued.

Satirical techniques were commonly used by authors of the Restoration era to expose the vices and follies of the affluent. For instance, the superficiality, vanity, and lack of morality of the upper class were satirized in <u>The Comedy of Manners</u>. These plays frequently featured ethically dubious characters who engaged in witty and occasionally biting repartee while navigating the difficulties of societal customs.

Additionally, this time period showed a shift in moral values and a more open discussion of subjects that had previously been forbidden. The literature of the time reflects the moral permissiveness that characterized King Charles II's reign. Satire was a tool employed by writers like John Dryden and Alexander Pope to critique social injustice, governmental duplicity, and societal moral dilemmas.

2. Reimagining of Gender Roles

The Restoration Age led to a rethinking of gender roles in English literature and culture, indicating a change in how women and femininity were portrayed. The historical significance of the introduction of the first female actors on stage contributed to this transition.

Since women were not allowed to participate on stage in previous eras, young boys were frequently cast in female parts in theater. But during the Restoration, women started making their first stage appearances in England. This change had a significant influence on how women are portrayed in literature in addition to revolutionizing the theater.

In Restoration plays, female characters were frequently portrayed as clever, smart, and forceful, especially in the <u>Comedy of Manners.</u> These characters questioned established gender roles and expectations. One of the first well-known female playwrights, Aphra Behn, established strong, multidimensional female heroines who participated in witty banter and actively pursued their desires.

In addition to other literary genres, the theatre was not the only place where gender norms were being reimagined. Through their writing, female authors like Aphra Behn helped to reevaluate women's opinions and responsibilities in society. Themes of love, desire, and female liberty were frequently explored in Behn's writings, which challenged conventional ideas of femininity.

Notable Figures of the Restoration Age

A number of well-known figures who lived during the Restoration Period had a profound impact on English literature and drama.

The "Father of English Criticism," as John Dryden is frequently referred to, was a renowned poet and writer of the restoration period. He produced works in a variety of genres, such as poetry, drama, and critical essays. In poems like "Absalom and Achitophel" and "Annus Mirabilis," Dryden demonstrated his skill in political analysis and satire. His neoclassical approach to theater, which is apparent in works like "All for Love" and "The Indian Emperor," had an enormous impact on the conventional dramatic traditions of the time.

Aphra Behn stands as one of the era's pioneering female playwrights and novelists. Her writings disregarded conventional gender roles and revolutionized the literary representation of women. Behn's plays, like "The Rover," were renowned for their clever and audacious handling of love and desire. She was one of the pioneering female authors who made a living as a professional writer, shattering stereotypes and opening doors for ensuing generations of female authors.

William Wycherley, who was well-known for his witty satirical comedies, played an important role in the development of the Comedy of Manners. His skill at humorous dialogue and social commentary were displayed in works like "The Country Wife" and "The Plain Dealer," which criticized the manners and morality of Restoration society.

Another notable figure of the time, William Congreve, received recognition for his contributions to the Comedy of Manners. His works, such as "The Way of the World" and "Love for Love," are prime examples of the genre's emphasis on the difficulties of love, marriage, and societal behavior. Congreve gained recognition in the restoration period as a result of his extremely sharp wit and deft wordplay.

Conclusion:

In conclusion, the Restoration Age in English literature was a dynamic and transformative time marked by its witty comedies, sarcastic poetry, and a rewriting of social standards. Authors like John Dryden, Aphra Behn, William Wycherley, and William Congreve made a lasting impression on literature by creating works that are still enjoyable and thought-provoking.

Following the turbulent <u>Commonwealth Period</u>, this period, which was characterized by the restoration of the monarchy under King Charles II, saw a resurgence of vigor, artistic expression, and intellectual inquiry.

Restoration Theatre | Restoration Drama Characteristics

Under Puritan rigidity, the English theater underwent a particularly difficult time. After Charles I's deposition in the same year (1642), the theater, which had seen tremendous popularity throughout the reigns of Elizabeth and the Stuarts, was formally closed by an order of Parliament. Up to the reinstatement of the monarchy in 1660, theater was not permitted to be performed in public and was inactive.

Charles II was reinstated to the throne in 1660. After a long twenty years of official silence during the Puritan's rule, drama also formally returned to England. The English people's thirst for this was undoubtedly unaffected by the 20-year absence of theatrical entertainment. However, the plays that were performed for them were remarkably dissimilar from those of the Elizabethan era and the early seventeenth century. With the civil war, something in England perished. Particularly in dramatic writing, one could experience that intense yet frequently elusive sensation of loss.

Characteristics of Restoration drama

The Elizabethan theater's spontaneity seems to have vanished. The dramatist's personal perspective on life vanished. Drama has, in some ways, become arrogant, fake, and overly staged. The primary source of the dramatists' dramatic ideas became court life, with all its mannerisms, immorality, and illusory glory. Of course, this new trend in the theater was noticed over time rather than right once. Through Dryden's "The Wild Gallant" and Etherege's "Love in a Tub," it became blatantly apparent in the world of comedy.

Changes in theatrical technique also occurred. Stage equipment became necessary, and moveable scenery started to be utilized. Actresses were then brought in to perform female roles. Compared to the Elizabethan era, the Restoration era's audience had a different makeup. The Restoration theater became a hub of obscene behavior and cheap entertainment for dishonest courtiers and haughty royalists. As a result, the dramatic works—especially the comedies—were extremely licentious.

Heroic Plays of Restoration age

The heroic plays that replaced serious tragic dramas marked the beginning of the Restoration theatre's new fashion. The incredible adventures that certain heroic individuals undertook were the basis of heroic plays. Heroic feats, dramatic events, and bombastic reactions were performed in front of a crowded theater. Heroic playwrights include John Dryden, the principal architect, Sir Robert Howard, and Davenant, the pioneers.

As a middle ground between tragedy and romance, the heroic plays of the Restoration seem to be in a class by themselves. Chivalrous-honor, love, and conflict are the principal topics of these plays. A romantic scene is used to try to illustrate the tension between love and honor. In the heroic plays, heroic characters are shown as having superhuman abilities and acting or expressing somewhat differently from the normal. The fight between love and honor in a heroic character or personalities is the main focus of the entire action, to some extent.

The main honor of the Restoration theater, however, goes to Dryden, the greatest writer of the time. Between 1669 and 1677, he successfully continued his theatrical career with "Tyrannic Love" or "The Royal Martyr", "The Conquest of Granada" by the Spaniards, in two parts, "Aureng-Zebe" or "The Great Mughol". His famous play, "All for Love," is regarded as both a tragedy and a heroic play.

But in the English theatre of the Restoration, the heroic plays don't appear to have had a long and illustrious career. It reached its pinnacle with Dryden and nearly fell with him. Its supremacy was quickly displaced by the Restoration's social comedy of manners, which was more in line with the spirit of the time.

Restoration tragedy

However, despite being significantly overshadowed by the heroic, tragic plays are still represented in the history of the Restoration theater. The Elizabethan tragedy lacks both the elegant allure and tragic grandeur of the Restoration tragedy.

The Restoration tragedy was mostly known for Dryden. His "All for Love" (or The World Well Lost), which was written in emulation of Shakespeare's classic play "Antony and Cleopatra" in 1677, is particularly notable in the annals of English tragedy. The form of Dryden's tragedy is traditional, and it adheres meticulously to the idea of three unities. The play is without a doubt Dryden's best, and is perhaps the finest Restoration tragedy, despite contrasts from <u>Shakespeare</u>'s classic Roman drama in its concept and characters.

However, Thomas Otway stands out as the most notable figure in the Restoration tragedy because his two potent plays, "The Orphan" and "Venice Preserved", have enhanced the stature of this tragedy on their own. Otway has created tragic feelings using a fully human approach, as though he knows the key to the tragic emotion. A sincere tragic emotion takes the place of the foolishness of circumstances or of verbal bombast. In later times, Otway's tragedies garner more honor and fame than Dryden's. In contrast to Dryden's, they are not heroic tragedies. These plays are more closely related to the category of domestic tragedy that includes "Othello" by <u>Shakespeare</u> and <u>"The Duchess of Malfi"</u> by Webster.

Restoration comedy:

However, comedies are the main genre in which the Restoration theater excels. These comedies are discovered to have a variety of aspects, including farcical comedy, <u>comedy of manners</u>, comedy of intrigue, and comedy of humor. The clever, entertaining lighthearted comedies of the era may have best captured the sentiment of the people who had just been freed from the stringent restrictions of the Puritans.

Again, Dryden is at the center of the Restoration comedy with works like "The Assignation", "The Spanish Friar", "Wild Gallant", and "Marriage a la Mode". However, despite the fact that he uses excellent effects in dialogue, his achievement is limited.

It's been discovered that the Restoration comedies' humor mimics that of the Jonsonian comedies. Early Restoration comedists like Shadwell, Sadley, Crowne, and a few others appear to have been inspired by Ben Johnson's comedy of humor; yet, their feeble attempts to emulate the great Elizabethan master only serve to highlight their weak dramatic abilities.

Neoclassical Age in English Literature

Neoclassicism and romanticism are often considered to be opposing movements. The main difference between neoclassicism and romanticism is that neoclassicism emphasized on objectivity, order, and restraint whereas romanticism emphasized on imagination and emotion.

• What is neoclassicism ?

Neoclassicism is a movement in literature that drew inspiration from the classical age. The writers of this period tried to imitate the style of Greeks and Romans. This movement, which was a reaction against the renaissance, lasted from about 1660 and 1798. John Milton, Alexander Pope, Voltaire, John Dryden, Jonathan Swift and Daniel Defoe are some well-known neoclassical writers. Parody, essays, satire, novels and poetry are some popular genres in this movement.

Neoclassicism was based on classical themes and forms. Structure, restraint, simplicity, decorum, order, logic, and objectivity were the main features of neoclassical literature. These were classical virtues which neoclassical writers admired and attempted to imitate. In his "An Essay on Criticism", Alexander Pope describes the benefits of order and restraint as follows.

"Tis more to guide than spur the Muse's Steed;

Restrain his Fury, than provoke his Speed;

The winged Courser, like a gen'rous Horse,

Shows most true Mettle when you check his Course"

This movement can be typically divided into three periods:

The Restoration Age (1660 to 1700): This period marks the British King's restoration to the throne. It is marked by Classical influence.

The Augustan Age (1700 to 1750): The Augustans believed that their period was similar to that of Augustus Ceaser in Rome, which was a period of tranquility and stability.

The Age of Johnson (1750 to 1798): Also called the Age of Transition, this stage was marked by the upcoming Romantic ideals and influence and slow transition from neoclassical ideals to romantic ones.

An Introduction to the Neoclassical:-

The Neoclassical period, sometimes referred to as the Augustan Age, was characterized by the resurgence of classical forms and ideals that were taken from classical Greek and Roman literature. It lasted roughly from 1700 to 1798. In an attempt to imitate the harmony and clarity of ancient antiquity, this era places a strong emphasis on reason, order, and restraint. Neoclassical writers emphasized logical exposition and ordered forms; they frequently used wit and sarcasm to question moral principles and modern society. Their compositions followed the norms of classical art, fostering an aesthetic that valued accuracy, discipline, and harmony.

Historical Context

After the turbulent years of the English Civil War and the interregnum, stability and order returned to England during the post-Restoration era, which gave rise to the Neoclassical period. This was a response to the alleged emotionalization and excesses of the earlier Baroque and Renaissance periods. In an effort to bring balance and clarity back to both literature and social discourse, Neoclassical writers and philosophers looked to the classical virtues of moderation, reason, and formal structure.

Key Characteristics

1. Rationalism and Order

The Enlightenment values that emphasized reason and clarity are reflected in the Neoclassical period's emphasis on rationalism and order. Inspired by the literature of classical Greece and Rome, writers of this age followed ordered patterns and classical norms. Heroic couplets, a type of rhymed iambic pentameter that came to define Neoclassical poetry, are a clear example of this regard. "The Rape of the Lock" by Alexander Pope, for example, demonstrates the accuracy and refinement of this form by using it to deliver a sarcastic commentary on the fripperies of aristocratic life. Similar to this, the plays of John Dryden, whose "All for Love" exhibits a methodical approach to character development and storytelling, demonstrate how the dramatic works of this era conformed to classical unities of place, time, and action.

2. Satire and wit

Neoclassical literature relied heavily on satire and wit as literary devices for social criticism and thought-provoking dialogue. Satire is a tool employed by writers to highlight and ridicule the vices and foibles of modern politics, society, and human nature. This use of satire is best illustrated by Jonathan Swift's "Gulliver's Travels", which uses magical metaphor to expose the corruption and absurdity of human behavior.

Similar to this, Alexander Pope satirizes the petty worries of the upper classes in "The Rape of the Lock" by using witty language and blunt humor. The writings of Joseph Addison and Richard Steele, who used humor and perceptive observation to remark on social etiquette and standards through publications like "The Spectator", further demonstrate the era's dedication to wit.

3. Adherence to Classical Forms

One characteristic of Neoclassical literature that set it apart was its adherence to classical forms, which demonstrated a profound regard for the elegantly constructed works of the ancient Greeks and Romans. The heroic couplet, which consists of rhymed pairs of iambic pentameter lines, rose to prominence in poetry. This structure made it possible to express ideas in a structured but adaptable way, which was perfect for satire and philosophical thought. This technique is best demonstrated by Alexander Pope's "The Rape of the Lock", where the sardonic and in-depth analysis of societal vanity and triviality is mirrored in the poem's elegant heroic couplets. Neoclassical dramatists also followed the classical unities of time, place, and action, which dictated that a play had to take place in a single day, have a single narrative, and take place in a single location. The play "All for Love" by John Dryden exemplifies this rigorous devotion to these classical standards through its cohesive action and solitary dramatic moment.

4. Moral and Social Commentary

During this time, literature frequently addressed current events and societal mores, with a significant emphasis on moral and social commentary. In an effort to encourage moral behavior and societal change, writers have utilized their works to consider and critique society's moral foundation. In Jonathan Swift's "A Modest Proposal", for example, satire is used to reveal and critique the British government's callous disregard for the suffering of the Irish poor. In a similar vein, Pope's "The Dunciad" makes moral observations about the faults of modern society and the erosion of literary norms through scathing satire. Through these pieces, Neoclassical literature promoted a thoughtful and frequently critical conversation about the standards and values of the day while also engaging with the ethical and social issues of the day.

Themes and Motifs

1. Social Critique

Neoclassical writers frequently use satire and humor to highlight the flaws in human nature and society norms. Social critique is a major theme in their works. Satire was a common literary device used by authors of this age to question and criticize the current status quo, demonstrating their acute understanding of the social and political events of the day. "Gulliver's Travels" by Jonathan Swift, for instance, is a biting critique of many aspects of modern civilization, such as political corruption and the triviality of human concerns. Swift is able to critically examine British politics and social views while combining comedy and astute observation thanks to his use of magical settings and characters. Similar to this, Alexander Pope's "The Rape of the Lock" exposes the ridiculousness of the elite's obsession with appearances and manners by using humorous satire to attack their superficiality and pointless pursuits.

2. Human Nature and Morality

Together with social criticism, Neoclassical literature explores human nature and morals in great detail, frequently delving into moral dilemmas and ideals. Allegory and philosophical contemplation are often used to accomplish this exploration. For example, Pope argues for a moral philosophy that is consistent with reason and the natural order in "An Essay on Man", which addresses issues of human nature, virtue, and humanity's place in the greater scheme of things.

3. Classical References

Neoclassical writing is characterized by classical allusions, with authors regularly referencing the writings and myths of classical Greece and Rome. By establishing a link between modern writing and the renowned traditions of classical antiquity, these allusions gave their works additional depth and credibility. For example, "The Rape of the Lock" by Alexander Pope is replete with references to classical epics, especially Virgil's The Aeneid and Homer's The Iliad, which he adapts to parody the frivolous interests of eighteenth-century British nobility. In a similar vein, the incorporation of classical mythical characters and ideas into literary masterpieces such as Jonathan Swift's "Gulliver's Travels" serves to both enhance the story and establish its connection to the rich cultural and intellectual legacy of classical antiquity. These references functioned as a way to situate current difficulties into a larger, historically esteemed context, while also paying homage to the literary heritage.

4. Elegance and restraint

Neoclassical literature's stylistic approach is characterized by elegance and restraint; it emphasizes a polished and refined method of expression while rejecting the excesses and emotionalism of earlier periods. A dedication to balance and clarity, together with a focus on crafting a refined and measured style, characterize this era's writing. As shown in poems like Pope's "The Rape of the Lock", where each line is painstakingly created to achieve both beauty and precision, the exact usage of heroic couplets in poetry, for instance, required a controlled and artistic expression. Likewise, the Neoclassical theater stayed true to classical principles, emphasizing coherence and unity while rejecting the dramatic excesses of previous eras. This dedication to grace and moderation demonstrates a literary style that favored nuance and control above flamboyance and emotional excess, and it also reflects the larger cultural norms of reason and order of the time.

5. Major Figures and Their Works

Important writers of the Neoclassical era who made distinct contributions to its literary canon included John Dryden, Richard Steele, Jonathan Swift, Alexander Pope, and Joseph Addison. Dryden made a name for himself as a master of satire and the heroic couplet with works like Absalom, Achitophel, and Mac Flecknoe. His works had a significant impact on the poetic form of the time. The heroic couplet became a defining characteristic of Neoclassical poetry with Pope's "The Rape of the Lock" and "An Essay on Man", which demonstrated his mastery of intellectual and sharp language. Through "Gulliver's Travels" and "A Modest Proposal", Swift established his reputation as a master of incisive prose satire, wittily critiquing social and political issues. With "The Spectator" and "The Tatler",

Addison and Steele, on the other hand, invented periodical essay writing. By providing social and literary commentary, their writings shaped public debate and reflected the issues of the day. Collectively, these individuals represent the era's dedication to well-reasoned criticism, refined style, and classical influence.

Conclusion

Reviving classical ideas with an emphasis on reason, order, and restraint, the Neoclassical period, which lasted from the late 17th to the late 18th century, is what makes it noteworthy. As a result of poets like John Dryden and Alexander Pope employing the heroic couplet to create satirical and philosophical works, this age saw a noticeable trend towards ordered forms and devotion to classical standards. A major factor in the literary identity of the century was the mastery of satire by Dryden and the refining of poetic form by Pope. While Joseph Addison and Richard Steele pioneered periodical essay writing and provided insightful social criticism, Jonathan Swift tackled political and social issues with his razor-sharp literary satire. Together, these authors and their works represent the Neoclassical movement's dedication to refinement, moral contemplation, and intellectual integrity. They also shaped the literary scene of their day and had an impact on other literary movements.

A detailed note on periodicals in the Neoclassical Age :-

A periodical is a publication that appears at regular intervals, such as daily, weekly, monthly, or annually. It contains articles, stories, research, or other types of content. Common examples of periodicals include newspapers, magazines, and academic journals.

Each periodical issue often has a consistent format and covers various topics. Periodicals are essential in providing readers with updated information, entertainment, and scholarly content, depending on their type and purpose.

Periodicals in the Neoclassical Age

The Neoclassical Age, spanning the late 17th to early 19th centuries, marked a transformative period in English literature. During this time, periodicals like journals and magazines became very popular. It was a prominent feature of that period.

These periodicals became vital platforms for writers, thinkers, and the emerging middle class to discuss literature, politics, manners, and societal issues. Pioneered by eminent writers like Richard Steele, Joseph Addison, and Samuel Johnson, these publications blended news, essays, satire, and literary criticism.

They not only shaped the literary norms of the time but also played a pivotal role in shaping public opinion, fostering debates, and reflecting the cultural zeitgeist of the age.

The popularity and influence of periodicals during this era highlight their significance in the evolution of English literature and journalism. The following are the famous periodicals of the time:

The Tatler (1709–1711)

The Spectator (1711–1722)

The Guardian (1713)

The Freeholder (1715–1716)

The Old Whig (1719)

The Rambler (1750–1752)

1- The Tatler (1709–1711)

The Tatler was a famous British magazine that combined news with fun stories. It started in 1709 and ended in 1711.

Founder

Richard Steele started it, and Joseph Addison also wrote for it.

Publication Frequency

The magazine was published three times a week.

Content Focus

It covered topics like society gossip, politics, literature, and deep thoughts.

Pseudonyms and Style

Some writers used fake names for their writings. This way, readers only sometimes knew who was behind each piece.

Fictional Framework

Stories sometimes came from made-up places like the Trumpet Coffee House or White's Chocolate House, making the magazine unique.

2- The Spectator (1711–1712)

The Spectator was a famous magazine in London. It started in 1711 and went on until 1712. It came back in 1714 for a short time.

Founders

Two men, Richard Steele and Joseph Addison, established this magazine and wrote many of its stories and articles.

Publication Frequency

The Spectator came out every day except Sundays. So, people have a lot of new things to read.

Focus of Content

The magazine wanted to be fun but also teach suitable lessons. It did not talk much about politics but more about being a good person.

Contributors

Other than Steele and Addison, famous writers like Alexander Pope also wrote for the magazine. They added more ideas and stories to it.

3- The Guardian (1713)

The Guardian was a short-lived periodical that began publishing in 1713 in London, following the successful model of The Spectator.

Founders

The key figures behind "The Guardian" were Richard Steele and Joseph Addison, who had previously collaborated on "The Tatler" and "The Spectator."

Publication Frequency

It was a daily publication, offering fresh content to its readers daily.

Focus of Content

The Guardian aimed to discuss societal issues, manners, literature, and more, providing readers with both entertainment and moral instruction.

Contributors

While Steele and Addison were the primary writers, "The Guardian" also saw contributions from notable writers like Alexander Pope.

4- The Freeholder (1715–1716)

The Freeholder was a periodical that emerged in 1715 and made its mark in the early 18th-century London literary scene. It ran for a relatively short duration, ending in 1716.

Founders

Joseph Addison was the leading mind behind The Freeholder. Known for his previous successful ventures in periodicals, Addison took on this project with a specific vision.

Publication Frequency

The periodical was published twice a week, ensuring regular content for its readers during its run.

Focus of Content

The Freeholder was primarily political. It championed Whig beliefs and showed topics like constitutional monarchy. It also addressed the risks associated with Jacobitism, reflecting the political tensions of the time.

Contributors

While Addison was the primary contributor, writing most of the essays, other writers might have made occasional contributions. However, Addison's voice and perspective were dominant throughout the publication.

5- The Old Whig (1719)

The Old Whig was a periodical that emerged in 1719, entering the political and literary landscape of early 18th-century London.

Founders:

The periodical is attributed to both Alexander Pope and Joseph Addison, two prominent literary figures of the time.

Publication Frequency:

Specific details about its consistent publication frequency are less widely documented, but it was not a daily publication. Given its nature as a response piece, its issuance might have been more sporadic, aligning with the ongoing debate.

Focus of Content:

The core content of The Old Whig revolved around political discussions, particularly opposing the views presented in "The Plebeian."

Contributors:

While Alexander Pope and Joseph Addison were the primary minds behind the periodical, other writers and thinkers of the era might have contributed either directly or through influence. However, Pope and Addison's voices were dominant, shaping the narrative and direction of "The Old Whig."

6- The Rambler (1750–1752)

The Rambler was a significant periodical introduced in the mid-18th century. From 1750 to 1752, it offered readers a blend of essays on various topics, making a notable impact on the literary scene of its time.

Founders

The primary force behind "The Rambler" was Samuel Johnson, a towering figure in English literature.

Publication Frequency

The Rambler was published twice weekly, ensuring its readers received regular content throughout its run.

Focus of Content

The Rambler's content was diverse, with essays covering various subjects. While some pieces delved into moral and philosophical discussions, others explored societal observations, manners, and everyday life.

Contributors

Samuel Johnson was the main contributor and penned most of the essays in the periodical. His unique voice and perspective shaped the narrative and themes of The Rambler.

Conclusion

Periodicals in the Neoclassical Age played a significant role in shaping ideas and culture. Magazines like The Tatler and The Spectator introduced new topics to the public, from politics to daily life.

They helped people discuss big issues and also enjoy light stories. Many famous writers, like Samuel Johnson, shared their thoughts in these papers.

These periodicals made a lasting impact; even today, we look back at them to better understand that time. They show how powerful writing can influence and change society.

Eighteenth Century is the Age of Prose Reason: An Advancement of Human Mind:-

Introduction: "Age of Prose Reason"

The 18th century viewed as a whole has a distinctive character. It is definitely the Age of understanding, the age of enlightenment, where a literature which had become pellucid (clear) began to diffuse knowledge among the growing public. The supremacy of reason was unchallenged – there reigned a general belief in the advancement of human mind. This flourishing of enlightened idea and the escalation of reason and logical thought found its best articulation through the triumph of English prose in the 18th century. As such, the 18th century has often been designated as "Age of Prose Reason."

This era, also known as the Enlightenment, was characterized by a remarkable shift in intellectual thought and a renewed emphasis on reason, logic, and empirical evidence. During this period, prominent philosophers, writers, and thinkers championed the power of rationality and sought to advance human knowledge through scientific inquiry and critical thinking. The Age of Prose Reason marked a significant departure from the preceding era's reliance on tradition, authority, and superstition, and it laid the foundation for modern scientific, political, and social thought.

Widespread Promotion of Rationalism

One of the key features of the Age of Prose Reason was the widespread promotion of rationalism. Rationalism, as an epistemological stance, asserts that reason is the primary source of knowledge and truth. It posits that through the exercise of reason, human beings can understand and comprehend the world around them, uncover universal truths, and develop logical systems of thought. This emphasis on reason led to a profound transformation in various fields of study, including philosophy, science, politics, and literature.

Empirical Observation and Experience

In the realm of philosophy, thinkers such as René Descartes, John Locke, and Immanuel Kant played pivotal roles in shaping the Age of Prose Reason. Descartes, known for his famous maxim "Cogito, ergo sum" (I think, therefore I am), emphasized the power of human reason as the foundation of knowledge. He argued that by doubting everything and engaging in systematic doubt, individuals could arrive at certain knowledge. Locke, on the other hand, focused on the role of empirical observation and experience in acquiring knowledge. He proposed that the mind is a tabula rasa, a blank slate, upon which sensory experiences imprint ideas. Kant sought to reconcile rationalism and empiricism by asserting that knowledge is shaped by both innate cognitive structures and sensory experiences. These philosophical developments propelled the idea that human reason is a potent tool for understanding the world.

Scientific Progress

Scientific progress also flourished during the Age of Prose Reason. Prominent figures such as Isaac Newton and Carl Linnaeus revolutionized the fields of physics and biology, respectively, through their application of reason and systematic inquiry. Newton's laws of motion and universal gravitation, formulated through rigorous experimentation and mathematical calculations, laid the foundation for classical mechanics. Linnaeus, through his work in taxonomy and classification, introduced a systematic method for categorizing and understanding the natural world. These scientific advancements demonstrated the power of reason in uncovering the laws that govern the physical universe.

Political Thought and Governance

The Age of Prose Reason also witnessed significant developments in political thought and governance. The Enlightenment thinkers sought to challenge traditional notions of absolute monarchy and divine right, advocating for the principles of individual rights, separation of powers, and social contract theory. The writings of philosophers such as John Locke, Baron de Montesquieu, and Jean-Jacques Rousseau provided intellectual frameworks for the establishment of modern democratic systems. These thinkers argued that political authority should be based on reason, consent, and the pursuit of the common good, rather than on hereditary privilege or religious dogma.

Literature and Literary Criticism

Literature and literary criticism also underwent a transformation during the Age of Prose Reason. The emphasis on reason and rationality led to a shift away from the highly ornamental and allegorical style of the preceding Baroque period. Writers such as Jonathan Swift, Voltaire, and Samuel Johnson adopted a more direct and accessible prose style to convey their ideas and critique society. Swift's satirical novel "Gulliver's Travels" critiqued human follies and explored political and social issues of the time. Voltaire's works, such as "Candide," challenged religious intolerance and championed the power of reason. Johnson's "A Dictionary of the English Language" paved the way for linguistic enquiry.

Jonathan Swift

Jonathan Swift's works are a monstrous satire on humanity. Swift, who hated all shams, wrote, with a great show of learning famous Bicerstaff Almanac containing "Predictions for the year 1708 was determined by the emerging states," which first brought sift into prominence This work appeared under the pseudonym of Isaac Bickerstaff was preeminently focus because of his satiric worlds . Ligaments any case of hypocrisy or by notice , he sets up a remedy which is atrocious , and defuse his plan with such seriousness that the satire overwhelms the readers with a sense of monstrous falsity . Swift's two greatest satires are A Tale of a Tub and Gulliver's Travels . The Tale began as a grim exposure of the alleged weaknesses of three principle forms of religion beliefs, catholic, Lutheran and Christin as opposed to the Anglican; put it ended in a satire upon all science and philosophy. In Gulliver's Travels the practice grows more unbearable strangely enough , this book upon which swifts' literary fame generally rests , was not written from any literary motive , but rather as an outlet of the author's own bitterness , against fate and human society .

Joseph Addison

Like swift, Joseph Addison despised shams, but unlike him he never lost faith in humanity; and in all his satires, these is a gentle kindness which makes one think letter of his fellowmen even when he laughs at their little vanities. Addison stripped off the mask of vice, so much upheld by restoration literature, to show its ugliness and deformity; put to reveal virtue in its own notice loveliness was Addison's main purpose. Further prompted and aided by the more original genius of his friend Steele, Addison seeds upon the new social life of the clubs and made it the subject of endless pleasant essays upon types of men and manners. His journals The Tatler and The Spectator are the beginnings of the Coverly essay; and their studies of human character as exemplified in Sir Roger – De – Coverly , are a preparation for the modern novel . The most enduring of Addison's works are Essays collected from The Tatler and The spectator. To an age of fundamental coarseness and artificiality his essays came with a wholesome message of refinement and simplicity. He attaches all the little varieties and all the big circles of his time not in substantial way, but with a finally ridicule and a gently humour which appears.

His Essays are the best picture we possess of the new social life of England; they advanced the art of literary criticism to a much higher stage than it had ever reached before; they certainly led English men to a better knowledge and appreciation of their own literature; and finally they gave us characters that live forever as part of that goodly company which extends from Chaucer's county power to Kipling Huluancy . Addison and Steele not only introduce the modern essay but their character forfeiture, they herald the dawn of the modern novel.

Steele was a rollicking, good – hearted, emotional, lovable Irishman. He was one of the few winters of his time who showed a sincere and unswerving respect for womanhood. Even more than Addison, he ridicules irks and makes pursue lovely. He was the origination of The Tatler and journeyed with Addison in creating The Spectator – the two periodicals which did more to influence the subsequent literature than all the magazines of the century complied. Steele was the original genius of Sir Roger and of many other characters and essays for which Addison usually received the whole credit. But the majority of the cities hold that the more original parts the characters, the overflowing kindness, are largely Steele's creation while Addison polished and perfected the essays.

Dr. Johnson

Dr. Johnson was probably the most significant intellectual stalwart of the time. His Dictionary and his Lives of the Poets are worthy to be remembered through both of these are valuable not as literature, but rather as a study of literature. The Dictionary as the first ambitious attempt at the English lexicon is extremely valuable, notwithstanding the fact that some of his derivations are incorrect. Lives of the poets are the simplest and the most readable of his literary works. As criticisms they are often misleading, giving undue praise to artificial poets like pope and abundant injustice to nobler poets like Milton, but as biographies, they are excellent reading, and we owe to them some of the best power picture of the early English poets. Bowell's Life of Jonson was one of the most famous prose works of the century. It is an immortal work where , like the Greek – sculptures the little slaves produced the more enduring work than the Greek – masters .

Edmund Burke

Edmund Burke in famous for his best known political speeches "On Conciliation with America , " American Taxation', 'The Impeachment of Warren Hasting' and also for his famous book of prose Reflection on the French Revolution which are still much studied as models of English prose . Characteristic of the classic age, they abound in fine rhetoric but lack simplicity. But his works reveal the stateliness and the rhetorical power of the English language and because of the poetic prose so rich in images and symbols and the musical cadence of his sentences, and also because of his profound sympathy for humanity and his purpose to establish the truth, Burke won a significant place in the History of English literature.

Edward Gibbon

Only Edward Gibbon remains to be mentioned, His famous prose work is a historical treatise, entitled. The Decline and Fall of Roman Empire spanning Roman history from 98 A.D to 1453 A.D. It gains little recognition because of his imposing style characterizing by the sinuous roll of his majestic sentences. gibbons style has been characterized as finished , elegant , splendid, rounded , massive , sonorous , elaborate , ornate , exhaustive etc .

Novel Writers

The flourish of prose in the 18th century like a tune is also evident in the rise of novel, bought into vogue by Richardson, Fielding, Smollett and Sterne. But since the novel is a distinct literary genre a discussion on the 18th century novels remains outside the scope of this essay. As a whole it can safely be concluded that because of the growing tendency of prose in the contemporary satires and periodicals, essays which catered to the public tastes increasingly the 18th century lonely triumphs in prose literature.

(The major prose writers of the age include Jonathan Swift (1667 -1745) Joseph Addison (1672 -1719), Richard Steele (1672 -1729) and Samuel Johnson (1704 – 1784). Other prose writers of significance are James Bowell (1740 – 1795), Edlemund Burley (1729 – 1797) and Edward Gibbon (1737 – 1794).)

The Rise of the Novel: A Social and Literary perspective (Neo-classical Period)

The 18th century is generally considered to be the first literary age during which we can speak of the novel as a well-established genre in British literature. The period is difficult to name; it was called by its contemporaries the Augustan or Neoclassical Age (as writers strove to identify themselves with the classical Roman model), or by other names such as Enlightenment, the Age of Reason. 18th century philosophers, such as Locke, Berkeley, D. Hume, Diderot or Voltaire stated the significance of the rational, positive spirit. In their opinion, human knowledge is empirical, based on the perception of the senses, hence its subjectivity and limits. Order was another first-rate value in the Augustan hierarchy. It was associated with thoughtful conduct, efficiency instead of complexity, scientific discoveries, acquiring connotations such as unity, harmony, precision, and clarity.

On the literary scene, the most influential genre that developed during the period was the novel. It was influenced by similar developments on the continent, among which Cervantes's Don Quixote, which was translated in 1700, the writings of Rabelais, or of Lesage, particularly Gil Blas. The ordinary man became the norm, consisting of a variety of individuals, such as the energetic merchant, the country gentleman directing his farms or estates, the lady in her social calls, the doctor, the lawyer, soldier, servant, labourer, in their occupations, the traveller observing life at home and abroad, and the writer including all these as his public and characters. Economic specialization provided a particular kind of audience - the lower and middle classes saw their lives and interests represented with a sympathy and seriousness that had hitherto been accorded only to their betters on the social scale. As A. Sanders has shown in his Short Oxford History of English Literature, the new style emphasized for the most part the everyday experience of men and women in society.

Enlightenment philosophy required a simple, unequivocal instrument of expression, making use of a plain, native language to record experiments and conclusions. No rhetoric, exuberant prose was permitted to obscure common sense, as writers (such as D. Defoe) wanted to communicate their ideas without aiming at a literary distinction. As Ian Watt also shows in his study The Rise of the Novel, the appearance of writers such as D. Defoe, S. Richardson, H. Fielding within a single generation was probably due to the favourable conditions of the time. 18th century literary historians have seen realism as the defining characteristic which differentiates their work from previous fiction (the term was apparently used as an aesthetic description in 1835 to denote the "vérité humaine" of Rembrandt as opposed to "idéalité poétique"). Primarily used as the antonym of "idealism", the term would trace down all possible continuity to earlier works that portrayed low life and where the economic and social motives were given a lot of space in the presentation of human behaviour. Fiction is not a new invention; there are a great number of Middle Age prose stories, of Renaissance romances, allegories, character-studies or picaresque tales. Yet, fiction's relation to life was peripheral, a mere idealization or satire.

Defoe and Richardson are the first great writers in English literature who did not take their plots from mythology, history, legend or previous literature. In this respect, they differ from Chaucer, Spenser, and Shakespeare who used traditional plots. However, besides the plot, much else had to be changed in the tradition of fiction: the actors in the plot and the scene of their actions had to be placed in a new literary perspective. The plot had to be acted in particular circumstances, rather than as had been common in the past - by general human types against a background determined by the appropriate literary convention. The novel is distinguished from other genres by the amount of attention it generally allots both to the individualisation of its characters and to the presentation of their environment. It is also related to the epistemological status of proper names as the expression of a particular identity (medieval or Renaissance writers preferred either historical or type names).

The principle of individuation accepted by Locke was that of existence in space and time; Northrop Frye has seen "time and Western man" as the defining characteristic of the novel compared with other genres. Philosophical and literary innovations must be seen as resulting in "a circumstantial view of life", a feature of the new prose. The narrative method that embodies this view is called formal realism, the premise that it is an authentic report of human experience, giving its readers details concerning the individuality of actors, particulars of their actions, through a more referential use of language than is common in other literary forms. The difference to earlier fiction consists in the fact that such passages were relatively rare, while the plot was traditional and highly improbable.

The Decline of Drama.

Drama had grown artificial, unnatural and immoral during the earlier part of the eighteenth century. It was the decline of drama during the first half of the eighteenth century that made way for the novel. The latter part of the eighteenth century was the golden age of the novel. A true novel is simply a work of fiction which relates the story of plain human life, under stress of emotion, which depends for its interest not on incident and adventure, but on its truth to nature. Richardson, Fielding, Smollett and Sterne, known as the —four wheels of novel‖- all seem to have seized upon the idea of reflecting life as it is, in the form of a story, and to have developed it simultaneously.

The Four Wheels of the Novel. Richardson, Fielding, Smollett and Sterne are known as the —four wheels of the novel‖. They brought this new genre to such maturity that it became the glory of England. Let's see, in short, these authors and their works as follows:

(i) Samuel Richardson (1689-1761). Richardson's first novel *Pamela* tells the story of the trials, tribulations, and the final happy marriage of the heroine. It is written in the forms of letters. It is also known as an epistolary novel because the novel is developed with the exchange of letters between the characters. It was instantly successful. In it the moral and social purposes are successfully blended. Pamela's character is well drawn. The plot, though simple, is well developed. It is considered as the *first novel in the modern sense.*

His *Clarissa* or *The History of A Lady* in eight volumes is a sentimental novel. It gave Richardson European reputation and —it is still regarded as one of the greatest of the eighteenth century novels‖.

Clarissa's character is realistically drawn with psychological insight. It also contains the most remarkable study of the scoundrel, Lovelace. In it the dramatic element is strong. It is characterized by pathos, sincerity and minute realism. Richardson's novels are stories of human life, told from within, and depending for their interest not on incident and adventure, but on their truth to human nature. Reading his work is, on the whole, like examining an antiquated work of a stern wheel steamer, it is interesting for its undeveloped possibilities, rather than for its achievement. Richardson's place in the history of English novel is very high. —Richardson‖, writes Rickett, —introduced sentimentality into English novel and popularized it forever. Without his influence we never have had *Tristram Shandy*, we certainly should have been without *Joseph Andrews,* ... Then the feminine standpoint taken in his writings stirred many able women to continue and amplify the feminine tradition. Fanny Burney and Jane Austen are indebted to him and a host of lesser names‖. In *Clarissa* he introduced the epistolary form of novel. He was the first novelist to show the real and vital knowledge of human heart, its perversities and contradictions.

(ii) Henry Fielding (1707-54). Fielding was the greatest of this new group of novelists. He is called —the father of English novel‖ because he for the first time propounded the technique of writing novel. He had a deeper and wider knowledge of life, which he gained from his own varied and sometimes riotous experiences. As a magistrate he had an intimate knowledge of many types of human criminality which was of much use to him in his novels. His first novel *Joseph Andrews* (1742) began as a burlesque of the false sentimentality and conventional virtues of Richardson's *Pamela*. In it Fielding humorously narrates the adventures of the hero, Joseph Andrews, and his companion, Parson Adams. From the very beginning we see the stamp of his genius- the complete rejection of the epistolary form and moralizing, the structural development of the story, the broad and vivacious humour which was denied to Richardson, the genial insight into human nature, and the forceful and pithy style. In Joseph Andrews Fielding emerges on a pioneer of the novel of manners. In *Jonathan Wild* he gives us new and piercing glimpses of the ruffian mentality.

Fielding's masterpiece, *Tom Jones,* takes an enormous canvas and crowds it with numerous characters. It gives us the fullest and richest picture of English life about the middle of the eighteenth century. Although the picaresque element is strongly marked in this novel, it is more than a picaresque novel. Fielding calls it —the comic epic in prose.‖ *Tom Jones* stands unrivalled in the history of English novel for its coherent and well-knit structure, richness of characterization, vivid and realistic presentation of contemporary society, sane and wise point of view. *Amelia* is the story of a good wife who, in spite of temptation,

remains faithful to a good-natured but erring husband, Captain Booth. It is at once a searching criticism of contemporary society and a mature. It soberly conceives story of everyday life, is rich in incident and, like *Tom Jones,* is remarkable for its insight into human character. Fielding has rightly been called —the father of English novel‖. He for the first time formulated the theory of novel writing in the prefaces of *Joseph Andr*ews and *Tom Jones,* and followed his own definition with utmost consistency. Other novelists followed his example. He gave a definite form and shape to the novel. In the words of Richard Church: —He is the first writer to focus the novel in such a way that he brought the whole world as we see it, within the scope of this new, rapidly maturing literary form.‖ Fielding is the first great realist in the history of English novel. Common life is the material of his novel but it is handled as Raleigh points out, —with the freedom and imagination of a great artist.‖ He presents a complete and comprehensive picture of contemporary society. His realism is epical in its range, sweep and variety. He is the founder of modern realistic novel and the novel of manners. Fielding's realism is connected with his comic point of view, his wise, tolerant acceptance of things as they are. He had nothing to do with the prudish morality of Richardson. He threw it aside and presented man in full length as he found him. Though he portrayed men with no reservations, he never forgot that he was one of them. From this inborn sympathy comes his large, tolerant way of looking at things, a view of life that often finds expression in raillery but never in cynicism. He laughs, but his laughter is always ready to give place to tenderness and pity. For him the tragedy of life lay in the presence of virtue and innocence in a world of evil, cruelty and deception. In the presentation of tragedy, Fielding is always direct, simple and sincere. Fielding was the first to infuse the novel —with the refreshing and preserving element of humour.‖ He was capable of presenting pure comedy in such characters as Adams and Partridge and lower and more farcical comedy in characters like Mrs. Slipslop and Square Western. He effectively lashes out his satire at affectation, vanity, pedantry, hypocrisy and vice. But he is always human and humane. Irony is a great weapon of his satire. Fielding's aim was to replace Richardson's morbid morality by a healthy commonsense morality. This commonsense morality gave him a shrewd insight into the weakness of his character. Fielding was a superb craftsman. He changed the concept of plot construction. In his novels we get for the first time a closely-knit organic plot. Other novelists learnt the art of plot construction from him,

He is the creator of the novel of character. He peopled his novels with lively and interesting characters. He endowed his characters with life and vitality. He has vividly portrayed all kinds of characters like Shakespeare. Like Shakespeare he has a sympathetic yet maturely detached view of human comedy. The forces which guide his characters are; for the most part, natural human needs, for it were these that Fielding knew best. Settings in Fielding's novels are realistic and recognizable. His narrative is energetic and effective. He initiates the practice of the omniscient narrator, which has been universally followed, by many following writers. As a stylist he broke away from the mannered, artificial style of the earlier novelists. It is fresh, clear, direct, unaffected, vigorous and easy. It gives vitality to his characters.

(iii) Tobias Smollett (1721-71).

Smollett, who wrote *The Adventures of Roderick Random, The Adventures of eregrine Pickle,* and *The Expedition of Humhry Clinker,* added new feathers to the cap of the craft called English novel. His novels are simply strings of adventures which are not organized into an artistic whole. He conceived the novel as a —large diffused picture of life. It is the personality of the hero which has the semblance of unity to various incidents and adventures. His novels are called episodic or panoramic novels. As a panoramic novelist Smollett has never been surpassed. Smollett's characters are types and not individuals. He had a genius for depicting oddities and he excels as a caricaturist. He describes his characters in terms of externals. His characters are grossly exaggerated and distorted. Smollett's presentation of the harsh and ugly realities of life and society makes him a forerunner of the novel of purpose. Hudson writes: It has, however, to be remembered that Smollett wrote expressly as a satirist and reformer, and that his purpose was to paint the monstrous evils of life in their true proportions and colures that he might thus drive them home upon the attention of the public, and we must certainly set it down to his credit that the sickening realism of the ship scenes in *The Roderick Random* led directly to drastic changes for the better in the conditions in the naval service. He, thus, anticipates the novel with purpose. Smollett followed the tradition of the picaresque novel, which presents a union of intrigue and adventure. His style is vivid and lively. It is forceful and masculine. His method could be easily imitated. Dickens followed him. There was a spurt of picaresque him.

(iv) Laurence Sterne (1713-1768). Sterne's first novel *The Life and Opinions of Tristram Shandy* won him immediate recognition. It records the experiences of the eccentric Shandy family. —Its chief strength lies in its brilliant style,...and in its odd characters like Uncle Toby and Corporal Trimm, which, with all their eccentricities, are so humanized by the author's genius that they belong among the great —creations‖ of our literature.‖ His second novel *A Sentimental Journey* combines fiction, sketches of travel, miscellaneous subjects and essays. It is remarkable for its brilliant style. Sterne defined all conventions of novel writing. He contributed to the development of English novel in his own peculiar way.

He is a skilled master in creating brilliant effects. Plot is non-existent in his novels. There is neither chronology nor progression. —His novels are one long parenthesis – a colossal aside to the reader. Yet despite the chaotic incoherence of his method of storytelling, his effects are made with consummate ease.‖ Sterne's prose style, which is characterised by brilliance, force, precision, force, melody and sensuousness of the highest order, helped him to create brilliant effects. His technique of creating striking effects influenced the school of the Stream of consciousness. Sterne's greatest contribution lies in the field of characterization. Cross writes: —He enlarged for the novelist the sphere of character building by bringing into English fiction the attitude of the sculptor and the painter, combined with a graceful and harmonious movement, which is justly likened to the transitions o music.‖ His characters are drawn with an economy of strokes, and they are utterly solid, three-dimensional characters. He develops his characters by subtle and minute analysis of gesture, expressions, intonations and a hundred other details. He imparted humanity to his characters. His methods of characterisation is impressionistic, a method which he introduced for the first time. This method of characterisation was followed by the novelists of the Stream of consciousness school. Sterne is the most original of English humorists. He deftly intermingles humour and pathos. He smiles at sorrow and finds matter for pathos in the most comical situation. He was the first to use the word, —sentimental‖ to indicate —the soft state of feelings and the imagination.‖ He used this word in the sense now attached to it. He made the word classic and current in the record of his continental travel, *The Sentimental Journey*. He could tell and distinguish between fine shades of feeling, and could communicate them to his readers in a way that aroused both compassion and mirth. Sterne is the pioneer of modern impressionism. His impressionistic narrative method is very close to that of modern impressionists like Virginia Wolf and James Joyce. He is regarded as the first of the impressionists. —Richardson had given sentimentality, Fielding humour, Smollet liveliness‖ and Sterne impressionism.

(v) Other Novelists. Oliver Goldsmith's *The Vicar of Wakefield* stands in the first rank of the eighteenth century novels. Its plot is simple, though sometimes inconsistent, the characters are human and attractive and humour and pathos are deftly mingled together. Goldsmith has adopted the direct method of narration through the principal character. Goldsmith for the first time depicts the picture of English domestic life in this novel. It is also unique because it gives delightful and idealistic picture of English village life. The blend of humour and pathos makes it all the more charming. Hency Mackenzie's *The Man of Feeling* is a sentimental novel which shows the influence of Sterne. William Godwin (1745-1831) wrote *Caleb Williams* or *Things As They Are* in order to give —a general review of the modes of domestic and unrecorded despotism by which man becomes the destroyer of man.‖ Miss Fanny Burney (1752-1842), the first of the women novelists, is an important figure in the history of English novel. She wrote four novels: Evelina, Cecilia, Camilla and *The Wanderer* but her fame rests mainly on the first two. She was endowed with considerable narrative faculty and great zest for life. She has successfully created the novel of domestic life. In *Evelina* she reverts to the epistolary method of Richardson, and in broad humour it follows the tradition of Fielding and Smollett, but without their coarseness. She for the first time wrote from a woman's point of view and, thus, brought feminine sensibility to English novel of the eighteenth century. —She has presented a large gallery of striking portraits‖, writes Edward Albert, —the best of which are convincing and amusing caricatures of Dickensian type. Her observation of life was keen and close and her descriptions of society are in a delightfully satirical vein, in many ways like that of Austen.

Why does Arnold call the 18th century an age of prose and reason?

In his essay "The Study of Poetry" (1880), Matthew Arnold (1822 – 1888) describes the 18th century as an "age of prose and reason." This period is popularly known as "The Neo-classical Age" (1660-1785). During this time, people cared more about clear thinking, order, and reason in poetry than about deep feelings and imagination.

Focus on Logic and Order: In the 18th century, writers focused a lot on logic, clear thinking, and balance. They liked everything to be neat and organized. Arnold says writers like Pope and Dryden wanted,

regularity, uniformity, precision, balance.

While this made the writing clear, it made poetry less imaginative and less emotional.

Prose Over Poetry: People started to prefer prose writing during this time. Arnold says that even the poetry of this age was more like prose with rhymes. He explains,

Dryden and Pope are not classics of our poetry, they are classics of our prose.

This means their writing was more about clear and careful expression than the beauty of poetry.

Shift from Imagination to Reason: The 18th century shifted from the imaginative poetry of earlier times to rational thought. Arnold states,

We are to regard Dryden as the puissant and glorious founder, Pope as the splendid high priest, of our age of prose and reason.

This shows that even though they wrote in verse, their work was more focused on logical argument than poetic inspiration.

In conclusion, Arnold calls the 18th century an "age of prose and reason." Literature then focused on logic and clear thinking. Imagination and emotion were secondary. Structured thought was valued more than the beauty of true poetry.